A Woman's Place Is On The Water

AND HOW TO BEAT MEN AT THEIR OWN GAME

Marjorie B. Sandell

Cover design by Bob Zieper. Illustration by George Karn.

Published by Muskie Memories Press
P. O. Box 44400, Eden Prairie, MN 55344

Library Of Congress catalogue number: 92-061615
ISBN 0-940107-06-6

Printed in the U.S.A.

II

DEDICATION

My inspiration to assemble the information contained within the covers of this book has come from two men whom I have never met, but both of whom my abiding husband has permitted me to consider as close friends.

The first is A. J. McClane, whose magnificent writings for more than forty years have taught us all so much about fish, and fishing. Many of his books have been around our household almost as long as the Holy Bible, and are referred to with almost as much reverence.

The second is Lee Wulff, who has helped us really understand what fishing is all about, and how we can pass that exhilaration along to others, just by releasing many of the fish we catch. Perhaps his greatest message is in the following passage from "The Wealth Of Age," originally published in the March, 1983, issue of OUTDOOR LIFE:

"There is a wealth in having sat around many campfires in a multitude of camps. It lies in the friends you make. When you have lived with them on the waters and in the woods and time has seasoned the friendship, it is far more satisfying than those that develop casually, each person showing the other only a part of what he is. It may be that the greatest wealth of all lies in our friends."

Both of these giants of men have now left us for The Great Fishing Grounds in The Sky. I shall miss them both very much.

M. B. S.

FOREWORD

"She Forgot The Basil..."

Some years ago I was associated with a large group of home-makers who had the responsibility for staging monthly congregational dinners for our church. For one of those events, the main course was a dish which I had affectionately dubbed "chicken cacciatore a la Marjorie."

After the multitude had been served, I joined the other ladies pouring the coffee in the dining room. In the process, I overheard two women guests discussing the entree. As one seemed to be praising it to her neighbor, the other woman turned to her and complained, "Yes, but she forgot the basil."

In the pages ahead, I have attempted to include all of the essential ingredients to provide you with a hearty meal of information about the wondrous sport of fishing...for women. That effort, however, has a likely possibility of overlooking "the basil,"...some key ingredient which you had hoped to savor.

Thus, in advance, I apologize for any such oversight. With what I have included, I sincerely hope that it will sharpen your appetite to find your way out on the water, and to share in the enchantment of just being there, and perhaps to catch a few memorable fish.

Marjorie B. Sandell

CONTENTS

MEN ARE SO DUMB!

"It's no accident there are more women than men on Earth. They're the sturdier, healthier sex. Heart disease, cancer, homicide, and pneumonia attack men at twice the rate of the supposedly weaker vessel. Women have more stamina and psychological resilience than men. "Men out-stutter women 4 to l. Men go bald, and sprout hair from their ears to make up for it. They're more likely to be color-blind, 16 to l, and are especially prey to ulcers and hernias and back problems. Faced with such a list of defects, any conscientious manufacturer would have issued a product recall. Men get heart attacks and strokes. Women are sick, but men are dead."

-Edward Dolnick, HEALTH magazine, July-August l99l.

Men are so dumb that they honestly believe that they are the only ones who can drive a truck, fly an airplane, run a computer, hunt for deer, shoot pheasants...or catch fish.

The truth of the matter is that women have come to excel men in many fields of business and sports today... and can jolly well hold their own in many others.

You can find women today in military combat, flying huge commercial aircraft, running large business enterprises, playing championship golf, beating men in many of their own games, and holding down hundreds of world-wide fishing records.

The fact that there aren't more women out on the water today, enjoying the immensely refreshing sport of fishing is due to many factors, but none that we can't overcome with just a little planning and determination.

Many wives will tell you that the major reason that they are not into fishing is because their husbands refuse to invite them along. Others will contend that they have yet to take up angling because there are no easy ways for them to learn the fundamentals, or that they feel a sense of inadequacy or insecurity in even thinking about it because of their lack of knowledge about where to go, how to prepare, what to expect, and what to do about it.

But that is all in the past.

The mission of this book is to erase all of your fears, to give you enough basic knowledge, to teach you the language, and to give you the courage to jump into it with all of the determination and energy that you would direct towards preparing a seven course dinner for your husband's boss and his wife.

That women are the equal, or better, of men in the business of fishing is probably best documented the fact that the first known book of any significance on the sport was written by a woman: Dame Juliana Berners (a.k.a. Barnes). Almost five hundred years ago, way back in 1496, when Christopher Columbus was just completing his second trip to the shores of the New World, Juliana published "The Treatise Of Fishing With An Angle."

Juliana was quite a lady, attributed to having been (at various times in her career) both a nun and a noblewoman. She was also a writer of essays on hunting, although it is not known that she was a huntress. Her writings, the historians tell us, were compilations of treatises written by others, but which she was able to assimilate in such exciting form as to titillate her British readers.

One researcher of the time tells us that Juliana was an illustrious female who regarded the sports of the field as a source of virtue, honor, and nobility. Others have testified that she was not the burly boot-and-mackinaw-clad outdoor type that you might expect, but was, indeed, "a gentlewoman endowed with excellent gifts both of body and mind."

Still another described her as "a Minerva in her studies and a Diana in hunting." And she certainly was a pioneer in the lore of fishing. Her treatise on fishing attracted far more attention than her other works on hunting, and is said to have dominated the angling world for two centuries.

It was then that Izaak Walton came on the scene. And, if you are really going to get into the fishing action, you will have to remember name of old Izaak. He is the guru to whom male anglers will refer when they are in a philosophical mood, and when they want to sound wise about the sport and its true origin.

Izaak got into the act in 1653 with the publication of an odd book called "The Compleat Angler." This was not one of those "how to" books such as we see in all of the sporting goods emporia today. Rather, it was a rambling tale of two characters, Piscator and Viator (later changed to Venator).

In their conversations while angling they touched on the basic elements of the pursuit, providing readers with exactly the kind of information they seemed to need to be successful with the fish they sought. In its detailed reportage of live bait fishing it was fascinating enough to create an intensive interest in the business of angling.

You should know, too, that it was his long-time friend Charles Cotton who collaborated with him at a later date to add the delicate details of fly fishing, the elite faction of this sport with which he's most associated today.

To get back to Juliana, it is Important for us ladies to note that, while she was there first with all of the facts, the male historians are loathe to give her credit for that one-upmanship. Few, if any of the men you speak fishing with, will ever admit that there was such a lady...and, even if there was, she couldn't have been the first person to document the details of their favorite outdoor sport.

But as women living in this male-dominated world, we have become inured to such manifestations of the masculine ego. It is now over seventy years since we were given the right to vote by the nineteenth amendment. But there are still a lot of men out there who believe that was a bad deal...for them.

I saw a quip in one of-my husband's golf magazines last month where one country club good old boy was saying to another: "I'm all for women's rights. I just don't believe that they should be allowed to vote or play golf. "But men aren't really standing in the way of women going fishing. They just aren't helping it along.

Way back in 1988 FISHING TACKLE TRADE NEWS carried a special report on the national conference of the Outdoor Writers Association of America held that year. A major topic on the agenda of that meeting was the question of whether or not the suppliers to the sport of fishing were doing a responsible job in marketing to women. The conclusion, reporter Tim Jones tells us, was "No."

Tim's article reports on sixteen of the attendees (13 of them women who issued their own individual indictments of manufacturers for overlooking the potential represented by the women who are not yet into the sport). Their statements were directed at refuting the perception which most suppliers seem to cling to:

1-Women don't fish.

2-Women don't buy fishing tackle, and

3-Women want "different" merchandise.

Jan Fogt, outdoor columnist for the PALM BEACH POST responded to the first perception by stating that "A woman needs to be taught how to fish. A learn-to-fish program for women sponsored by a tackle company, or, better yet, an industry association, would pay tremendous dividends." Outdoor personality Adele Dovey of Johnstown, PA., agreed. "I'd love to see more educational programs. A husband cannot teach a woman to fish. It would be bucks in the pocket of the tackle industry to organize classes at the local level."

Yet many of the assembled women writers and other fishing experts in attendance reported that they had never been approached by a local retailer or distributor to give classes or seminars for women anglers. Sharon Rushton, education coordinator for the AFTMA (American Fishing Tackle Manufacturers Association) Sport Fishing Educational Foundation commented that the time to promote women's fishing was long overdue. "Even though a higher percentage of men than women fish, I think manufacturers need to wake up."

In reference to perception number two, a report from the National Sporting Goods Association showed that women buyers accounted, for 17% of all rod-and-reel combinations and 12% of all reels, which is an important share of any market. Those figures could be higher, too, many of the women present figured, if it weren't for the fact that they are usually invested with the hand-me-downs of their husbands.

And as for perception number three, Sugar Ferris, president of Bass'n Gal (the first organization to consistently promote women's fishing) told it as she saw it: "I've spent the better part of 12 years trying to convince national fishing manufacturers that women are not seeking a feminine fishing product, packaged in pink and white... We only ask that the manufacturer realize...he needs to promote what he has. Design is not the problem."

Writer Liliam Larsen stated that she had spent considerable time looking into the subject, but added that she didn't see any clear solution. "I've had manufacturers tell me it's a waste of time to target women with advertising because women don't make the buying decisions," she concluded. But Maryjeanne McAward, another writer, stated that she felt that "Tackle companies should use women in their advertising—women fishing by themselves, women driving the boat. Not bikini-clad models; just ordinary women. A woman on her own and who hasn't fished can picture herself in that role."

As will be pointed out in rich detail in later chapters, those manufacturers and their advertising agencies haven't yet got the message. To them, we are an Invisible market yet to be discovered.

But we don't have to wait for the men who run those businesses to discover us. We need to go fishing, and we will go fishing. That fact that so many of don't fish today is simply that we haven't put our minds, and our effort, into it. But we can do it!

According to the Aircraft Owners and Pilots Association, there are 42,299 female pilots in the United States. That's 6.1% of all licensed pilots!

This is one of my all-time favorite advertising illustrations. It appeared in the August 29, 1988 edition of THE WALL STREET JOURNAL in an ad for SABRE Travel Information Network. The photo, it told us, is the flight deck of one of the world's most advanced jetliners and operated by American Airlines. And right there, in the co-pilot's seat, is a woman. A woman pilot! While good news to us ladies, it might have shook up some of those corporate biggies who sit up there in the First Class section, sipping their scotches. A woman in the cockpit? You bet, and there are many more of them up there today...and some of them sitting in the chief pilot's seat!

In May of 1991, the House Armed Services Committee voted to allow women pilots to fly combat missions in the Air Force, Navy and Marines. By that time many female helicopter pilots had ferried fuel and troops throughout the combat zones of the Gulf war, It has taken 43 years to recognize what we women can do when it needs to be done.

There is also the story of the little girl in a Sunday school class who was asked to tell the story of Adam and Eve. "First God created Man," she said, "and then He looked at him and said "I think I can do better". So He created Eve."

Getting into fishing isn't as difficult as many believe. For me, it came easy. My husband returned from one of his early angling ventures into Canada some twenty-five years ago, and then made the mistake of telling me what a great time he had, in exquisite detail.

When he had finished his saga, I told him that the trip sounded just like something I would enjoy doing. He took me up on it just a few months later, and we have been fishing together ever since.

Best of all, he hasn't really seemed to mind, and I have even got the idea that on many of those excursions that I have provided him with many evenings more entertaining and enjoyable than those old games of nickel-ante-five-card-stud-jacks-or-better-to-open-dueces-wild poker games.

That all husbands, or other male companions, will not respond in such a compassionate manner is understandable, given the perverse nature of the species. Indeed, there is a great deal of literature on the subject (most of it in those chauvinistic "outdoor" magazines), wherein men continue to console themselves with exaggerated stories of their derring-do in the wilderness.

One writer in FIELD & STREAM put it this way: "A man doesn't belong in an aerobics class where he is the only one without a bustline. And a woman just flat-out doesn't belong in a camp where everybody else is a man."

Fiddlesticks!

The writer apparently is unaware of the many women who have flown shuttle missions with crews made up largely of men. There also is the female British chemist who flew in a Russian mission to join the all-male crew of the Mir space station. That lady was probably as welcome as a woodchuck in your lettuce patch during the early hours

6

of her visit. But flight commander Anatoly Asterbarsky soon warmed up to her. "She can change her clothes in our presence," he told a reporter. "She has no barriers that are known to our women."

For some strange reason, the biological differences between men and women cause many men to panic when they consider the awful prospect of having a member of the opposite sex in their fishing boat or cabin. Yet these are the same biological differences which draw men toward women under different circumstances. And I, for one, say "Vive la difference!"

In later pages you will learn of many (make that hundreds) of women who have acquitted themselves with honor in the sport of angling. Fish, it seems, don't really care what gender a person is on the other end of the line when an attractive bait is presented to them at the right time, and in a tantalizing manner. But the need for skill sets in when the fish discovers his mistake and registers his displeasure by jumping, running, sounding, or heading for those rocks, logs or other obstructions which can help set him free.

Those are the skills which will come to you with experience, just as surely as they have come to those men who have preceded you in this sport. There is delicious excitement in the fight with a fish, regardless of its size. Men have thrilled over this contentiousness, this "moment of truth", from their very first exposure to a stubborn trout or all bellicose tarpon.

Winning the struggle, whether the fish is kept or not, is the true exhilaration of the game, and you can experience that same exuberance from your very first day on the water. This is the raw material from which fishing stories are crafted and garnished. It is the fire that flames your desire for more. In many ways, I have found fishing to be absolutely intoxicating; much from the thrill of the catch, but just as much in the excitement shared with my fishing partners, wherever we are.

Fishing will take you to many places where you will feel more at ease, more a woman, and more a part of the natural world. You will share in an unfettered tranquility of spirit never known before, and, perhaps best of all, you will discover the warmer, unbridled camaraderie that comes with being with friends in God's great outdoors.

All of the above represents my determination to convince you that fishing is for you, that you will enjoy it, be refreshed by it, strengthened by it, and enjoy the self-confidence which it brings. Later chapters will discuss the varieties of our most popular species...both fresh water and saltwater...plus the equipment with which to catch them, the boats and motors to take you where they are, and the people with which you will most enjoy the sport. They will not, however, relieve you of doing much of the planning for yourself.

The time has come for more women, you among them, to get out on the water and benefit by having been there. And; whether you do a lot of it, or just do a little (but talk a lot about it) you will be pleasantly-astounded by the new respect which it will bring for you among other women, and especially among the men with whom you live and work.

Our public libraries are packed with many books which probably never needed to be written, but which are still read avidly by people of all ages. This, I believe, is one book which needed to be written for the unfishing women of the World, and could conceivably be the third most important book that they will ever own, right behind the Holy Bible and the Betty Crocker Cook Book.

IT CAN HAPPEN TO YOU!

"I realized I'd created a monster. This woman, who once threatened to break every graphite rod I owned if I didn't devote a weekend to her family reunion, was a converted bass fisherman....I really can't complain. Our 17 years of marriage was rocky in the early going, due largely to a conflict between my fishing obsession and her interest in other things. It's been a lot different the past four years, since she picked up a rod. "If I had to do it over again, I would have started her many years ago. Teaching a wife to bass fish is easier than it sounds. The tactics are the same as if you're teaching a youngster or a grown man who's never held a rod. The only difference is in the reward you'll enjoy for many years to come."

-Louie Scott, GONE FISHING', March 1987

Friends often ask me why I am so hung up on fishing, and what it is about the sport that has captured my enthusiasm so completely.

"Why not bowling?" they ask. Or quilting. Or painting, or just plain old biking?

The answer is somewhat complex.

My principal reason for being so enthusiastic about fishing is that it takes me outdoors, away from the house, away from the kitchen, away from the laundry room and the unmade beds. It puts me right smack in the middle of God's great outdoors, on pleasant waters, surrounded by the magnificent beauty of cool, clear-water lakes, running streams and calm backwaters.

It makes me neighbor to waterfowl of many kinds, the noisy loon, the circling gulls, protective covies of ducks, and even the majestic bald eagle.

Fishing brings me to the community of busy beavers, solemn moose along the shoreline, watchful deer at the water's edge, and even the odd bear shepherding her cubs along the shore.

As Keith McCafferty wrote in FIELD & STREAM, "I have begun to see fishing as a restorative sport, a matter of getting out of the house, of letting my mind unwind."

And, as Erma Bombeck has told us, "Motherhood is the longest running continuous production of your life. Every day. Seven days a week." Clearly, we need something else to broaden our understanding of life, and to fulfill our days on earth.

We are all dreamers of a sort. We are confined to our homes, andor our employment, in a harsh environment that becomes the boundary of our lives. We dream of being someplace else, doing things that we are sure we would enjoy more...if we would only do them.

And fishing, I have discovered, provides a release and pleasant excitement that makes life all the more worth living. George Will, a philosopher on many aspects of life, describes it this way: "Fishing is a way of life...democratic in that it is open to all. Adequate equipment is not expensive, and the fish are broad minded."

Like president George Bush, I have fished enough to know that there is a reason that it is called fishing, rather than catching. It is more the thrill of outfoxing a scrappy bass, of feeling him on the line, and the joy of seeing him swim away to fight another day after he is released.

Heady stuff, fishing. Fun. Excitement and spiritually refreshing. But more than all of that, fishing builds a sense of competence within you. The ability to successfully participate in a sport which men have so zealously held to themselves for so many years...even centuries.

Being there in the boat, rigging your rod and reel, tying on the right bait for the right fish at the right time, casting it out with practiced precision...and then bringing your catch to the boat with all of the skill of a journeyman angler. That builds respect. Confidence. And exhibits competence in a male-dominated world where we need all of the respect we can muster.

It begins with understanding the language of fishing, speaking it glibly with other anglers (mostly male), and being dressed in the clothes which reflect a keen understanding of what a true fisherman should look like out on the water.

Going to a fishing camp or fishing with a professional guide are both challenges to which we can respond with an obvious appearance of knowing the game, how it is played, and how it is won.

All of these achievements will bring personal satisfaction a thousand times more important than having the whitest wash on the block, the best-dressed kids, or making the world's best ravioli. And, best of all, it is easy to come by...and there is no one out there who can really keep us from it.

Indeed, government figures tell us that already 15% of all American women are into fishing. That's almost ten million of us who have discovered its joys and have dared to share in its rewards in spite of the preponderance of menfolk who still believe that it was invented for them, alone.

That figure, then, ought to indicate that the time has come for you to put aside the dust mop in favor of a 5-foot, nine-inch casting rod and a quality casting reel.

Later chapters, as advertised earlier, will equip you with adequate intelligence to master the chore of properly equipping yourself for the adventure, and certainly none of it can be more complex than making the right decision on which refrigerator, washer, dryer or microwave to purchase for the household. Automobile dealers tell us that women play an active role in 80% of all new car purchases...and make the final choice in 51% of those transactions.

And if women can cope with the typical new car salesman, they will find the average tackle hustler a genuine pussy cat.

In addition to the enjoyment that fishing brings, and the establishment of competence which it conveys, there is also the unique fellowship that it affords, both with other women, and even with men, in the boat or in the cabin.

Some social scientists have tried to convince us that anglers are basically loners, that they go fishing to get away...away from other people, from the workaday problems, and even the kids. But it is a safe bet that those social scientists have never been in a fishing boat, in an outpost cabin, or even in the spartan cabin of a "bush" plane headed for a wilderness experience.

Those are the true centers of human companionship, superior in every way to an Elks Club meeting or an afternoon around a bridge table. Unlike the Elks Club hall or a card club room, a boat is a rather hard-scrabble environment, 14 to 18 feet long, and maybe six feet across at its widest point. There are no powder rooms, no lounging chairs, no telephones or handy cupboards or refrigerators loaded with snacks and endless other refreshments.

A salt water, deep-sea charter boat is another matter, and we will get to that later. But, even at an overall length of 42 feet, it generally affords a conversation pit of no greater area than the average fresh water fishing hull.

Among the few million of us ladies who love to fish, a few have even had the courage to put their thoughts into articles for those outdoor magazines that men love to read. Some of those treatises which I have read taunt the male readers with such titles as "Wake Up Guys, Women Fish, Too," "Take Your Wife Fishing...PLEASE," and even "An Open Letter To Fathers Of Daughters."

These fearless writers, with unconditional emancipation on their minds, have rubbed the noses of those male-readers in the facts of women's competence in the sport, and their capacity for sparkling good companionship. Bobby Tuomi, author of the "Wake up!! article, tells those boys that she has "discovered the existence of dyed-in-the-wool female anglers." And, further, that "They are, admittedly, scarce, but they do all the things male anglers do, and do them with style. After they catch a fish, they clean and cook them to perfection. In fact, these women aren't about to concede that there's any reason to take a male along on their fishing expeditions."

Good on you, Bobby!

Dawn Marie Horn, who wrote the "Open Letter" for ANGLER & HUNTER magazine, tells us that her husband "still insists that the only reason he married me was because I could bait my own hook, take off the fish I caught, clean that same fish and cook it." And then she adds, "Isn't that romantic?"

Romantic or not, it shows that fishing competence can lead to greater things than just week-end seminars at your local tackle store.

R.T. "Bill" Robinson, who classifies himself as a "Master Manitoba angler", has written a book called "Rather Fish Than Eat." In it, he seems to confess that there are, in fact, women anglers such as those Bobby Tuomi wrote about. "The lady anglers," he writes, "can be roughly divided into two classifications:
- The casual ones who regard the whole business as a bore, and are only fishing because of the hubby or the kids; and
- Real dyed-in-the-wool lovers of the sport"

It probably never occurred to old Bill that even that first group could perform more effectively if they had had even a modicum of encouragement and instruction from those hubbies.

Married or single, women today don't have to wait for such encouragement and instruction from their married partners or male friends.

They can just jolly well make up their mind that they are going to learn and enjoy the sport, and then put a little dedicated effort into it.

There are many fishing clubs to join, dozens of magazines and thousands of books to read on the subject, all of which are discussed in enduring detail in later pages, but there is no known or effective substitute for getting out on the water and actually <u>doing</u> it.

You can begin just as soon as you have finished reading this book, have equipped yourself properly, and selected your quarry and the waters where you will go in its pursuit. Or, you can today by asking your husband or other male acquaintance for the opportunity to go along on his next fishing excursion. As I mentioned earlier, that tactic worked for me and the results surprised both my husband and myself.

The benefits to an acquiescent husband can be both pleasant and startling, as detailed in a letter written by a Missouri housewife to the editor of FIELD & STREAM: "It's very rare to see a story about a woman who enjoys fishing, as we are most often shown as wives trying to keep their husbands on dry land. I love everything about fishing, and recently when the subject of buying a fishing boat came up, my husband said that maybe we should wait as I needed a new carpet and curtains right now."

And here's the kicker: "I told him to forget it, that if he thought I wanted to stay home all summer and look at carpeting, he was wrong. We now have a boat, motor, trailer, and trolling motor. Carpeting and curtains can wait!"

What we have witnessed here is a modern day family miracle, accomplished because the husband had taken his wife along fishing, and because she had come to enjoy it every bit as much as he does. That's a pretty good return on the investment of a little confidence in a woman who had been wiping his kids noses and washing their clothes for many years.

The husband who ignores that condition faces the prospect of an unfulfilled and contentious marriage, whether he realizes it or not. If he is a persistent, hard-riding angler who can't stay away from the water, he probably is a compulsive bait and tackle buyer, feels driven to have the finest, biggest boat and motor he can buy, and takes the whole business out every week-end. The costs of all of that indulgence have a seriously depressing effect on the family budget, and the wife soon becomes the major victim.

And wives can quickly become distressed over its apparent unfairness toward the total business of running a home. If, on the other hand, the wife is taken in as an active and voting partner on the fishing activity, the two of them will soon find a way to handle things in a more equitable manner.

Actress Meredith Baxter Birney has been quoted as saying that despite the advance of the women's movement, women still get shortchanged in matrimony. "At best," she said, "marriage is not an institution that favors women. Whether we stay at home or whether we have jobs, it remains a given even today that the kids, the house and making one's husband comfortable are all our responsibilities."

If even half of that is true in your life, it is time to seek a change. And you can do it just by going fishing!

It isn't essential that you go fishing often. It is just important that you know how, and that you pack up and go whenever the spirit moves you, and whether your partner goes with you or not.

Out on the water there is a peace that sort of surpasses all understanding, a calm that soothes the nerves, and a strengthening excitement that comes when you bring that feisty bass or pike to the boat. There is an ecstatic delight that comes from sitting around an open fire for shore lunch, or for reminiscing at the end of a day. There are awesome visions of the mysterious northern lights to tuck into your bank of memories of life, and the total wonder of the great outdoors to warm your spirit.

Days on the water come in many varieties and flavors. There are cool, breezy days that totally refresh you; there are hot, humid afternoons which challenge your staying power, and there are even rainy days that will both soak you to the skin and invigorate you thoroughly.

I can clearly remember on summer afternoon, up on a Canadian wilderness lake, when we were having an absolutely remarkable time catching plump, scrappy bass. Every time my frog entered the water, there was a lunker bass waiting to attack it.

Then the rain came. Cold and drenching, coming down in sheets. I put on my rain hat and jacket, but still the rain poured in under my collar, and soaked my entire backside, right down to my derriere.

But I kept fishing, and the bass kept obliging. Our stringer was full, and we began releasing every new catch. It was fishing such as I had never before experienced. Then I took a look at myself. Soaked to my bones, my hair hanging in heavy water-soaked strands, rain invading my boots, and menacing clouds above trying to convince me that it was time to head in. And I just kept fishing.

Then I looked at my husband and said, "If my brothers could see me now, they would think I had gone bananas!"

That's fishing!

I remember reading a letter from an Ohio wife to another outdoor magazine editor who had a similar experience. "I've been called obsessed with fishing, since there aren't many like me who would sit all day in a pouring rain trying to see how many perch they could catch. What glorious fun! We had 2 inches of water in our 12-foot boat and caught the fish so fast we just let them splash around in the bottom. And then listen to this: "I'm a fifty-two year old grandmother and could spend the rest of my days fishing for yellow perch."

Yes, that's fishing.

Izaak Walton's famous volume rewards us with some pleasant observations on the sport which put it in clear terms for those who are skeptical of its benefits:

- "Angling is an employment for idle time, which is then not idly spent, a rest to the mind, a cheerer of spirits, a diverter of sadness, a calmer of unquiet thoughts, a moderator of passions, and a procurer of contentedness."
- Doubtless God could have made a more calm, quiet, innocent recreation than angling, but doubtless He never did."
- Angling is like the virtue of humility, which has a calmness of spirit and a world of other blessings attending it."

Quite likely, however, even these endorsements won't persuade those more sophisticated women who already feel secure and satisfied in what they are doing, in their jobs and their home life. When you talk fishing to them the only visions they can call up are those of twisting, a slippery earthworm on a fishing hook, or handling an elusive, slimy fish with threatening jaws. To their credit, those are some of the true facts of angling, but not all of them.

Worms generally go with the business of going after panfish, and the handling of a slick, scrappy bass or pike obtains only when you don't have a male companion, or a guide, to remove that fish from your line. Which is the best way to solve that undetectable chore. No need to be overly concerned about that $15.00 manicure if you are clever enough to find someone else to handle that critter for you.

Those of us who have worked our way up the ladder of fishing expertise have all gone through those stages, and it hasn't hurt us a bit. The exhilaration of winning the fight with our quarry has more than compensated for the minor uneasiness which comes from those somewhat unladylike experiences.

Sigmund Freud, who is quoted as often as Betty Friedan on the drive of women to achieve personal success, is credited with this classic inquiry: "The great question that has never been answered, and which I have not yet been able to answer, despite my thirty years of research into the feminine soul, is 'what does a woman want?'"

The answer which we most often hear is that a woman wants everything that a man wants, such as status, power, money, love, marriage, happiness and fulfillment. Somewhere in that group of responses we can find the contentment and acceptance which evolves from those purifying, fascinating experiences which are a part of the sport of fishing.

Throughout these pages you will find precious, reassuring notes about individual women anglers who have achieved magnificent success at the sport, many even with world record catches, and without the help of male companions. These are all ordinary ladies, with backgrounds no different than yours and mine, and who have achieved that success because they made it their business to become competent anglers.

While you won't find my name among them, I can confidently tell you that I have accomplished my own personal triumph within my immediate family. The largest fish hanging on our household walls is a 65-pound white marlin caught years ago off the shores of Florida, and which generously outweighs the 42-pound muskie of my much more experienced husband, and the 30-pound wahoo taken by my younger son.

Do they tell their friends about it when they talk fishing with them? Not a word! But it's there, and is not likely to be outdone by father or son in the foreseeable future. My husband continues to pursue only the cantankerous muskie, and only one 65-pounder has been landed in the past 30-odd years. And, as for my son, he has finally given up the chase, and now directs his water-based outings to windsurfing.

I make no promise to you that you can accomplish similar dominance within your own family, or circle of friends, but that doesn't mean that it can't happen to you. Consider Sandy DeFresco of southern California, who recently caught a 21-pound, 12-ounce bass In Lake Miramar, only 10 ounces short of the world's record for that species. Sandy might have been a candidate for large sums from tackle

There's 21 pounds, 9 ounces of bass hanging from Sandy DeFresco's wrist, caught in Miramar Lake near San Diego, California, on March 14, 1988. The weight was documented on a certified scale and Sandy was on her way to National Glory. But then a male taxidermist discovered a 2 1/2-pound skin diver's weight in its belly. From there on, everything went down hill. The boys who keep the record books told her, "No way, Sandy. You've got a 19-pound, 1-ounce bass, and that's all." Sic transit gloria Sandy!

endorsements, magazine and television deals. But when the taxidermist and a state biologist (both men) opened up the fish they discovered a large skin diver's weight in its belly. But they still gave her credit for a 19-pound, 1-ounce bass, a true lunker in anybody's record book.

This book won't tell you how to catch 19-pound bass, or 800-pound sharks, but it will acquaint you with much of the mechanics, the language, and the gear associated with those kinds of catches. By leaving the discrete details for you to discover, I hope to motivate you to talk with the experts and amateurs alike, to the tackle dealers, the guides, and the charter boat captains to broaden your understanding, and heighten your desire to make your time on the water an enriching part of your life.

FISH THAT FOSTER
FISH STORIES

"If one has to die, I should think November would be the best month for it. It is a gray, stormy month: the salmon are dying, and the year is done. I should think there is nothing very bad about dying except for the people one has to leave and the things one hasn't had time to do. When the time comes, if I know what it's all about, I suppose I shall think, among other things, of the fish I haven't caught and the places I haven't fished. I shall, of course, do my best to meet such regrets ahead of time and I keep in my mind, as I suppose most fishermen do, an often-changing list of the places I should like to fish and of the fish I should like to catch."

-Roderick L. Haig-Brown,
"A RIVER NEVER SLEEPS"

It has never seemed terribly important for me to know exactly how many species of fish there-are out there in our lakes, rivers, streams, reservoirs...and even oceans. McCLANE'S STANDARD FISHING ENCYCLOPEDIA goes on for over one thousand pages, most of them listing nothing but the various kinds of fish that anglers around the world have found exciting enough to chase after.

The National Fresh Water Fishing Hall Of Fame annual book of record catches carries reports on over 125 species which are found in the waters of North America alone. The International Game Fish Association's yearly volume of "World Record Game Fishes" details another 86 species which are peculiar to saltwater and are native to the oceans of the world.

From the Hall Of Fame annual you will learn that there are fish within the waters of the United States which travel under such names as amur, carpsucker, inconnu, mooneye and burbot. The I.G.F.A. record book lists such strange names as horse eye jack, kawakawa, dogtooth tuna, Pacific dog snapper, tautog and even little tunny. While they all sound odd to me, there are anglers in our midst who have sought them out and have their names on the world's records for each of them. But the anglers of our fifty states focus their attention most heavily on an assortment of some fifteen species which generally have three

19

important characteristics which make them so attractive:

1 - They are generally available in nearby waters,
2 - They offer the angler a scrappy fishing experience, and
3 - If kept, they make tasty meals.

In alphabetical order, here are those fifteen:

Black Crappie	Coho Salmon	Rainbow Trout
Bluegill	Flathead Catfish	Smallmouth Bass
Brown Trout	Largemouth Bass	Striped Bass
Channel Catfish	Muskellunge	Walleye
Chinook Salmon	Northern Pike	Yellow Perch

If you have had any social intercourse with the anglers of your community or workplace some of these names will be readily familiar to you. It's almost impossible today to escape knowing a cadre of bass enthusiasts, or walleye followers. Your earliest fishing expeditions will quite likely be heavily influenced by those close to you who have already come to enjoy the sport of angling and who will want to assist in your baptism into their particular choice of quarry.

The state in which you live will also have a major influence on the species on which you set your sights for your initial adventures. By writing to the Department of Natural Resources or Division of Wildlife for your state (see "Marge's Handy Household Shopping Guide For Fishing Adventures" at the back of the book) you'll receive complete information on those fish broadly available in your area, how many you are permitted to catch and keep, and perhaps a few hints on how to go after them.

To save you some time (in respect to the fifteen most popular species which are detailed in chapters 14 through 18) you will find a comprehensive table for all of them, listing the states within which they are to be had, included in this chapter. A quick review of those pages will reveal that the largemouth and smallmouth bass lead most other species in availability, and can be caught almost everywhere.

Panfish (bluegill, black crappie and yellow perch) are second in distribution, and are found in all but a very few states. Surprisingly, rainbow trout are also now found in 44 of our states, and browns are reported in 41. The popular walleye and the sleek northern pike attract anglers in at least 40 states.

Channel catfish might not appeal to you during your early days of

CURRENT RECORD CATCHES, BY STATE, OF FIFTEEN POPULAR FRESHWATER SPECIES

	Largemouth Bass	Smallmouth Bass	Striped Bass	Bluegill (Sunfish)	Channel Catfish	Flathead Catfish	Black Crappie	Northern Pike	Muskie	Yellow Perch	Brown Trout	Rainbow Trout	Walleye	Chinook Salmon	Coho Salmon
Alabama	16-8	10-8	55-0	4-12	40-0	80-0	4-4	—	19-8	1-11	—	7-2	10-14	—	—
Alaska	—	—	—	—	—	—	—	38-8	—	—	—	—	—	97-4	26-0
Arizona	15-14	7-9	59-12	3-5	35-4	65-0	4-10	24-3	—	1-10	17-0	21-5	12-12	—	—
Arkansas	16-4	7-5	53-0	2-1	38-0	80-0	4-9	16-1	13-13T	—	40-4	19-1	22-11	—	—
California	21-12	9-1	66-0	3-8	48-8	55-0	4-1*	—	—	—	26-8	27-4	—	88-0	22-0
Colorado	10-6*	5-8*	12-13	2-4	33-4	—	3-4	30-1	27-3T	2-5	30-8	18-5	16-8	11-0	—
Connecticut	12-14	7-12	75-6	2-2	17-3	—	—	29-0	—	2-13	16-14	12-4	14-8	—	—
Delaware	12-5	4-15	—	2-0	18-0	—	4-9	—	—	2-11	—	—	—	—	—
Florida	20-2	—	38-9	2-15	44-8	25-7	3-12	—	—	—	—	—	—	—	—
Georgia	22-4	7-2	63-0	3-5	44-12	53-0	4-4*	18-2	38-0	2-8	18-2	15-0	11-0	—	—
Hawaii	8-0	3-11	—	0-8	43-13	—	—	—	—	—	—	5-10	—	—	—
Idaho	10-15*	7-5	—	3-8	31-0*	36-4	2-8*	34-4	—	2-9	26-6	19-0	15-9	42-0*	5-6
Illinois	13-1	6-7	31-0	3-8	45-4	64-0	4-8	26-15	28-12	2-8	28-8	24-13*	14-0	37-0*	20-0
Indiana	14-12*	6-15	26-0	3-4	37-8	79-8	4-9*	28-14	30-0	2-8	22-8	18-8	14-4	38-0	20-12
Iowa	10-12*	7-12	—	3-2	31-0	64-13	4-9	25-5	40-5	1-15	15-4	19-8	14-8	—	—
Kansas	11-12	5-5	43-8	2-5	33-12	87-8	4-10*	24-12*	—	0-12	—	9-5	13-1	—	—
Kentucky	13-10	11-15	20-8	4-3	22-5	97-0	4-3	9-8	43-0	—	18-8	14-6	21-8	—	—
Louisiana	13-6*	—	44-8	2-8	—	98-0	6-0	—	—	—	—	—	—	—	—
Maine	11-10	8-0	—	—	—	—	3-4	26-12	22-12	1-10	19-7	—	—	—	—
Maryland	11-2	8-4	—	3-0	27-0	—	4-4	22-13	20-0	2-6	11-9	14-13	11-4	—	—
Massachusetts	15-8	8-2*	—	2-1	26-8*	—	4-10	35-0	19-4T	2-12	19-10*	13-0	11-0	—	—
Michigan	11-9	9-2	—	2-7	40-0	47-5	4-12	39-0	62-5	3-7	34-3	26-5	17-2	46-0	30-5
Minnesota	8-9	8-0	—	2-13	38-0	70-0	5-0	45-12	54-0	3-4	16-12	6-6	17-8	33-4	10-6
Mississippi	14-15	7-15	33-8	2-5	45-8	65-0	4-4	—	—	—	—	—	9-10	—	—
Missouri	13-14	7-0	51-0	3-0	34-10	66-0	4-8	18-9	41-2	1-0	23-4	16-1	21-0	—	—

The numbers within each box indicate the weight of the current state record catch for each species. Thus 22-4 indicates 22 pounds, 4 ounces. A "T" indicates a tiger muskie catch (also known at "hybrid").

CURRENT RECORD CATCHES, BY STATE, OF FIFTEEN POPULAR FRESHWATER SPECIES

	Largemouth Bass	Smallmouth Bass	Striped Bass	Bluegill (Sunfish)	Channel Catfish	Flathead Catfish	Black Crappie	Northern Pike	Muskie	Yellow Perch	Brown Trout	Rainbow Trout	Walleye	Chinook Salmon	Coho Salmon
Montana	8-2*	6-0	—	2-6	25-8	—	3-2	37-8	11-1T	2-3	29-0	29-0	14-14	31-2	4-14
Nebraska	10-11	6-1	44-10	2-13	41-8	80-0	4-2	29-12	35-8	2-10	20-1	14-2	16-12	2-8	5-12
Nevada	11-0	4-11*	53-2	—	31-1	—	3-2	27-0	—	1-8	27-5	16-4	14-11	—	—
New Hampshire	10-8	7-14*	—	1-5	—	—	2-8	20-9	11-11T	2-6	16-6	14-3	12-8	—	—
New Jersey	10-14	7-2*	27-12	3-0	33-3	—	3-8	30-2	38-4*	4-4	18-5	13-0	12-13	—	—
New Mexico	12-7	6-8	54-0*	3-1	29-8	78-0	4-9	36-0	—	—	20-4*	16-0	16-9	—	4-6
New York	11-4	—	—	2-4	28-0	—	3-9	46-2	69-15	3-8	30-5	26-15	15-3*	47-13	33-4
North Carolina	15-14	10-2	54-2	4-5	40-8	62-7	4-15	11-13	38-0	2-9*	15-13	16-5	13-8	—	—
North Dakota	8-7	5-1*	18-0	2-12	33-4	29-6	3-1	37-8	26-5	2-15	15-12	25-4	20-7	31-2	10-2
Ohio	12-2	7-8	35-2	3-4	30-0	76-8	4-8	22-6	55-2	2-12	14-2	7-9	15-2	20-7	13-10
Oklahoma	13-8	6-14	46-8	2-6	30-0	70-14	4-10	36-8	—	—	—	10-4	11-4	—	—
Oregon	11-7	6-14	64-8	2-5	36-8	41-0	4-0	—	—	2-2	35-8	28-0	19-15	83-0	25-5
Pennsylvania	11-3	7-10	53-13	2-9	35-2	43-9	4-1	33-8	54-3	2-6	17-0	15-6	17-9	38-15	15-5
Rhode Island	10-6	5-15	70-0	2-1	—	—	3-0	35-0	—	2-4	7-5	11-0	—	—	—
South Carolina	16-2	6-12	55-0	3-4	58-0	74-0	5-0	—	—	3-4	17-9	9-6	9-3	—	—
South Dakota	8-14*	5-9	—	3-4	55-0	54-0	3-4	35-0	40-0	2-6	24-8	19-4	15-3	20-3	3-5*
Tennessee	14-8	11-15	60-8	3-0*	41-0	65-8	4-4	20-12	42-8	1-12	28-12	14-8	25-0	—	—
Texas	17-6	7-7	45-0	3-2*	36-5*	98-0	3-6	18-2	—	—	7-1	6-2	11-8	—	—
Utah	10-2	6-12	48-11	2-3	32-5	—	2-11	22-0	—	2-11	33-0	26-2	15-9	—	—
Vermont	10-4	6-12	—	1-0	32-4	—	1-13	30-8	29-8	2-2	22-3	15-4	12-8	—	—
Virginia	16-4	7-7	42-6	(4-12)	28-12	56-0	4-3	27-12	45-0	2-2	14-12	12-9	12-15	—	—
Washington	11-9	8-12	—	2-5	32-8	—	4-8	18-6	7-2T	2-12	22-0	22-8	18-7	—	—
West Virginia	10-8	9-7	21-0	2-7	27-13	70-0	4-0	22-0	43-0	1-8	16-0	11-5	17-2	—	—
Wisconsin	11-3	9-1	—	2-6	44-0	65-0	3-6	38-0	69-11	3-4	32-8	24-4	18-0	43-3	24-6*
Wyoming	7-2	4-12	—	1-4	23-1	—	2-3	23-1	28-1T	2-2	25-13	23-0	15-5	—	—

This is the second group of 25 states. All data has been supplied by the Fresh Water Fishing Hall Of Fame through its annual record book published in 1992, with the exception of three catches which were made in 1992.

angling, but they are in abundant supply in 46 states, and in three of those the state record catch was made by a woman. Flathead catfish (which grow even bigger that the channels cats) turn up in just 32 states, most of them in the South, and record catches run near the 100-pound mark.

Striped bass, the largest variety of that family, are found in 31 states, which is the same number as for muskellunge (more commonly known as "muskie"), the fighting king of the pike family.

Finally, thanks to the great work of many Great Lakes area fisheries scientists, the United States angling resource for coho and chinook salmon reaches into 19 and 17 states. Twenty years ago these species were found in a much smaller region and their fishing was enjoyed by only a very limited number of American fishermen and women.

As I assembled these tables I was especially impressed by how lucky we are to have such bountiful waters in every state of the Union. Five states; Illinois, Indiana, North Dakota, Ohio and Pennsylvania, offer all fifteen of these fish . And when I counted the total number of species available in all states I was surprised to find that South Dakota has a total of sixty! Minnesota, Tennessee, Missouri, Michigan, Nebraska and Wisconsin all have over fifty!

That ought to convince you that excellent fishing is close at hand, wherever you make your home. More than that, you could well be the next record holder for northern pike, walleye or rainbow trout in your state.

The asterisk (*) marks appearing at the right of thirty-eight of those individual weight records indicate that those were recorded by women anglers, Jennifer Schultz, for example, holds the largemouth bass record for Indiana with a 14-pound, 12 ounce catch; Gloria Eonatti is the Iowa walleye record-holder with her 14-pound, 8-ounce fish, Diane Zilian takes top Wisconsin honors for coho salmon with a 24-pound, 6-ounce catch. Mrs. Joe L. Cockrell has also proved that catfish in large sizes can be caught by women, and holds the Texas record with her 36-pound, 5-ounce monster.

All of these numbers should help convince you that fishing is for women, too. The U. S. Department of Interior in 1988 released its "National Survey Of Fishing, Hunting, and Wildlife Associated Recreation" to help identify trends in participation in outdoor sports, as well as expenditures made in the enjoyment of those activities. According to their figures nearly 20 million Americans are "hard-core" serious anglers, which means that they fish an average of 21 days per year. Those who get out on the water only 5 to 9 days each year are termed "occasional" anglers, and those who fish less often are "infrequent" followers of the sport.

Fresh water fishing is the first choice of 70% of those of us who fish, it tells us. But saltwater angling ranks more Number One with another 14 per cent, and we will get into that later in this chapter and again in chapter nineteen.

Independent of the numbers related to distribution of the various species throughout the states, tackle manufacturers, the hospitality industry, marina operators, boat and motor marketers and outdoor magazine publishers have a need to know just which fish we are most interested in (and willing to spend money to pursue). IN-FISHER-MAN magazine, which is rapidly becoming a major concordance of the whole fresh water fishing business, has published the results of a survey conducted among its readers on their fishing preferences. The final numbers surprised them, as they did many industry suppliers.

The figures will be useful to you as you contemplate your own entrance to the sport since they will tell you just what kinds of fish are getting the top attention of your friends, neighbors, your husband, or your significant other. Here is how they came out:

1 - Largemouth bass	75%	7 - Catfish	37%
2 - Walleye	67%	8 - Lake trout	21%
3 - Crappie	67%	9 - Stream trout	21%
4 - Smallmouth bass	64%	10 - Salmon	19%
5 - Other panfish	60%	11 - Muskie	18%
6 - Northern pike	51%	12 - Rainbow	
		(steelhead) trout	12%

This list has one major difference with the tables presented in this chapter in that it includes lake trout. I have omitted that species from my own list of the fifteen "most popular" fresh water fish because of the limited number of states in which it is found in large numbers, plus my own perception that it is sought more for food than the excitement of the catch.

All that aside, both tabulations identify those fish which will provide the most entertaining action for you when you get out on the water...any water...and join the ranks of us who have already come to enjoy this sport.

Many women have a vision of fishing as something that elderly grandmothers do with a cane pole, whiling away the time on the bank of a quiet stream. This may have been true half a century ago, but not today. FISHING TACKLE TRADE NEWS estimates that 60% of today's anglers are between the ages of 18 and 34, and only 40% of those fishing now are over 35. Whatever your age is, you will find many pleasant companions who have reached the same point in life, right up through your retirement years.

One industry publication, promoting the need to get children interested in fishing, recently forecast that individuals who are not happily exposed to fishing before the age of 18 will be unlikely to take up the sport later. That prediction might well apply for boys, but how many fathers have ever taken a young daughter on a fishing trip? Boys (if well-mannered) are often accepted for participation in an all-male fishing expedition, but girls just wouldn't fit in, would they?

For that reason, alone, most women have their first exposure to fishing when they are invited by a husband, other friendly relative, or a male suitor testing her staying power. Others have their first angling experience after having joined a local fishing club which has a substantial number of women members. However many years you have been waiting for an invitation to get into the sport, the time to do something about it is right now.

After digesting the full contents of this primer you will be well-prepared for that first adventure. But as in cake baking, it is better to start on something humble like a chocolate sponge variety before attempting a delicate angel food. Which translates to say that a modest foray after some type of panfish can provide an adequate learning experience before getting into the chase of a lunker smallmouth bass. Linda England, recognized as a high-level fishing authority, has stated that "fishing on small waters is a good idea as a woman is being introduced to fishing....She needs to have something pulling on the other end of the line, even if it is only a bluegill or crappie."

The total fishing experience can be understood and effectively joined in only after you have been there, observed the deportment of your companions in the excitement of a sizable catch, and listened to the language which goes with success, confusion, and despair. Sportsfishing is unlike anything you have attempted before, but learning comes easy if you have the spirit. And those words apply to saltwater (or ocean) fishing as well that done on our inland waters.

Very little is written about offshore fishing in our outdoor journals in spite of the fact that 30% of all anglers actively participate in it. Many of those, as the record books attest, are women, just like you and me. They come from the 18 states which border on the Atlantic and Pacific oceans, the Gulf of Mexico...or sit out there in the middle of the Pacific, as Hawaii does.

The women of those states have the same zeal for the fish they go after as their sisters who go after bass, pike, panfish or trout in their fresh water lakes and rivers. They enjoy the tussle with a husky bluefish, a scrappy dolphin, the tough wahoo or grouper, and even a variety of marlin and sharks. In total, these coastal waters ladies have their names on over 200 records for 55 species.

These are fish that you will delight in just as much as those women do, once you have had them on your line. The 56-pound, 12-ounce dolphin landed by Rita L. Pierce in Florida's Gulf Stream is one that you could handle, too, and which would provide a glistening memory for the rest of your life. Gale E. Cozzens of Virginia holds a line-class record for the 25-pound, 4-ounce bluefish she captured off Chesapeake Bay in 1986, but you are capable of handling an equal challenge, once you put your mind to it.

Charlene Mascuch of New Jersey and Erin M. Burks of Louisiana both hold I.G.F.A. records for wahoo catches of over 100 pounds, which is a lot of fighting fish. Yet there are many more of those scrappers out there just waiting to test your skill when you slip into the fighting chair on your charter boat.

It may be difficult for you to believe that there are also women anglers who get their kicks from fishing for sharks, but there are legions of them, most of them in boats patrolling the waters off the coasts of New York, Florida and California. They have their names on records for porbeagle sharks, mako sharks and even thresher sharks.

Audrey Cohen's 911-pound, 12-ounce mako shark taken off Palm Beach, Florida, taken on a charter boat in April of 1962 is the largest shark catch that I can find credited to an American woman angler. Elsewhere around the world many larger ones have been caught by women from such faraway places as Australia and New Zealand. But you could become the talk of your P.T.A. just by bringing home a harrowing, unembellished story of a hammerhead shark catch off the beach of Boca Grande, Florida. Connie L. Cora did it in 1986...and the monster tipped the scales at 750 pounds!

So there you have it. Small fish, feisty lunkers and real monsters of the deep, all being caught by those women who have already found their way into the sport of fishing, and who are having the times of their lives lasting them out, bringing them to boatside, and registering indelible memories.

In the next chapter we will chat about why you should become one of them and what it can do for your self-confidence, your joy of living each day...and your status within the household.

TOO LITTLE TIME...
TOO MUCH STRESS

"Americans are starved for time. Increasing numbers of people are finding themselves overworked, stressed out and heavily taxed by the joint demands of work and family life......Full-time workers put in, on average, 138 more hours a year in 1989 than they did in 1969......And women took on a bigger work burden by working a greater fraction of the year."

-Juliet Schor and Laura Leete-Guy, Case Western University.
"THE OVERWORKED AMERICAN:
THE UNEXPECTED DECLINE OF LEISURE." 1992.

If the foregoing passage does nothing else, it should persuade you that:

A-Women need to go fishing.

B-Women deserve to go fishing.

And, when I speak of fishing, I rush to clearly detail just what fishing is all about.

"Fishing" is not just the fish described in the previous chapter. It is about adventure, about getting away from the kitchen, the laundry room, the vacuum cleaner, the P.T.A., the job, the bills and the neighbors. And everything else that crowds our every day at home, or at work.

Valerie Cravens, one of the few female writers to be published on the pages of SPORTS AFIELD, wrote an essay entitled "The Silent Society which appeared in the October, 1991, issue of that publication. Fishing, she writes, "is dependability. Not necessarily comfort, it is warmth. It's the glow of having a passion to grow old with, alone or with friends who share that passion. It is the fulfillment of having something to care about, to protect. Fishing. Having an interest and learning not to be compelled to perfect it, but to accept and appreciate and age with it.

There is no sense of disappointment or longing when I realize that the outdoor world is still not a fully integrated one. The pain of discrimination is felt only by those who don't understand nature's ability to transcend divisions of gender. Fortunately, I have found my unprejudiced musty. I can feel it while I am on the water: on perfect days with crisp, untainted air, and when I am miserable and wet in foul weather, lips blue and boots soggy. But better perhaps, I feel it when I need a soothing image to clear my mind of insurmountable problems."

My own personal dreamful reverie of the fishing experience is somewhat more annotated. "Fishing" (the fishing trip) begins the moment that the door is shut behind me. It includes the expectant travel along forested roads, necessary stops at small town diners where lumberjack breakfasts and fresh-from-the-oven baked goods are waiting, inquiring conversation with the "locals", a visit to a tackle shop where cascading displays of kaleidoscopic baits of every description and mechanical construction tempt me, the funky clothes, the high spirits, free-swinging conversation, a continuing sense of escape and "awayness" which continues for every mile along the way, some times a final leg on a well-worn bush plane, and finally arrival at our destination: the base from which we shall do our fishing...on our own time, and only as long as we care to.

The fish, you see, come only at the end, and are not the total element of the escape.

Fishing in Canada is an experience that many American anglers will spend heavily to enjoy every summer. Legendary fish of the fightingest fresh water species inhabit the countless lakes and rivers which cover half of the Dominion's surface, and the fabled Indian guides add to the aura of such an expedition. Yet, in the most recent "Survey Of Sportsfishing In Canada" conducted by the Canadian Department Of Fisheries And Oceans, anglers reported that the top factor influencing the gratification of such an experience was their enjoyment of the environment.

Kim Chadwick, a woman reader of ANGLER & HUNTER magazine, wrote in a letter to the editor that "There is nothing more beautiful than going out onto the lake, listening to the birds, hoping to see a glimpse of any wildlife, listening to the loons at the end of the day and being serenaded by bullfrogs at night. The food tastes better over a fire, the fresh air helps you sleep better and I get a great tan sitting in the boat. How can anyone say this is only for men?...Ladies, leave the makeup and curling iron at home. Get a good pair of jeans, a warm sweatshirt. Plan to get a little dirty but, most of all, have a great time!"

Hyatt Hotels Corporation recently conducted a study entitled "Time Off: The Psychology Of Vacations." Darryl Harley-Leonard, Hyatt president, stated that "Vacations have taken on increased priority in today's stressed-out society." And the results of their survey showed that 92% of those interviewed reported that vacations help avoid burnout, and 86% believe that vacations "recharge you psychologically," while 79% said that vacations "improve your outlook on life." And that goes double for a fishing vacation.

Charles Bradford, writing about "Trout Truths" in "The Armchair Angler", tells us that "The desire for fishing is like some diseases, in attacking a man with great severity without notice. It can be no more resisted than falling in love can be resisted, and, like love, the best treatment is its gratification."

And here's a bit of philosophy from a woman, Gladys Taber: "The curious thing about fishing is you never want to go home. If you catch something, you can't stop. If you don't catch anything, you hate to leave in case something might bite."

The common thread which runs through all of these references is that fishing can, indeed, bring a new level of enjoyment into your existence. Do you need it? Of course you do. A recent edition of the Mayo Clinic "Health Letter" reports that one major key to relieving anxiety is to "do something you enjoy...a pleasant activity will help relax you." Fishing fits that prescription perfectly.

I personally know of no woman who has dropped out of fishing because it failed to fulfill her expectations. Rather, it is the broad spectrum of angling opportunities that heightens your interest from year to year. There are more varieties of fish to go after ("more fish to fry"), and in more challenging waters, making new friends everywhere.

No wonder a national poll commissioned by SPORTS ILLUS-TRATED reports that Americans are almost as interested in fishing as they are in professional football and baseball. Fishing ranks third overall at 43%, and ahead of college football. And a survey conducted by the National Sporting Goods Association reports that freshwater fishing is the third most favored sport among people 55 and older, led only by exercise walking and swimming .

Those figures, you must remember, are taken at a time when only

15% of American women are into fishing. When the rest of you join us, fishing can well become Number One, and we will all be enjoying life more, having more fun, and caring less about the tangled fabric of today's living. Our lives will be less messed up, many marriage counselors will be looking for work, and those high-flying family psychologists will begin to wonder what happened to all of our unhappiness.

The Gallup poll of 1988 which reported that only 44% of women were satisfied with their lives will quickly be outdated. Consider that we make 72% of all supermarket purchases, purchase 47% of all cars, own more than 28% of all U.S. small businesses, occupy over 18,000 elected offices in the country, live 7.8 years longer than our male counterparts, fill 69% of the teaching positions in our schools, tend 93% of the teller counters at our nation's banks, occupy 29 seats in Congress, 2 in the Senate, sit on the boards of many Fortune 500 companies, serve with the Army, Navy and Marine Corps, and still make all the beds, wash the dishes, do the laundry and keep a reasonably clean house for our husbands and kids to return to ruins every week.

That we can get out on the water, share the fishing camps, enjoy the same shore lunches, bait our own hooks, catch and release our own fish is a genuine given. We win more Olympic medals than men, drink less booze, tell fewer lies, cause fewer automobile accidents, work harder to keep our families together and lose our cool a lot less often.

While my principal thesis is that more women don't get into fishing is because they aren't being asked, there are many who will retain-a firm conviction that the sport really isn't for them. Their adopted life style is so orderly and satisfying that they can't picture themselves in a pick-up truck charging away to a remote lake alongside an unshaven husband in stained trousers and a shirt which should have been in the laundry three months ago.

Materialism has driven many of us into a pattern of living which dominates most of the decisions related to what we do with every hour of our lives. A survey conducted in 1991 by the Massachusetts Mutual Life Insurance Company reported that two-thirds of those interviewed were "very" or "extremely" satisfied with their lives. But an almost equal number said that across the country "family values have grown weaker."

Susan Schwartz, writing for the Santa Rosa, California, DEMO-CRAT tells us that "Trendists, for some time, have been predicting the end of materialism and a return to family values." And Mary Ann Limauro of the NEW YORK TIMES' adds that "Couples are now working a lot harder to save their relationships."

Can fishing help save family relationships? Sure it can. Just give it a chance. It's sort of like what my friend Phyllis told me: "Fishing is a good deal like sex. The first time is not so enjoyable because you are so filled with expectation and anticipation. But once you get over that, it adds spark to your life...and is a whole lot more fun than Canasta."

There is an intoxication in being in God's great outdoors which sneaks up on you, and gives you a great new feeling of being a player in nature's way of things. Anthony Acerrano, one of the fishing editors for SPORTS AFIELD, conveys all of this in his story of a visit to a favorite fishing spot. "I needed to get away. I needed it desperately," he wrote. "As soon as entered the stream's narrow little valley, a verdant, mountain-rimmed span of sweet water and fluttering cotton-woods, I felt the tension begin to ease and dissipate. This was more like it. The early-evening sun was low and its light was generous to all that it touched. The thick firs were as dense and textured as velvet, and along the water it seemed that each cottonwood leaf twinkled, every vesicle and serration calling for attention."

That's where we need to be more often. Away from the classic suburb, "an agglomeration of houses, shops and offices connected to one another by cars...not the fabric of human life," as described by Elizabeth Plater-Zyberk in the WILSON QUARTERLY. Men like Accerano understand that, and so does Nick Lyons, one of the foremost chroniclers of the sport. In an article entitled "The Family That Fishes Together" written for FIELD & STREAM Nick talks of a family visit to a cabin on Maine's Great Pond. "All the way upcountry I dreamed of us all together...me, my wife, and our four children...catching huge smallmouth bass. It would be a kind of wholesale baptism: at last we could share my deepest love together...As we were settling in, I saw a flight of wood ducks cleave the light blue, cloudless sky. Then I heard the loon call from somewhere back in the pine forest."

Many of the millions of women who do fish today have experienced the same type of pleasure, but we rarely see anything written by them about it. Tom Paugh, editor in chief of SPORTS AFIELD tells me this is the result of so few of us taking the time to put our thoughts together, and in a form which meets the editorial standards of magazines such as his. "We do have to go looking for them and they are hard to come by," he says.

In a nation of over 253 million people, some 30 million of us paid $260,000,000 on fishing licenses last year, but men were by far the biggest benefactors of that expenditure. Yet the cost of a license, as low as $8 to $15 in many states, is no reason to deny yourself the joy of a fishing experience. There are other costs, too, as we shall examine in additional chapters, but the total cost is relatively small compared to the expenses of such community-centered activities as golf, bowling or even aerobics exercising, none of which get you out where you can refresh your soul and drink in the natural beauty which is so close at hand.

And, as Kathryn Zuckerman of Cambridge, Massachusetts, wrote to the editors of FIELD & STREAM, there are the traits "of kindness and communicating, teaching and patience, traits that those who fish appear to have in greater abundance then the average commuter or basketball player."

I began this chapter reviewing the stress that crowds our lives. and I hope that these warm, vivid remembrances of so many others who have come to know the release of fishing will persuade you to become part of it. And to remember that fishing is not just fish alone, but represents the complete sensation of living in and with nature. Perhaps Henry David Thoreau, the great nineteenth century naturalist, said it better than anyone in his highly-praised work, "Walden: or, Life In The Woods," published in 1854: "Many a man goes fishing all his life without realizing that it is not the fish that he is after."

Now that I have burdened you with all of this philosophy, let's move on to a subject that every woman can relate to: clothes, and how they identify you as a true angler.

OF COURSE, YOU DRESS FOR FISHING!

"Clothing makes a statement about who and what a person is. People just like clothing that shows they are on the water a lot or that they are engaged in some sport."
-FISHING TRADE TACKLE NEWS, July, 1990.

For most of us women, the enjoyment of any activity is often measured by the way in which we can dress for it. We want to look good. Some of us feel we need to look good. And clothes are what it is all about.

Clothes may not make the man, but for a woman they can be the true nirvana...the supreme spirit. We anguish over our wardrobes. We build them to match what we consider to be our special life style. We pack them with everything imaginable...and then we sort them out, and sometimes completely demolish them as we see a new image in our mental mirror.

We intuitively know that every costume we affect, every ensemble, makes a "statement." A statement of what we are, or want to be perceived as being. Some statements which we dress to affirm include:

1 - "I am into fitness."
2 - "I am an executive."
3 - "I love dining out."
4 - "Rock music is my thing."
5 - "I do all of the important work around here."
6 - "As long as I am driving a Harley, I might as well look the part."
7 - "I really care for you."
8 - "I am the teacher here, and I deserve your respect."
9 - "My body has some neat geography, and I thought that you ought to notice it."
10 - "I'm collecting for the Red Cross, and you can trust me."
11 - "I am at this meeting to help shape the decisions."
12 - "No, I am not pregnant, and it's none of your business."
13 - "Yes, I am pregnant, and I am married."
14 - "I really enjoy taking care of these kids."
15 - "I dress like this because I want to, and I really don't care how

you feel about it."

And this is a great time for clothes-conscious women to be alive. Designers are giving us more colors, more styles and more fabrics than ever to choose from. And, whatever our size, there always seems to be a style which makes us look just like the person we imagine ourselves to be.

Dressing for fishing is a stimulating new experience because of the fun styles, the relaxed fit, and the adventurous range of fabrics and colors which are not in the ordinary mix of clothes worn by today's businesswoman or homemaker. And it's not all just because they lean heavily toward men's styles, but because so many manufacturers have long sensed our need (and want) to escape into another world more full of freedom and self-expression than afforded by our everyday outfits.

L. L. Bean, the great Maine mail-order merchandiser, was probably the first to perceive the need, and the opportunity. From a modest program of selling a limited selection of specialized outdoor clothing for sportsmen, Bean has now become a multimillion-dollar enterprise which regularly tempts men and women alike with a continuing series of catalogues throughout. You can order their "Spring Home & Camp", "Spring Women's", "Spring Sporting", "Fly Fishing", "Holiday Preview", "Christmas", or just plain "Spring" catalogue by just calling their toll-free telephone number (1-800-221-4221).

Each volume presents over a hundred of pages of clothing items which you will rarely find down at your neighborhood mega-mall. Where else can you order a "barn jacket", "ridge trail pants", "Penobscot shorts", "windy ridge jackets", Wicked Good slippers", or "wildberry turtlenecks"?

Colors, patterns, styles and fits that you have never experienced before jump out of almost every page. And they are rich in pockets where you always wanted them, but couldn't find them in the clothes offered by your local retailers.. And, if you don't like what you see when you open the box, you can pack it right up and ship it back. But you probably won't.

Other mail order purveyors have now jumped on the bandwagon, and companies like Gander Mountain (1-800-558-9410), Cabela's (1-800-237-4444), Bass Pro Shops (1-800-227-7776), and even Orvis (1-800-548-9548) have colorful catalogues which will brighten your

35

evenings as you page through them, discovering new-ways to send your bank account into overdrive...but also to brighten your life.

And to properly equip you for your new role as a woman angler.

What do you want to shop for? Well, first of all you need to recall that there are at least two facets to the business of fishing. One of these involves the hours which you actually spend on the water, on a fishing pier, or at streamside. Those hours call for the wardrobe elements which will withstand heavy wear, some soiling, and generally informal packing in duffle bags...plus protect you from the elements of rain, heavy sun, chilling cold and slippery fish which may intrude on your person.

Then there are the "other" hours of the fishing experience; those "social" hours when you are travelling with other anglers, meeting with them at local fishing clubs, or swapping tales with them in front of the fireplace at a comfortable resort or a spartan wilderness lodge. And you can include in this category your visits to the local tackle shop where you will want to become known, and taken for a knowledgeable practitioner, of the sport.

In either case, house dresses are out, as are exercise pants and "business" outfits. You will want comfortable cotton blouses and shirts, light on the decoration, but heavy on comfort and utility. Pants (slacks) that fit without binding, plenty of hip and thigh room. Plenty of pockets, cotton or chino for good leg protection, supple, not stubborn to movement. Choose an elastic waist, if you prefer...but select those with belt loops because you will certainly be hanging something from a belt when you get into full field uniform.

Catalogue shopping for shoes will be a special treat. Today's outfitters offer some of the funkiest footwear ever worn by mankind. From the classic leather camping moccasin through a whole gamut of leather-and-rubber and leather-and woven-nylon, you can pick some of the most comfortable and at the same time, dramatic shoes the world has ever witnessed. They offer a wholesome escape from the crowded field of those me-too exercise shoes which seem to get more bulky and clumsy with every new version.

While your new environment may not seem to call for the "dressing for success" that dominates so much of our lives, you are still dressing for acceptance, recognition and respect. And in a somewhat indifferent or hostile environment of males who may take a little time to appreciate your presence. But if what you have selected makes you feel good all over, you will fit right in, and, when you acquire a thorough grasp of their language, you may even be accepted as "one of the boys."

There is, however, one other element of your ultimate outfit which also needs to be discussed here. The fishing vest.

The fishing vest, if you accept tradition, is the corporate property of only those who fish with flies ("fly fishermen", "fly fisher women"), for it was conceived by such an angler, and has been seized upon by countless thousands of his followers over the past forty years or so. But how it came into being is not sufficiently important for us to be spending any time on its history in these pages.

Fly fishing folks <u>needed</u> the vest, and so it was born. They needed it because most of them do most of their angling while wading...in lakes and streams...with water up to their private parts, and beyond (all of which are generally protected by waders: those long rubber-like Dr. Denton's which are secured over their shoulders with husky suspenders).

And, being out on (make that "in") the water without any handy tackle box to warehouse their tackle, they adopted the vest as a satisfactory alternative, covering its surface with clusters of pockets and "D" rings to store and secure their peculiar needs. These essentials included such items as a line snipper, net and net retractor, lines or "tippets", flyboxes, a flashlight, forceps, various hardware and spares, plus even a light-weight rain jacket. Plus sandwiches, candy bars and other snacks.

For many years, the fishing vest was respected as being peculiar to, and an integral part of the uniform of those who tied their own flies and tossed them at dimples they detected on the water's surface. Whenever you saw a photog\ph of such an angler, you invariably saw such a vest, embellished by ti nkets of all kinds, dangling down to and around the waist of the wearer.

I n more recent years, the vest was also adopted by a number of those who chose to call themselves "ultralight" anglers because of the delicate nature of the tackle they employed: smaller spin-cast type reels, long and light casting rods, and line as delicate as your daughter's hair. The vest felt good. And they felt <u>good</u>.

Now, to the delight of the manufacturers, the fashion has spread to an even broader spectrum of the fishing universe. Many more courageous anglers, who piously hoped that the wearing of the vest would elevate their station in the society of fishermen and women have taken to it. And they like it, too. Which is why you now find it more commonly on display in the tackle bazaars of our neighborhoods.

"Are your customers hide-bound traditionalists, trend-chasers, or a little of both?" Richard Alexander asks dealers in FISHING TRADE TACKLE NEWS. "Either way," he tells them, "there are going to be vests that appeal to them." And retailer Bob Marriott of Fullerton, California, tells us that "About 30% of our customers are now women. Women are far more color conscious than men, and we sell many vests in non-traditional colors."

Some of this, Gene Hill writes in FIELD & STREAM is because "More and more women are taking up fly fishing. I'm positive this is because a lot of the women have watched the head of the household for awhile and become convinced that they can do it as least as well, probably better."

Of course we can. And we will dress to look the part.

But first let's look at the anatomy of the fishing vests which are being offered today, by manufacturers and retailers such as Orvis, Cortland, L. L. Bean , Gander Mountain, Bass Pro Shops, Cabela's, Columbia, Simm's, Browning, Patagonia and Stream Designs.

Only a few of those offer the vest in "women's" sizes, while most of the rest tailor the item strictly for the male torso, and invite us ladies to "order one size down. Example: "Women's medium order Men's size small" (L. L. Bean). No thought that our upper bodies might be just a bit more well-favored than their flat-chested men customers!

Not all of these odd garments are for the fishing novitiate who will wear it both professionally and socially. You must study the literature, and examine each model to make sure that you will be impressively adorned but not over-equipped. For example, Orvis says of its "Super Tac-L-Pak" model that it "has been built with unprecedented pocket capacity...There are 33 pockets in all. On the outside, four large 5" x 9" pockets will handle the largest fly boxes, and they are zippered for extra protection. Two additional zippered maximum security pockets are ideal for small, easily lost items like pocket knives and keys. There are _nine_ (italics mine) other outside front pockets with Velcro tabs to carry everything from small fly boxes to floatant." That baby goes for $72.50.

Cortland, as a more delicate choice, offer its "Deluxe" model, with only 14 pockets, but still plenty of storage spaces for all of the whips, whistles and balloons you might want to take fishing. Price just $39.95. It's their best-seller.

But it is Stream Designs which offers what must be considered the most authoritative, truly woman's vest: the Joan Wulff model (named after the wife of the recognized inventor of the vest). But this unit still has 22 pockets! The fact that it comes in powder blue color identifies it conclusively as a ladies' model. It sells for $59.95.

At the bare essentials end, and certainly adequate for those purposes described earlier, is the "Angler Fishing Vest" offered by L. L Bean in its "Fly Fishing Catalogue." Check this brilliant description of its features: "Rugged, well-constructed vest designed by our staff to offer just the right amount of storage. Nine exterior pockets hold fly boxes, leaders and other gear. Eight interior pockets include 6 tippet spool pockets and zippered pocket for wallet and car keys. Large rear bellows pocket can be overstuffed without affecting natural shape of vest. Net ring. Pin-on lambswool patch. Self-healing nylon coil zippers. Velcro closure on all pocket flaps. Made from a durable, easy-care blend of 60% polyester/40% cotton poplin. Bar-tacking throughout for durability. Imported. Machine wash."

With a $34.50 price tag, it should fit your budget just fine. Less than most sweaters today, and a lot more fun to wear. With all of those pockets you will find plenty of room for lipstick case, combs, tissues, mascara, change purse-or wallet, nail polish, powder, brushes, and those other essentials that you just wouldn't go anywhere without.

The importance of this purchase cannot be over-stated, and it should be approached in a planned manner. The first step would be to visit your nearest dealer in fishing tackle and clothing, Browse carefully. Avoid the clerks while you handle and try on the merchandise. Check all those that you try on in the closest mirror. If you find one that you like, and that doesn't fit you like a potato sack, is priced right, and isn't overly pocketed, buy it.

If you can't find one that you like, try another store. Failing there, at least note that size that fits you best, so you can order one by mail with full confidence that it will make you look just great.

One final note about the vest. You absolutely <u>cannot</u> wear it right out of the box, or off the hanger! Throw it in the laundry. Wash it two, three times. Lay it out to dry, and be sure not to iron it.

I have heard my husband tell stories about newly-commissioned officers in the Navy who would soak their gold braid and status pins in salt water for several days before wearing them aboard ship. The last thing they wanted to do was look like they just stepped off the academy graduation platform. And you will want to affect the same deshabille...or casual affectation. The experienced look. Not the interloper.

All that done, you are ready to wear the vest out into polite society of most descriptions. Maybe not to church, but certainly to P.T.A., Business Women's Club, the Garden Club, your fitness center, on most shopping trips, and absolutely on a cruise ship.

Here's a true lady's fishing vest, styled by Joan Wulff for Stream Designs. "Stylish and crisp," is how they describe it, "yet function is not compromised." Loaded with pockets, and zippers. And you can have it in tan, green, blue or grey!

Your costume now makes the statement, "I am into fishing. Want to talk about it?"

A few words need to be added about hats or caps before we dispense with the subject of your wardrobe for joining in the sport of fishing. Few women these days wear a hat when engaging in most activities of the home or their business circle. The same rules apply when you move about in any of these elements when attired in the angling costume, or ensemble. On the water, or enroute to a fishing destination, other considerations kick in.

The most common form of headpiece for such parts of your adventure is the baseball-type cap. The Headwear Institute Of America tells us that 300 million of these caps were manufactured in America last year, and that at least that many more were imported. As a style, they account for 70% of all hat sales in any year, although their full share of the hat-wearing business is even greater when you figure in those endless numbers that are given away in sales promotions or advertising ...for every kind of business from DeKalb Seeds to Barney's Bowl & Tap.

That, of course, is what calls for caution in accepting a baseball-type cap as the crowning element in your statement of style. To stand above the crowd, you must be selective. If someone thrusts Barney's Bowl & Tap cap at you, take it home and give it to the kids. Then repair to your desk, open your library of outfitters catalogues, and select one less gauche. Orvis will supply you with one of aristocratic quality, design and in an assortment of tan, red or navy for just $11.50. And the embroidered Orvis logo will announce that you know your way around the cosmos of respected suppliers to the sport.

The International Game Fish Association (referred to in a later chapter) will supply you with one of equal distinction, carrying their famous logo, for a mere seven bucks.

The same cap will provide adequate protection for your coiffure out on the water, but if the sun is intense, you will want to add a colorful kerchief of large dimension to avoid annoying sunburn, all the while adding to the full flavor and timbre of your total outfit.

If you become so taken with the sport that you find yourself venturing out in more inclement weather, particularly the cold, you can add further dash to your appearance by switching to one of those "woodsman" or "hunting" caps, which come in khaki and blaze orange colors, as well as subdued camouflage patterns. Any one of these will add conviction to the impression that you are, indeed, a serious angler, and warrant the respect which goes with such distinction.

You may not get it, but you deserve it.

In any, event, you are now properly uniformed for the world of fishing, further described in the chapters ahead.

ALL DRESSED UP,
AND NO PLACE TO GO?

*"The unifying theme today is the new confidence of women as they make
and deal with choices, and balance the opportunities and pressures of being
a woman in the last decade of the twentieth century."*
                                        -Market researcher Judith Langer,
                                            president of Langer Associates,
                                                SELF magazine, 1989.
*"We've had the 'me' decade, the 'we' decade. The 80's was the 'me'
decade. The 90's is the 'she' generation."*
                                        -Dr. Joyce Brothers, September 1992.

There is a little bit of "school teacher" in every woman. Most of us
instinctively know that we can teach others how to learn the alphabet
faster, how to cook better, and to dress more elegantly. We just know
that we can teach men more about the world than they ever learned in
school. And, especially, we can teach them how to approach us more
effectively.

All of which is why, for many years, I have fantasized that the
suppliers to the fishing business would one day call me (make that "beg
me") to address one of their annual gatherings to tell them what really
goes on in the female mind. But the call never came.

And now it's too late.

I have read in their trade magazines that they have passed the buck
to other social psychologists and alchemists by forming a growing
number of "councils," each charged with determining why their
business continues to falter on the Brink of Despair, and why their
merchandise doesn't jump faster off the racks of their appointed
retailers.

The problem, they tell each other is their lack of "demographics,"
which is a high-sounding term for all of the data which will tell them
which side of the tracks their prospects live on, what their sexual
arrangement is, how much more money do they spend than they earn,
and which fork they eat their salad with.

43

But the real demographics which they ought to be looking at are simply these two:

1 - There are 5% more adult women than men in this country.

2 - There are many more millions of women than men who have yet to accept fishing as a viable outlet for their recreational drive.

To put it in a form that even a schoolboy can understand; If you are looking for more customers for whatever you have to sell, take a careful look at the vast market which women represent.

One of the major outdoor magazines recently marked its Golden Anniversary year by reprinting some of the advertisements placed between their covers half a century ago. There were ads for tackle, boats, motors and fishing destinations... all peopled with nothing but pipe-smoking men, fondling their rods and reels, admiring their fishing craft, and holding up amazing strings of freshly-caught bass, pickerel and trout.

Exactly the same as they are today. Only their uniforms have been changed. They still show nothing but men enjoying the great outdoors. You are supposed to take it for granted that their womenfolk are back home, wiping the kids' noses, making their beds, and doing the laundry. And enjoying every wonderful minute of it!

Now, before we convict the industry decision-makers alone for these grievous mistakes, we need to reflect on the unhappy fact that they are joined in, or led, in their advertising resolutions by that flashy group of "image makers" known as advertising agencies, and which are generally positioned as inhabitants of New York's Madison Avenue. Not all of them abide there, but that venue is highly-regarded as the mother-lode of their thought processes.

Each of these agencies is richly endowed with active young Masters Of Business Administration ("M.B.A."-types) who specialize in the numbers game of identifying high-spending prospects, and creative types (generally with lesser academic credentials) whose special talents rest in the business of writing the words and assembling the art which make the advertiser's proposition irresistible.

These are the folks who generate the demographics and then "package" their commercial literature into a form which they promise the manufacturer will lead them into The Promised Land.

Their presentations are made to the innocent advertiser by a team leader who travels under the name of "Account Executive". This presenter is a seasoned professional in the Art Of Persuasion, and with more raw flamboyance than the most polished trial lawyer.

Whether said account executive has ever spent a day in an outpost camp, whooping it up with the boys out on the water is not really germane to the matter at hand, he will tell the client assembly.

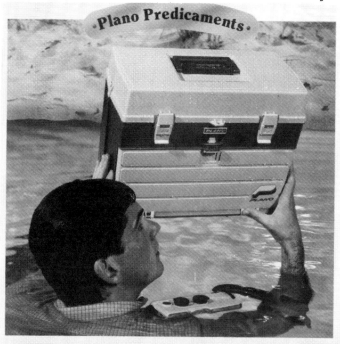

Plano Predicaments

"Take this—I'm going back for my wife."

There really isn't a predicament. The new Plano 787 is the fisherman's perfect mate.

After all, you know no one else can match Plano's innovative styling and durable, lightweight construction. No one else can help you put so much into so small a place. And only Plano lets you choose from so many styles. From traditional swing-back, hip-roof, and drawer boxes to classic Magnums and trendsetting Phantoms.

And, once you've experienced a Plano adventure, you know that nothing else will do. That's why fishermen love their Plano tackle boxes.

Create your own predicament with three new innovations from Plano: Phantom 1466, Plano 707, and Phantom 1468.

Number One by Design

PLANO

Plano Molding Company, 431 E. South St, Plano, IL 60545-0189

My friends at Plano Molding Company have told me that they thought this ad was "kind of cute" when they ran it in a bunch of outdoor magazines few years ago. Then they received some letters from women readers who straightened them out, and they have behaved better since. Imagine, a tackle box as "the fisherman's perfect mate"!

What is really important, he will tell them, is that they <u>like</u> the ads presented, run them in all of the magazines read by men...and run them often. They will build "product recognition,", establish "brand prefer-

Here is a dandy example of an ad from the "Har har!" school of marketing. "Perfect female...big gut." Absolutely repulsive, but indicative of the way some folks in the advertising business think about women. I have crossed out the name of the advertiser, just in case it wasn't really their idea.

ence, win "dealer support" and "make the cash registers ring."

The client (the manufacturer), infinitely wiser in how to manufacture his product at low cost than how to sell it, nods his head. The deal is done, and the entire group retires to cocktails and a prime rib dinner.

While back at the agency's office, the M.B.A. group and the creative types consider the opportunity to ask for a generous raise.

That's how it all happens. That's why the ads in the hundreds of issues of outdoor magazines which I have labored through for this treatise showed me nothing but men; one, two, three or a whole cabin full. All having a whee of a time.

Is that fair? Is it smart marketing? Does it make you feel like you are wanted?

Of course not!

The March, 1992 issue of GLAMOUR magazine carried a story by Jon Tevlin entitled "Why Women Are Mad As Hell." The source of his material is a 1990 poll conducted by the respected Gallup poll organization. From its findings, Jon observes "Men just don't get it....Women are seething...they are fed up...even angrier at men than they were 20 years ago."

The poll produced data which established, once again, that men were perfectly satisfied that the role of their betrothed was "to help around the house."

But that won't do today, the ladies countered. They believe that they deserve more. They have "a sense of entitlement", and they expect more from men, and want more out of their relationships. I couldn't have said it better!

The study confirms that many manufacturers "don't read the newspapers...let alone the ladies magazines." Women have arrived at the point in time where they are ready to say "I've had it, and I am not going along with it any more."

An executive of one of the leading tackle manufacturers whom I contacted about this study told me that "ads in LADIES HOME JOURNAL do not make sense...compared to fishing publications," but maybe the publishers of GLAMOUR should send him a copy of their story, along with an advertising rate card He can read it, and then send it along to the folks at his advertising agency.

Thanks to their innate sense of humor and their good-natured forbearance, many women have ignored the lack of a formal welcome and have deigned to intrude on the sport anyhow, and with many of them performing admirably well, as will be revealed in later chapters.

But more, we all know, would join in the fun and excitement of fishing...and spend all of the money that it demands ...if the industry forces would just show us that they wanted us, or that there was room for us out there with the boys.

Successful advertisers to women know how and where to sell us, how to turn us on, get our erogenous glands churning, and make our lips quiver. The dress merchandisers do it, the perfume brewers do it, and even the pots and pans peddlers know our hot buttons. As Erma Bombeck put it so beautifully, "We can read and write, and some of our sisters are heavy hitters in industry."

Those state bureaucrats whose empires grow with the expansion of outdoor sports should know that, too. Each year, they publish and distribute millions of copies of their fishing regulations and handbooks, many embellished with what they consider to be enticing pictures of anglers at play. But if you were to pick up one card for each state that placed a picture of a woman angler on its official publication, you would still be one card short for a game of five-card-stud. Arizona, California, Minnesota and Arkansas are the only states with departments of natural resources which consider women as important participants in their lakes, rivers and streams, if you are to believe what you see.

Some states, however, do supply other literature, produced by commercial operations in the hospitality business, and which include a welcome photo of a woman or a family finding fun in nearby waters. On the whole, however, there is monstrous room for improvement if any of them are serious about getting more of us into the game.

As recently as March of 1992, Vin T. Sparano, editor-in-chief of OUTDOOR LIFE, wrote that he had-attended a fishing trade tackle show and "I didn't like what I heard. The message was that fishermen have been decreasing in numbers for the last five years or so....Why? Here are some of the reasons given. No one to fish with..."

Much of the answer to that problem lies within the pages of his own publication. In that same issue I counted ten full pages of full-color advertising which depicted men (and men only!) in fishing situations, with no signs of a woman angler anywhere on their separate horizons.

That is quite likely the way that many of our boys like it. No sound reasons to invite the ladies along to break up their fun. It occurred to me,

EDITORIAL TRAILS By Vin T. Sparano, Editor-in-Chief

Get People Back Into Fishing

I n January, I attended Catch '92, a fishing tackle trade show where manufacturers exhibit the latest in rods, reels and everything else you would use to catch a fish. I listened to many people in the fishing business, and I didn't like what I heard. The message was that fishermen have been decreasing in number for the last five years or so. Why? Here are some of the reasons given. No one to fish with. Not enough time to fish.

...should be thousands. Don't wait for someone else to get the ball rolling. If you're a member of a sportsmen's club, initiate a program to start children fishing. If you don't belong to a club, contact your local recreation center, fish and game department, sporting-goods dealer or anyone else who will listen. Organize a fishing event for children. You can do it!

There are other ways to get people back into fishing. First, we can make it easier to go fishing. Let's start with a fishing license, for example. Ever try to get one on a weekend or when you arrive in town at 6 in the morning? It's almost impossible!

...censes, how about one federal fishing license for all national parks and forests, regardless of which state they are located in? I know this will raise hackles in many states, but our primary purpose is to make fishing more accessible. State and federal compatibility has to be secondary.

I think we can count on Washington for some support. During the past year, I met with Secretary of the Interior Manuel Lujan and his staff. Secretary Lujan has developed a recreational fishing initiative to increase fishing opportunities on the 440 million acres the Interior Department manages, as well as a similar initiative on Forest Service lands. You can learn more about Secre-

...ary Lujan's fishing initiative and how you can be a part of it by writing directly to Secretary of the Interior Manuel Lujan, Department of the Interior, Washington, DC 20240.

I also get uptight when I hear people complain about not ...ugh fish to catch. I don't buy ...excuse at all. In fact, if some ...measures the success of a ...g trip by the number of fish ...ooler, he probably shouldn't ...hing in the first place. But ...s something we can do. ...ral years ago, my friend ...rrett from the *New Jersey* ...n and I tried to promote ...ept of releasing one fish ...m your catch. Fresh wa... water, it doesn't make ...ence. ...re are more than 65 million fishermen in the United States. If half of them agree to release one fish a day, I cannot even fathom how many fish would be returned to the water on a typical weekend. The late Lee Wulff said a fish is too valuable to be caught once. He was right.

When I finished this editorial, my first reaction was that I had put together a disjointed collection of thoughts and ideas. But that's not really true. My goal is to generate increasing interest in all areas of fishing, so that our sport can demand the attention it deserves and a fair share from all levels of government.

We will do our part at Outdoor Life. Will you do yours? Start by releasing a fish on your next trip. 🌲🌲🌲

You will enjoy reading OUTDOOR LIFE magazine, and its Editor-In-Chief Vin T. Sparano is generally on the side of Right and Justice for those who enjoy fishing and hunting. But he still doesn't seem ready to recognize the opportunity to help more of us to get out on the water.

as I surveyed that exclusiveness, that one neat way to shake them up a little would be for some of us girls to announce to our house partners that "Four of us girls have decided to take a little fishing trip. We are heading up to George Grisdale's camp near Georgian Bay in upper Ontario. We hear the place attracts a lot of hairy-chested men from Montreal."

After that news settles in, you might well get the first genuine, full-bodied invitation to go with the old boy, the next time he hitches up his boat to head out into the wilderness.

I was surprised that Mr. Sparano overlooked the mention of women in his editorial as a potential resource to fatten up the fishing numbers. His publication frequently includes articles by women writers, including Kathy Etling, who has written on every subject from bass fishing to cold weather underwear. Kathy, I am certain, could give his advertisers a pretty clear idea on where to look for more prospects for their baits, boats and batteries.

Many of those advertisers, however, have passed that responsibility to their "Sportfishing Promotion Council," which has as its mission "working to ensure the profitability of your business." Perhaps it has achieved that, but its programs to-date indicate that it has yet to discover the growth possible through those millions of would-be women anglers.

For a number of years the Council has directed its promotional efforts towards the business of getting kids (principally boys) into fishing. "Get hooked on fishing! Not drugs!" was one of its programs for the 1990's and was supported by more comprehensive activities than its earlier "Take A Kid Fishing" program, such as community fishing clinics and even a teaching curriculum for schools ...with a magnificent 102-page textbook.

The thrust of it all, according to its prospectus, was to reach into those 60% of all "fishing households" which contained kids who don't fish...and get them out on the water...with their fathers, of course.

Having had some experience with young boys, I could have told them at the outset that they were trying to bite off substantially more than they could comfortably chew. And not just because of the drugs hang-up, but because of the determination of youngsters today to do just those things which turn them on. Like cruising the streets in daddy's car, listening to "boom boxes" screwed up to full volume, watching wild videos, just "hanging out", dressing like ragamuffins, hitting the hamburger dispensaries, and "just doing it."

No doubt the program succeeded in introducing many of the kids to the intricacies of a rod and reel, the fun of out fooling the neighborhood crappies, or even tagging along on a camping/fishing trip with father. Kids need that persuasion, too, but they are a mighty-hard sell.

In 1992 the Council shifted gears and set out to generate more frequent participation in the sport by those anglers who appeared to falling away because they were enjoying it less. Their coup d'eclat to achieve that goal was to run a 13-week radio campaign of good old country music.

Now I don't have anything against country music, nor against those folks who prefer it to the "rap" stuff being aimed at kids these days. But I couldn't help wonder how much more effectively those dollars could have been spent if they had been directed at the women of America who have yet to hear any voice of the industry singing siren songs to get them into a boat and have their fair share of fun out on the water.

Does it make sense to advertise to women...to promote activities which will make them feel more comfortable in their perhaps fumbling entry into the sport? Listen to what the National Shooting Sports Foundation is doing:

While I perceive that this "Foundation" is similar in support and direction to that of the fishing industry, it appears to have a much stronger grasp of the demographics of its market. Recognizing a latent interest in fire arms among us ladies, they are working to convert this interest into sales through at least three approaches yet to be tackled by the greater forces of the angling suppliers.

First of all they are advertising in a women's magazine (Women's Sports and Fitness). Secondly, they are sponsoring women-only shooting events. And thirdly, they are sponsoring a series of seminars for women only called "Removing The Barriers To Women's Participation In The Outdoor Sports" at the University of Wisconsin.

Wow! And right on! They are complimenting women everywhere by telling them that they understand their need for help in getting started, and they are getting it to them. Help is also coming from large retailers like Houston-based Oshman's, a leading merchandiser of outdoor gear of all kinds. Its "Women And Sports" programs based in its local outlets have been organized, they stated, to counter the feeling held by many female customers, that sports in general constitute a male-oriented environment.

Women-only seminars are being conducted in their stores, with women experts conducting demonstrations and answering questions... with crowds numbering in the thousands. No doubt the cash registers are ringing a happy tune, not to be confused with country music.

No doubt some of the high-rollers in the fishing industry will be reading the reports of those successes, and word will also come back to them from their field representatives who make regular stops at those stores. This could lead to a better understanding of the true demographics of their market today, including recognition that women appreciate being recognized, have money to spend, and can make their own decisions on what they do in their spare time.

Finally, manufacturers ought to be looking in on the University of

As living proof that men can still have a good time fishing while their ladies are along I submit this picture of Mary Jane Getter, Kathy Perkins, Linda Widham, Linda Vaughn, Susan Pontak and Joyce Lewis, all of Missouri, Texas and Tennessee...with their happy male companions behind them. Pictured at the Canadian wilderness camp in the summer of 1992.

Wisconsin-Stevens Point College of Natural Resources. Located just eight miles east of the quiet village of Tomahawk is the school's Treehaven Field Station, where women are invited to attend a three-day seminar bearing the name "Becoming an Outdoors Woman." At

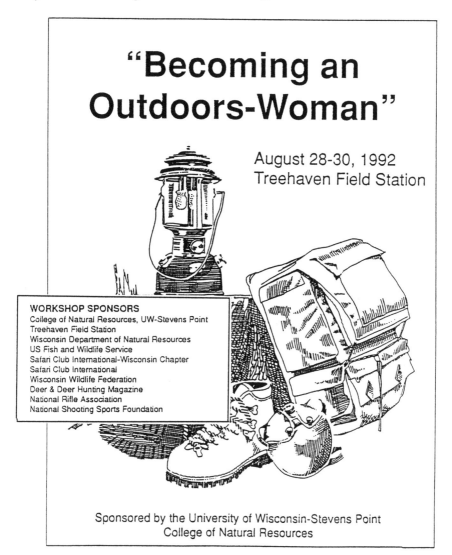

"Becoming an Outdoors-Woman"

August 28-30, 1992
Treehaven Field Station

WORKSHOP SPONSORS
College of Natural Resources, UW-Stevens Point
Treehaven Field Station
Wisconsin Department of Natural Resources
US Fish and Wildlife Service
Safari Club International-Wisconsin Chapter
Safari Club International
Wisconsin Wildlife Federation
Deer & Deer Hunting Magazine
National Rifle Association
National Shooting Sports Foundation

Sponsored by the University of Wisconsin-Stevens Point
College of Natural Resources

This is the cover of the course outline for Treehaven's trailblazing new school to help women feel more at home-out on the water or in the woods. Note the list of sponsors, and the absence of names of fishing industry suppliers.

this comfortable winterized facility, complete with residence halls, a classroom center, and a main lodge with a friendly lounge, cheery fireplace and excellent food service, women over the age of 18 can learn "outdoor skills usually associated with hunting and fishing, but useful for many outdoor pursuits."

There are classes on basic fishing skills, beginning flyfishing, fly-tying and on-stream and on-lake angling exercises. The ladies are also taught how to prepare their catch for the fire, and how to turn it into a gourmet meal. Instructors are both male and female, all seasoned veterans of the sport.

For icing on the cake, there is even a class in dressing for the outdoors, complete with a fashion show of "clothes that work."

Certainly the most creative and promising effort of its kind, the course is funded primarily by affiliates of the sport-shooting industry, with some help from Wisconsin's Department of Natural Resources and the U.S. Fish and Wildlife Service. Manufacturers and "councils" within the fishing industry have yet to recognize its work, or respond to requests for support.

Which shouldn't surprise you at this point. Those folks are either mighty slow learners, or scared to death that one day we will outnumber the men in the sport.

While the staff at Treehaven tells me that their classes fill up fast (enrollment limit is 100), you might want to write for their prospectus and get on their waiting list. The address is: Treehaven Field Station, 2540 Pickerel Creek Road, Tomahawk, WI 54487. You could mention this book, and ask for more information on class schedules.

Support for the interest of women in fishing is growing, led by imaginative women with leadership ideas. It's up to you to follow their lead, put on your whole new outfit of fishing fashions, zip up your fishing vest, and announce to all of those within earshot: "I'm going fishing."

And then do it.

WORLD CLASS WOMEN !

Women "fish with utter determination, especially if there are men on the water, too. Nothing diminishes their concentration. Foul weather will not discourage them nor physical discomfort quench their spirit....The ability of women to beat the men on the same day in the same water occurs time and again."

-Hugh Falkus, Introduction to SALMON AND WOMEN,
by Wilma Peterson & Professor Peter Behan, 1990.

When most men think of a woman with a fishing rod, they visualize a midget-size bluegill sunfish flopping on the end of it. And they would be eternally grateful if those were the true facts of the case.

But take my word for it, boys, that's not the way it is . Listen, my dears, and you shall hear of some catches that most of you can only dream of.

We can begin by chatting politely about that 1,314-pound tiger shark caught by Mrs. Bob Dyer off the shores of Australia back in 1953, setting a new world record for 130-pound test line. And then there was Linda Ciletti, whose first marlin catch, made off the shores of the Big Island of Hawaii in 1990, registered a neat little 995 pounds.

Not bad for openers, fellows?

You could also take a lesson or two from Heidi Mason whose 87-pound amberjack in March of 1991 made her a tournament champion. And if you have never had your hook in a Gulf Stream amberjack, you just can't appreciate what an herculean feat that was. Eighty-seven pounds of stubborn dynamite!

Over in the British Isles, even the most resolute male angler will agree with the national position that the 64-pound salmon caught by Georgina Ballantine back in 1922 is a record which will never be beaten. The 54-inch fish had a girth of 28 1/2 inches! Just monstrous. And caught by a 32-year-old female!

And then there is Dana Ross, the lady who took over the top spot for muskie catches in her home state of New Jersey with a 38-pound, 4-ounce catch in 1990. Up on the Columbia River, south of Longview, Washington, Mrs. Renee Furikawa created quite a stir with the sturgeon she battled for almost for four hours before beaching it and then releasing it. The monster measured 9 feet, 8 inches, and was estimated to weigh 500 pounds. Guide Ted Howell said it was the largest he has ever seen, and that it bettered the old 468-pound I.G.F.A. all-tackle record. Howell should know, too. He has fished those waters for more than 50 years.

Older ladies do it, too. Witness 80-year-old Ann Miller who brought

Linda Ciletti was fishing in the 1990 Lahaina Yacht Club's Spring Wahine Tournament in Hawaiian waters when she hooked into this 955-pound blue marlin. It was her first marlin and it took first place and set a new state women's record. The fight lasted for one hour and 45 minutes but Linda never gave up.

a 52-pound sailfish to boat off Islamorada in the Florida keys. And we can't overlook Mrs. Louis Marron, whose 772-pound swordfish set a new record back in 1954...caught on 80-pound test line. Most swordfish caught these days are under 100 pounds, handy size for the men who generally catch them.

Folks around the shores of Lake Ontario can also tell you about a 41-pound chinook salmon caught in those waters by Diana Warren in 1986. The neighbors of Marie Vanderstel will also tell you about her 60-pound, 8-ounce king mackerel which-was a first place winner in the International Game Fish Association's 1991 competition.

Quite likely there are many more outstanding catches made by women angler which have not come to our attention. Not being as competitive-minded as most seasoned fishermen, they are probably unaware of how to get a possible record-breaker registered. As referred to throughout these pages, the five major routes to recognition are these:

1 - The International Game Fish Association's annual listing.
2 - The Fresh Water Fishing Hall of Fame's yearly report.
3 - The SPORTS AFIELD annual fishing awards program, presided over by Homer Circle.
4 - The annual Master Anglers Awards competition conducted by IN-FISHERMAN magazine, and
5 - Individual citation projects of many state conservation and fisheries departments.

Each of these has its own set of rules, its own special application forms to be filled out and witnessed, requirements for samples of line used in the catch, and (in some cases) verification of the species by a state biologist.

Somewhere in the circle of fishing friends you will come to have there will be someone who can assist you in finding the proper paperwork and preparing the proper documentation when your Day Of Glory comes and you have a true world-beater on the end of your line. I urge you not to overlook this exercise because it will put your name in print for all to see, bring a certificate, trophy or plaque to display in your home or office, and establish the incontestable fact of your competence.

In all of the years which I have shared a boat with my husband I have

Certificates like those above will look good on your home or office wall. And they are yours for the asking when you catch a notable fish...which you certainly will when you get enthusiastically into the sport.

never deliberately conspired to out-fish him. Long years before we were married, my dear mother gallantly responded to any hardship we faced with this quiet counsel: "The Lord will provide." And He certainly has. I have consistently caught more bass than my more-seasoned housemate. I have caught and provided the food for shore lunch on many occasions in which he demonstrated long, heaving casts, jabbered constantly about where the fish were, but brought up none to nourish us.

The six-foot white marlin which hung on our walls for many years has also reminded him that his largest muskie is still in second place on the premises.

We are living in a fantastic era of opportunity for women. The reason? Probably because we have more women of greater skill, deeper wisdom, and more passionate determination than the world has ever seen. We crave due recognition and success. The old artificial images no longer apply. British actress Glenda Jackson deserted the stage to seek a role in Labor Party politics. "Women," she told the press, "are seen almost always in terms of the emotional life of the story's dramatic engine, which is invariably a man. We are slotted in pigeon-holes: beddable, which means wives or mistresses: or non-beddable, which means mothers, grandmothers or aunts...And I am certainly not going to hang around to play the nurse in 'Romeo and Juliet.'"

Glenda should also try fishing. She has the spirit for it.
But then, so-does Josephine Stevens, the 83-year-old youngster who brought down a 12-point bull moose at 80 yards in the Fall of 1991. So does the delightful Margaret Thatcher, who has proven to the world that a woman could hold her own in a tough political environment over-populated by men.

Women have also won a few merit badges in the financial world. The September 1991 issue of FORTUNE magazine carried pictures of six of our wealthier sisters on its cover, with the headline: "The Billionaires...and many of them are women." Among those shown were Estee Lauder and Liliane Bettencourt. Estee has an accumulated piggy bank of over five billion dollars from her cosmetic empire, and and Liliane has scratched together over two billion promoting her Ralph Lauren, Lancome and L'Oreal merchandise.

Among the thirteen lady billionaires there is also one Heidi Horton, widow of the founder of the Horton department store chain in Europe.

Heidi's nest egg is a neat 1.9 billion dollars, but her ever-loving husband's will stipulates that she may spend only $150 million per year...and that she may not give her fortune to three types of men: kidnappers, blackmailers and future husbands.

FORTUNE tells us that Heidi has been a reasonably good girl, and hasn't yet married her 40-year-old fiance. That obviously means that she has plenty of cash to go out and do a little fishing!

But we have other role models, too. You may remember Olive Beech, the clever lady who ran the Beech Aircraft Corporation for so many successful years after the death of her husband. Olive made her way to the FORTUNE magazine list of America's ten top business-women, and was cited by the NEW YORK TIMES as one of our twelve most distinguished women.

Then, too, there is Sandra Day O'Connor, who now sits on the Supreme Court. And spunky Sally Ride, who became our first woman astronaut. Add to that list Lyn St. James, the first female driver to finish the Indianapolis 500...and was named "Rookie of the Year" in doing it.

Up in Ontario, Canada, another Lyn is making her presence known as Minister of Natural Resources. In that role she directs all of the hunting and fishing support activities for the province which attracts the largest number of anglers from the United States. She is Lyn McLeod, and has won the support and admiration of many observers who were sure that she could never handle the job.

There are thousands of other examples of successful women which ought to convince the men around us that we are a force, and a sex, to be reckoned with. And fished with.

Give us a chance and we will handle any boat, motor, or rod and reel with as much expertise and dexterity as any of those old boys who masquerade as "fishing pros"..

To further establish the facts of that claim, let's review a few of those remarkable catches made by women, and registered in the record compilations referred to earlier. We can begin with Nadine Anderson of Crystal, Minnesota, who caught and released both a 49-inch and a 50-inch chinook salmon in Alaska's Kenai River in June of 1990. Shirley Steinbach of Post Falls, Idaho, took top honors for her region in the IN-FISHERMAN 1991 rainbow trout category with her 19-

pound, 4-ounce steelhead.

In the SPORTS AFIELD awards list for the same year you will find the name of Gloria Foster who landed a 11-pound, 4-ounce rainbow in Lake Ontario. Cindy West of Georgia made the same register with a whopping 4-pound, 11-ounce crappie, and then there is that 65-pound flathead catfish credited to Julia (Judy) Hines on the Fresh Water Fishing Hall of Fame 1991 record catch re-cap. Catfish count, too!

For closers, I will mention Carla Waldholm of Proctor, Minnesota, who caught and released a 41-inch hybrid ("tiger") muskie on Island Lake (a fish which many men would consider a true trophy and hurry it to their local taxidermist), and Jackie Lalonde of Dowling, Ontario, who surprised many fellow Canadians with the 14-pound, 4-ounce walleye landed in Onaping Lake in her home province.

All of these exceptional catches represent the trail-blazing performed by women who have already taken to fishing, and who have proven that we girls are up to the rigors of the sport, that we can perform admirably, and that those men whom we love and live with should no longer leave us at home.

Canadian wilderness fishing provides uncommon exposure to wondrous natural beauty, plus sightings of eagles, loons, gulls, deer, bear, and even an occasional moose, such as the one shown above.

THE "P" FACTOR

"Because of their recessed plumbing, women have a special problem urinating hygienically in weightlessness. To solve this problem, NASA studied the issue in detail. This involved the photography of the urination function performed by a group of women volunteers. Based on their data, NASA developed a unisex toilet which is used on the shuttle."

-William R. Poague, astronaut,
"How Do You Go To The Bathroom in Space?"

In most areas of life, I am a rather easy-going person, and generally accept things as they are, or are reported to be.

That's why I pretty much took it in stride when I heard that Jeana Yaeger had decided to spend ten days in an experimental airplane, flying around the world, non-stop, accompanied by male co-pilot Richard Yutan. At just 116 miles per hour, it should be a reasonably pleasant flight. And while their total cabin space was not much larger than the cab of a Winnebago camper, the two of them would be able to attend to their separate eliminations without major inconvenience to the other.

Surely Jeanna wouldn't be nudging Richard at odd hours, suggesting that they put down at Andrews Air Force Base so that she could relieve herself in greater privacy.

She didn't, as we all know, and they concluded a rather uneventful but record-breaking flight. The flight log carried no notes about Jeanna dribbling over the maps, or experiencing any other notable discomfort.

How pilot Yutan handled the problem never really interested me. But with whatever grace it was accomplished, it was satisfactory unto their purpose, and they were broadly acclaimed for their achievement, together.

In the same calm manner, I accepted as reasonable Sally Ride's decision to ride along with four other astronauts in the summer of 1983 on a six-day mission scurrying around our planet at over 18,000 miles an hour. Surely, somewhere in that cozy little nose cone our eminent space scientists had provided means by which both the boys and Sally could respond to the call of nature without any embarrassment to the others.

Nothing in their flight plan called for intermittent road stops in Angola or Ashtabula, Ohio, to attend to those needs.

Quite likely, when those Conestoga wagons began to rumble over the Oregon Trail into the Golden West, I am content to believe that the stalwart young ladies who elected to go along for the ride, would be accorded adequate courtesy to attend to their needs to void in a manner which would not disturb or distract the trail bosses or other male companions.

And there is nothing in the literature to suggest that there were Standard Oil stations, or other "comfort stops" along the route to provide more private and comfortable facilities.

A study of the 65-day voyage of the Mayflower from the coast on England to the shores of New England in the Autumn of 1620 reveals that there were twenty women on board, in the company of fifty men

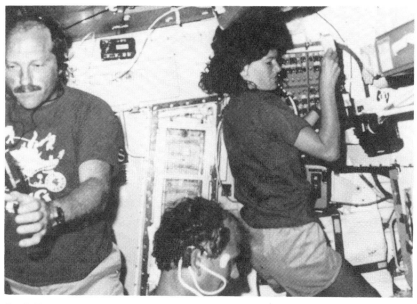

The folks at N.A.S.A. are a mite more understanding than B.A.S.S. about men and women traveling together in a confined space for long periods of time. Sally Ride, shown above, is much too busy with the work at hand to worry about what to do when nature calls. And the men with her enjoyed having her along for the ride, pioneering the way for many other women astronauts who have since followed.

and at least thirty young children. During their 65 days at sea, all on board were able to repair to the only "necessary" at hand (even though it is written "that the ship had only the crudest of conveniences and no sanitary facilities of any kind except the traditional bucket"). Among those, you will remember, was Priscilla Mullins, an 18-year-old lass, later to be betrothed to the muscular John Alden, a hired hand brought along to help in the heavy work ahead.

That Priscilla and John experienced no embarrassment over the lack of more adequate accommodations is certainly witnessed by their continuing fervent amity, resulting later in a marriage in which Myles Standish is alleged to have been an interlocutor.

All of the above being part and parcel of our rich history and heritage, it is utterly amazing to me that so many men feel ill at ease at being in a fishing boat with a person of the opposite sex.

That they are, and that many of them will fight it to the eradication thereof is documented in almost every tale you hear about fishing trips which self-destructed before they began. But nowhere is the data more clearly nonsensical than in the convolutions of those fishing "pros" of B.A.S.S. (the Bass Anglers Sportsman Society, an enormous fraternity of bass fishermen).

The annotated details of that organization's disconcerting suspicion that a woman's presence in a tournament boat could bring on filial disaster and communal shame are as follows:

1 - In the summer of 1989, the organization declared that its James River tournament would remain all-male "not because of any bias toward females, but to avoid the indelicate situation that could arise from two anglers of the opposite gender being together for long periods of time in boats devoid of toilet facilities." Said B.A.S.S, boss, Helen Sevier: "While I'm for women's rights, I've never been what you might call a women's libber. I'm not one of those who wants to go into the locker room. I've never tried to be one of the boys."

2 -In April of the following year, tournament director Ray Scott announced that the 1990 tournament trail would finally be opened to women angling competitors. But almost immediately, fighting words came spewing forth from the wives of the male "pros." They were not going to stand at the dock while their

husbands were out in their boats with other women. Their husbands joined the chorus and threatened to withdraw unless the rules were reversed once again. By a margin of 441 to 133 they defeated the "open boat" policy, and the ladies were once again on the outside looking in. Said spokeswoman Sevier: "The mandate is clear. They do not want women to compete." Organizer Ray Scott was right behind, insisting that the lack of private toilet facilities would threaten "the integrity of the rules" because contenders are required to stay within sight of each other. "If you are fishing with a lady, that could be a problem."

I am indebted to writer Deborah Morris for the authentic details of the above report. I was not there at the time, but Deborah's article (Guess Who's Coming To Deer Camp") in the December 1990 issue of OUTDOOR LIFE has kept me in both good humor and righteous indignation as I considered the nonsensity of the total debacle.

These precious, timid fishing professionals, who can cuss with the best of them when the fish don't respond to their baits, and whose knowledge of the female anatomay probably goes back to their grammar school days, just can't countenance the idea that a woman angling companion might get through an entire half day in their boat without having to attend to her renal needs, or wetting her fishing britches.

Rick Clunn, a four-time tournament champion quoted by Deborah, puts it in more convincing language. "The women I've fished with have been as professional, if not <u>more</u> professional, than 80 per cent of the men I've fished with....I suspect that the real issue is that some men don't want to risk being beaten by a woman. And that, of course, could happen." (Remember that?)

Putting those tournament "professionals" (they coined the term) aside, we need to recognize that the same bull-headed stubbornness exists in many of our own families, or circle of friends. What we have here is a whole fraternity of men who have watched female frontal nudity on their television tubes and neighborhood movie screens ever since they were able to ride a bike. They are rich in lustful, rugged language, and possess an abiding and thorough knowledge of the difference between the male and female organs employed in the process of urination, plus the inconvenience we must experience when we piddle.

There, I said it.

But someone had to. It is the Berlin Wall that has kept us out of too many boats, left behind on too many fishing and camping trips, and kept us captive to our homes, our kids, canning tomatoes and planting spinach. It may just be a convenient stalking horse to keep us "in our place", but it is not an acceptable condition to keep any of us away from the healthy enjoyment of God's great outdoors any longer.

This wholesale tentativeness about the subject of sex is absolute rot. Our schools have jumped higgeldy-piggedly onto the matter to such a degree that young girls today know more about the male sex organ at the age of thirteen than most of their mothers knew when they married. And the boys are smirking in classrooms all across America while their newly-profound instructors carefully detail the geography of the bodies of the girls in the next row.

Men can talk openly and confidently about their propagative glands, and even the menstrual cycle, but they just can't accept the possibility that they might be comfortable in a fishing boat with a female companion.

Get off it, boys! It's been going on for years, and it won't hurt even a little bit to try it. If your lady companion gets an uncomfortable urge during the fishing exercise, she can quietly announce that she has to "go," and you can head for the nearest shore...the same way that you would if the companion were Jack, John, Peter or Paul. It's as easy as that.

Any woman who wants to get along peaceably in the world that men have so over-complicated today recognizes the need for a continuing good sense of humor. The boys accuse us of causing trouble when we ask for a more equitable number of ladies toilets in their auditoriums and sporting arenas, and when some desperate female rushes into a "men's room" because she can't stand in line any longer, they want to arrest her and send her off to the pokey.

Is it any wonder that Kathie Jones of Florida felt so keenly about the matter that she has now invented the "She-inal"? That neat little device, she figures, can help reduce the time of a woman's-stop in the "ladies room" to a point almost approximating the few seconds that it takes a man do attend to his needs, zip up his zipper, and be on his way.

Kathie responded to the studies conducted by Cornell University and the Virginia Polytechnic Institute which determined that current practices take women 180 seconds to accomplish their objective on a typical "rest stop" while a man can achieve the same result in just 45 seconds. And you wonder what other amazing facts these esteemed academic institutions have been keeping from us all of these years!

Anne Richards, Texas' first female governor (and one of us) has told her state House of representatives that their proposed law to increase to ratio of ladies'-to-men's restrooms in sporting facilities to two-to-three may not be enough. She can't understand why we just can't be treated equally.

In the great outdoors there are no such sexual barriers. That clump of bushes on the nearby shore will provide equal privacy for either a male or female visitor. And then everyone can get back to fishing.

Any grown woman who has witnessed the covetous attention which her chosen male partner pays to her sexual arrangement just has to be comically confused by the way in which that same partner evaluates it as a nasty deterrent to a pleasant day on the water. Indeed, there are many men who consider an outdoor, wilderness experience with their wives as a catalyst to more exciting sex. Not necessarily more primitive, but somehow more free from restraint, "back to nature" and worth repeating.

The above is not intended to encourage sex in a fishing boat. While the infinite loneliness of being out there together, and the suggestive pounding of the waves against the sides of the boat could generate unanticipated passion, the meager comfort of a boat seat can quickly dampen desire. Over-enthusiastic indulgence could also provoke an overturned vessel, loss of property and further participation.

The cabin will accommodate such urgings in more appropriate coziness, with the added amorous *joie de vivre* provided by a crackling fire in the stove or fireplace.

But I digress. The sociological message of this chapter is that the sexual plumbing with which the female body is graced should be no deterrent to an outdoor experience-for-two, in which fishing may play either a major or minor role. Ours is a most sophisticated society when it comes to the matter of our body comfort and our practices to maintain it. History has proved that the differences in our orientation in elimination has not deterred us from rising from a primitive condition to a state of almost incomprehensible enlightenment.

And ambivalence. We are as comfortable in our private acts in that clump of bushes as we are on one of Mr. Koehler's most contemporary water closets. We sacrifice accustomed comfort to the rugged surface of a fallen log if that's what it takes to share in the enjoyment and beauty of God's great outdoors.

As Helen Reddy sang it so magnificently, "If I have to, I can do anything. I am woman!"

As a further reference to this turbulent subject, I cite the example of a young Shoshone Indian woman by the name of Sacajawea who (at the tender age of 17) was recruited by explorers Captain Meriwether

Lewis and Clark didn't carry any cameras on their expedition, so this drawing may have been made by one member of the expedition when Sacajawea pointed out the stretch of shoreline where she would like to put in for a rest stop.

Lewis and Lieutenant William Clark in the early months of 1805. On April 7th, carrying her two-month-old son on her back, she stepped into one of the three humble boats which had been especially made for the tortuous trip west toward the Pacific.

For sixteen months, the historians tell us, she travelled with a force of 31 men, all between the ages of 18 and 35, constantly facing the hazards of hostile Indian tribes, accidents, sickness, grizzly bears, rattlesnakes, exposure and near starvation. Through it all, you must believe, young Sacajawea attended to her fundamental need for elimination with no recorded discomposure by the all-male company.

Indeed, young Sacajawea is reported to have saved the entire party from attacks by Indian bands along the route by interceding for them. Further, she has been described as "an intelligent, lovable and useful addition to the expedition." And the respected Encyclopedia Britannica tells us that "her fortitude in the face of hazards and deprivation became legendary. More memorials have been raised in her honour than any other North American woman."

Finally, good sister Helen Sevier should consider the two women astronauts who spent 13 days, 19 hours and 30 minutes with five male members of the crew of the shuttle Columbia, traveling almost six million miles, circling the world 221 times...without having to pause along the way for a rest stop.

As with the others who preceded them, these lady scientists and explorers have acquitted themselves with great credit and have enriched our knowledge of the universe. All the while confined in a miniscule working space, and always outnumbered by male members of the same crews.

And nowhere in the records of these odysseys have there been reports of those ladies' husbands hunkering together on the ground, near the launchpad, gazing skyward and asking, "What is really going on up there?"

THE "SECRETS" ARE OUT!

"Twenty years ago fishing guides kept their mouths shut. Television fishing stars showed a bunch of fish being caught but didn't offer much detail...Now it's the Age of Angling Information. Now the country's best anglers are eager to tell it all. In seminars. On TV. In print. The more secrets revealed the better."

-Ron Schara, outdoor writer,
Minneapolis STAR TRIBUNE, March 1992.

"Nothing is secret, that shall not be made manifest."
-HOLY BIBLE, Luke 8:17

Just a week ago, one of our favorite outdoor magazines arrived in the mail, and right there on the cover in bright red ink it called out: "Secret Bass Tactics - America's Best Fishermen."

Secrets. I responded just as my husband had taught me. I went immediately to the basement, dialed open the wall safe which had been installed there just for this purpose. With the magazine carefully placed on top of the many other issues and books already in there, I closed the thick steel door, and spun the dial.

Upstairs, I quickly called the Ready Response Security Company to advise them of the increase in our inventory of sacred secrets in the vault. The sentry on watch took the news grimly, it seemed to me. We are near the top limit for secret storage on our current policy, he told me. But everything would be okay if I would just not disturb anything for the next few days, He would send a man out to microfilm the new information, catalogue it, assay it, and then release it for reading.

Sure enough, when I opened that magazine to its index page a week later, there was no such story heading. There was that article on page 103 entitled "Bassin' Big Time: 21st Century Tactics of America's Best Fishermen," which conveyed nothing really new or unusual enough to be labeled a "secret."

But it was fun to read. There were almost a dozen tournament anglers reporting how they had caught a fish or two, but not promising any sure-fire way to succeed on every body of water, at any day of the year. And it was reassuring, since those old boys were just doing what I had been taught by an Indian guide dozens of years ago.

That's what makes outdoor magazines so enjoyable to read. Their constant supply of tips, "hot" tips, tricks and tactics provide pleasant comfort in knowing that the old, tried and true methods of catching fish haven't gone out of style...and none of them are perfect.

Our mailbox has been a massive collection point for these outdoor journals for over thirty years. As of the date of this writing, we are down to subscriptions for just six of them, which pile up sixty separate-issues on our coffee table during the course of each twelve months. This is down somewhat since the early years, when we had more money to spend loosely in our frothy search for the Truth About Fishing.

We get along well with the few that remain on our list. They supplement my own list of cooking and home-making publications, which is also manifest. But those generally tread closer to the facts, and none of them have professed to share secrets. There's not much romance or

The Big Four of the outdoor publishing field...which sportsman Ted Williams to as the "Hook-and-Bullet Press". They still don't seem to believe that we are acceptable story material, but they are about all we have today.

adventure in them, and I never put one away sensing the pleasant smoke of a campfire, or hearing the waves wash against a boat.

In a world as crowded and busy as ours, in a life that is so full of incessant demands on our time and our patience, outdoor magazines are almost essential to maintaining an inner peace, and to recognize that there is a another world out there waiting to be discovered, shared and enjoyed.

From what I have been able to determine, there must be at least a hundred such periodicals available on our newsstands or by subscription. There are regionals, specific species gazettes, state-centered journals, and those true "national" magazines. Wherever you live, whatever you choose to fish for, I recommend at least a subscription or two to help you get your bearings, acquire at an entry-level vocabulary of the angler's language, and to broaden your awareness of what tools of the sport, and other embellishments, are out there in the market place.

Those which you will find on your supermarket racks, in most areas, include FIELD & STREAM, SPORTS AFIELD, OUTDOOR LIFE and IN-FISHERMAN. Pick any of them off the shelf. At least one "super special" subscription card will fall immediately into your hands. Replace the magazine. Take the card home. Study it for a quiet moment and you will discover that you can receive a full year's issues for about the same price you would pay for a pair of Danielle Steele's bedroom novels. The language may not be as pithy, but it will stick to your bones a lot longer.

Since much of this chapter concerns itself with the anatomy of a typical outdoor magazine, it is probably appropriate to begin with an examination of its cover. As a starting point, I did a quick review of the thirty-six (36!) issues still hanging around our fireside awaiting recycling to a local barber shop. I don't spend much time looking at their covers when these magazines arrive, but the word "secret" always stops me.

This minor deception is akin to some of the sensational headlines employed by the gossip tabloids which clutter most supermarket check-out lines. It's there to help sell copies, since all of these publications rely on these impulse-provoked sales to swell their total penetration into American homes. And I forgive them for that. If it takes a modestly exaggerated promise to get you to pick up an outdoor magazine, then so be it. You will be enriched by your purchase, and your budget will not suffer a greater blow than if you had purchased a couple of extra frozen dinners.

If you are interested in further detail, I can report to you that pictures of bass appeared on nine of the issues examined. Five of them displayed deer which had been killed, or were about to be; two showed handsome moose; another two featured bears (one brown, one black);

ANGLER & HUNTER magazine, the official publication of Canada's Ontario Federation of Anglers & Hunters, displays its ambivalence toward female anglers by placing the picture of this smiling lady on the cover of its June 1992 issue. I'm sure the picture had nothing to do with it, but that was the last issue it published. The magazine has now been merged with ONTARIO OUT OF DOORS, the Dominion's premier outdoor magazine.

and three gave us a look at a walleye. There were also one illustration each of a catfish, a turkey, a pheasant, a rattle snake, a hunting dog, and one fly angler.

The most important statistic, however, is that men were a part of thirteen of the covers...and there were no women to be seen anywhere.

This situation, we are asked to understand, is because the editors are convinced that women make up a relatively small portion of their readership. So it is the business of economics which keeps us off the covers.

But, to be fair to those editors, we can reflect on the fact that men rarely (if ever) are seen on the cover of BETTER HOUSEKEEPING or MADEMOISELLE. So forget the covers. Let's move inside.

If you are into philosophy, and enjoy examining the opinions of others (to see how they line up with yours), you will want to stop first at "The Editor's Page," wherein the particular C.E.O. (Chief Editorial Officer), will give you some "sound bites" of the material which follows, plus all of the nice things the magazine is doing for you.

In one notable issue, the C.E.O. promised "to broaden our editorial base to include features and departments that will complement and expand (our) hard-line coverage of hunting, fishing and related activities." That commitment was made over a year ago, and the level of that publication's coverage of women's fishing activities hasn't changed a lick.

I wrote that C.E.O. and asked him if we could expect more, but he elected not to reply to my letter. That was a mistake, since, if he had, I would have told him that I really like his publication because he does have one female writer who is given reasonably regular space. But her bag is more hunting than fishing, as mentioned in chapter six.

The next section you will come to in each of these journals is those pages of "Letters to the editor," and these are usually worth the price of-admission, alone. Here is the forum where the readers sound off, objecting to what they read last month, or cheering to ask for more of the same. Unlike the literature which appears on later pages, this sounds like your neighbor talking, and it brings you into the game. You feel like you are one of the family, and are permitted to complain about the coffee, or ask for another piece of toast.

It is the section which has been cited in earlier chapters, detailing letters from lady anglers who are fighting our battle to receive more of the attention which we deserve. If more of us write those kinds of letters, maybe some of those Madison Avenue C.E.O.'s would take us more seriously. But not to the point that it upsets their male constituencies.

Scattered through the next one hundred or more pages of each issue is the true main course of the meal they have prepared for us each month the fanciful mythology of modern day fishing, skillfully crafted by a seasoned stable of outdoor writers who transport us to such exotic venues as Alaska's Unalakleet River, Wisconsin's famous Chippewa Flowage, Lake Wawasee of Indiana, Florida's bass-rich Lake Kissimmee, the Ambergris Cay of Belize, the Allagash River of Maine, or California's Castaic Lake, today's most promising bass Valhalla.

Some ten to twenty articles, richly illustrated, will take us into the lilypads where monster bass await us, to the raging river rapids where trout struggle upward to their feeding pools, onto the deep-blue waters of the Gulf Stream, alongside a submerged rock where a giant muskie is lurking, or onto a quiet sandbar where fish of many species are feeding...often on each other.

This is true escape. We can feel the soft breeze on our face; listen to the quavering, plaintive call of a loon; catch a glimpse of a scurrying beaver, and sense the quick bend of the rod as a hungry fish awakes us from our lethargy. Excitement! We read it in bed as a nervous husband shifts around to look quizzically at us. "Not tonight," we tell him. "I'm float-fishing down the Umpqua River with Homer Circle."

Never mind that these are mostly folksy "old boy" stories inter-twined with the teller's effort to convince us that he has discovered a new "secret" method, discovered a "secret" new place, or is in the company of a wizened wilderness guide who has introduced him to rare paradise of fishing fulfillment. We are there. Without kids to get to the school bus on time, without a check-book that needs attention, a mother-in-law who is waiting for an invitation to dinner, or that hot dish to prepare for tonight's P.T.A. meeting.

The manuscript is convincing. Tomorrow we head for the tackle shop, call ahead for a reservation, and plan to get out on the water. We need the release, the change of pace, the pleasant companionship of other anglers, and the wind and the rain in our hair. The outdoor magazine has brought us out of servitude into serenity!

Well, almost.

Almost every sportsfishing publication, and not just the few mentioned in this chapter, has at least one writer who has missed his calling and should have been a nuclear physicist. They are the piscatorial know-it-alls who persist in over complicating one of life's most pleasant adventures. Their works are jammed with new definitions of some of the most homely elements of the sport. Old terms no longer apply. The simple adjective is now passe', and you now have to play the game on their terms to be _au courant._

The most bizarre example of this obfuscation is the word: "structure."

For centuries, anglers have been able to pursue their quarry ...and talk about it to their fellow folk...speaking of the type of "bottom" over which they fished. No more. "Bottom" is now "structure", and no self-respecting outdoor writer puts together an article without using that term almost as often as he uses the first person singular. It's "rocky structure', "sandy structure", "sloping structure" today.

It's a word you should carry around with you, written on a card you carry in your purse. Then, when you fall in with a group wherein a notable catch is being discussed, you can reach in your purse, glance at the note, and politely ask, "Over what type of structure?"

You will be immediately accepted as an articulate member of the modern fishing society.

But your challenge doesn't end there. Words like "piscivorous", "anadromous", "breakline", "stratification", "epilimnion" and "presentation" will pop out at you in many of the texts you attempt to understand and enjoy. It's really not that important that you understand them at all. I remember reading an article by Elaine Viets of the ST. LOUIS POST-DISPATCH on the subject. "Many women worry because we can't talk sports," she wrote. "We're afraid this is a handicap, if not socially, then professionally.... But I've just learned something incredible: There are men who don't understand, either. They know even less than I do, but they pass for sports experts at the office because they fake it."

You can do that, too. But being a smart-aleck has its dangers, too. You will be pleased to learn that social psychologist Linda Carli has written in the prestigious JOURNAL OF PERSONALITY AND

SOCIAL PSYCHOLOGY that a tentative tone can increase your influence in a male audience. "Men," she tells us, "have more resistance to women who are assertive and confident than to women who appear to be lacking in confidence and knowledge but who are at least not 'pushy'." And that can be a very important factor in getting yourself invited on a fishing trip with some of the boys.

So you don't have to become a fishing encyclopedia to be successful.

All of the above will not be totally pleasant news for Al Lindner, C.E.O. of IN-FISHERMAN magazine. His publication prides itself on its motto: "Teaching America How To Catch Fish Is Our Business." When I spoke to Al on the subject of my thesis I told him that I have long classified his publication as the NATIONAL GEOGRAPHIC of fishing magazines because its articles are so heavily-detailed and extensively illustrated.

As a woman reader, I told him, I find them somewhat difficult to follow, and more complex than the simple sport of fishing seemed to call for. As I recall, he told me that their "teaching system" required increased attention to techniques and principles, not all of which could be adequately attended to in four-letter words.

The somewhat astounding ascension of his publication into the top position among all pure fishing magazines today certainly supports his response. He did, however, tell me that his staff is becoming more aware of the disparate interests of their female audience, and that future features might reflect a less technical bend.

There are other forces at work in the fishing communication business which must be included in the curriculum of this chapter. The first of these is the fishing book.

No distinct inventory of the books in our family library has been recorded over the past two or three decades. If it had been, it would probably show fishing books outnumbering my cookbooks by a two-to-one margin, which I am resigned to consider acceptable. The difference in their value, and contribution to knowledge, however, is strongly on the side of those which tell me how to prepare a chicken fricassee, risotto Milanese, beef teriyaki, or veal parmigiana.

The fishing book is generally a one-time experience, to be quietly enjoyed in front of the fire on an off-season evening, savored and committed to memory. It satisfies a need to be a part of the action when circumstances prevent it in fact. Worth the price at the time, but nothing the bank will accept as collateral when you are in need of a loan to paint the house.

I except from that description the wonderful volumes of A. J. McClane, already praised in earlier pages. Charlie Waterman is a favorite, too, most likely because he says so many nice things about his wife in his writings. Witness his dedication of A HISTORY OF ANGLING: "For my wife Debie, who is really more interested in this afternoon's fishing than in all that old stuff."

Exactly where this brief book will fit into your scale of values has yet to be determined, since we have so much more work to do, so many fish stories to tell. Unlike so many of the others, however, it promises the revelation of no secret whatsoever, and promises nothing more than the enrichment of your life by getting out where the fish are. It carries no warranty of "limiting out" on every trip, or the imparting of divine wisdom.

The above books by A. J. McClane are excellent reference materials for any angler. For light-hearted, far-reaching fishing adventure stories, check out Charlie Waterman. For philosophical musings about fly-fishing, Nick Lyons is unbeatable. And for some real wacky fish stories, pick up any of those hilarious volumes by Patrick F. McManus.

That has all been done. And fishing is no easier today than it was when the kids were catching them with cane poles and bent hooks. But when the winter seems too long, the television dull, and family conversation doesn't satisfy, head for your favorite bookstore and pick up a fishing book. It will do well until the real thing comes along.

Other purveyors of fishing lore have rushed in to take a slice of the book market with fishing "videos". While many of these provide exciting substitutes for your regular television fare, most of them are direct descendants of that other element of angling education: the television "fishing special".

I am old enough to remember many of those exciting deep-sea adventure shows which appeared during the early days of television, and which showcased wealthy sportsmen at sea in their large cruisers, trolling the Atlantic and Pacific oceans for huge marlin and tail-dancing sailfish. They were exciting exhibitions of men subduing huge monsters of the deep...but also depressing in the realization that I probably would never be able to afford such an adventure.

But today it is different. Hardly a Saturday or Sunday afternoon goes by that there is not a folksy angler staring out at you from his boat on the Backwash River or Lake Piscatawney, cranking his reel, and exclaiming "Nice fish!" as he slops a small bass over the side of his boat. Or maybe it's a walleye, a northern, or even a catfish.

For twenty minutes or so he will tell you how easy it is, if you will only use the products advertised during the other ten minutes of his half-hour "special". The performer is usually a person of modest skills, but with the ability to spend more of his time on the water than you or I...and therefore much deeper into the "true facts" of where the fish are, and what will bring them to your stringer.

"Nice fish," he says as he pulls in another, whether it is or not in your estimation. But more often than not, he speaks with a friendly southern drawl, or a backwoods slang that is intimidating. You can tell by all of the embroidered patches on his jacket, and the bright decals on his boat, that he is a veteran of the fishing wars, the tournaments, and has more trophies at home than Sam Snead.

At the end of his show, he will probably offer you a copy of his book, or video, containing untold "secrets" which will assure you the same success which he is enjoying. You will henceforth be able to master everything that swims, bringing it over the gunwales as you turn toward the camera and say, "Nice fish , And all for only $19.95 a copy.

If you find the video attraction irresistible, consider first that many of them are available on rental from your local tackle shop, and even some from your neighborhood library. You may find their close-up action more satisfying than reading about it in a magazine or book. Whatever turns you on, strengthens your determination to get out on the water, that's what you should do.

This total communications business, however, is dominated by the magazines, and well it should be. You really don't need a book to learn the basics, and keep up with everything that's new. The same goes for the videos. But you do need a friendly outdoor magazine or two.

In addition to brightening your off-season reading, the magazines report regularly on new developments in the gear required for almost every type of species, and the vast variety of fishing waters to be enjoyed. What they don't cover in editorial matter will pop up in the ads of the manufacturers and other suppliers. That advertising, like the articles which it surrounds, doesn't have to be taken seriously, but it will help you build your shopping list when you head for your nearest outfitter or tackle shop.

All of this applause for the fishing journals should not be interpreted as a statement of unqualified support for them and their editorial staffs. The four publications referred to in the earlier pages of this chapter distribute well over four million copies into our homes in an average month. That works out to over fifty million copies a year.

When you add to those figures the numbers added by the scores of other outdoor magazines not included in this study, you can be assured that the total annual issue of all of these publishers amounts to something over sixty million magazines falling into the hands of anglers every year. Sixty million!

The FISH & WILDLIFE SERVICE survey cited on previous pages tells us that Americans spent over $70,000,000 on those magazines in 1985, averaging something under $2.00 per angler. That clearly indicates that not all anglers are readers. But those who do read will learn more, fish more successfully, and enjoy the sport even when they are not out on the water.

But what they won't find in those magazines, in any quantity, is the growing role that women anglers are playing in the sport, their prize catches, their adventures and fun in the pursuit of their favorite fish. Norma Brand, one of the better-known women tournament competitors, lays it right on the line. "Look through the fishing magazines," she tells us. "There are millions of female anglers out here, but it's like we're invisible."

I probably don't have to tell you that the same type of situation exists within the field of newspaper reportage. The University of Southern California's "Women, Men and Media" project released a study in 1992 which concluded that women (who make up 52% of our

There is really nothing special about this collection of full-page, full-color ads taken from some recent issues of outdoor magazines. They are all the same. Peopled with men only...because the advertisers and their agencies are still ignoring us.

population) show up just 13 per cent of the time in prime news spots in our newspapers.

Commenting on that report, BOSTON GLOBE columnist Ellen Goodman adds: "Lest you think this is just a reflection of reality, even the stories about breast implants quoted men more often than women." Ellen also tells us about Nancy Woodhull, a founding editor of USA TODAY who now owns her own consulting firm. Nancy puts it this way: "Women around the country really notice when the press doesn't report their existence. It's like walking into a room where nobody knows you're there."

With the cards stacked so heavily against us it is easy to understand why Jane Clifford didn't make the headlines in the sports pages of the COEUR d'ALENE PRESS, or find her picture on the cover of FIELD & STREAM when she landed the new Idaho state record chinook salmon back in 1987.

But our days are coming, ladies, and they will come a lot sooner when you join in the action. Life is short, and there is so much to be enjoyed, whether those editors know we are there or not.

A STARTING POINT

"Don't give (your wife) your old, beat-up rod and reel. If you don't want it any more, why should she?...A newcomer deserves the 'good stuff.'...Spinning equipment can be easier to learn to use, but today's baitcasting rods and reels are light and have become simpler to use as well...Get a woman accustomed to fishing with it right from the start, so there is no transition to make later."

> -*"Take Your Wife Fishing, Please," Jill Barnes,*
> *BASSMASTER magazine, January 1989*

"For years ice fishing has struck me as a contradiction in terms, like Los Angeles Lakers or casual sex."

> -*"Call Of The Iceman," Rent Cowgill,*
> *FIELD & STREAM magazine, December 1986*

In support of my position that husbands can often be as dumb as those "other" men, I submit file No. 2106-H (for "handbags").

In this report I call attention to a certain shopping trip from which my husband returned, triumphantly (he thought) carrying three purses which he had purchased for me at the clearance sale of a local emporium. "Cheap!" he exclaimed as laid them out for me to view.

And they certainly were. All in garish, out-of-style colors, and in fabrics not seen since Queen Victoria last displayed her carpet bag of knitting supplies.

It was at that point that I printed and posted Marjorie's Inviolable Law 2106-H, which emphatically states that "no husband of mine shall at any time in the future purchase handbags for his spouse, regardless of price or the bust size of the attending clerk."

With a similar respect for you, and your own perception of the form of fishing best for you, I will not try to push you into any of its various forms of execution. There are, however, some mechanical and seasonal matters related to the sport which need to be discussed to assist you in determining your initial orientation.

The classic view of a fishing person is that of an angler holding up a rod of some type in his or her hand, and flailing it in a forward motion as some type of fish attraction ("lure") flies off into space, connected to the rod by a frail line of fine denier spinning off dutifully from the reel located at the base of the rod.

It has been that way for almost a century, and, in its simplest form, it was known as "casting." But not today. It is now classified as "baitcasting," unless the reel is one which does not spin in the flight of the line.

In such a case, it could be "spin casting," or just plain "spinning."

All three of these exercises are generally embraced in the umbrella category of "casting," and serve to identify those millions of anglers who employ rods of no more than seven feet in length, and are content to let the mechanism of the reel thereto attached do most of the work: taking the lure to the fish, and bringing the captured fish to the boat.

Those who have adopted "fly fishing" as their game are of an entirely different religion. They disdain any object which goes by the name "lure". Their enticement to the fish they seek its almost exclusively a tiny hook surrounded by miniature feathers (make that "hackle"), hand-wrapped to the hook with an assortment of yarns.

These are delicately named "dry" flies or "wet" flies, and I am not sure why. Both will be abundantly "wet" when they hit the water, so why should it really matter?

The fly fisherman can also be identified by the length of the rod with which he pitches those flies. Few self-respecting practitioners of this method would want to be seen with a rod of under nine feet in length, and many carry rods as long as fifteen feet. "The longer the rod, the better one can control the line," they will tell you.

In an apologetic suggestion that a woman could not perform well with a rod of such extreme dimension, the folks at Orvis offer a model only eight feet in length, "made especially for ladies." Embellished with "reversed cocabella seat and Marbury grip." And it weighs only 2 5/8ths ounces!

Yet another very specific element of the fly angler's arsenal is the line he employs. First of all, it must float. To sink below the surface would betray its presence to the fish being stalked, so a "hydrophobic" line coating which actually repels water will make it even more acceptable for the purist.

Color is also important, and fluorescent yellow or fluorescent chartreuse are popular favorites. Construction of the fly fishing line is also more carefully studied than the simple braided or monofilament lines of the "bait casters". A first-class fly line may have a "shooting head" and it will certainly offer "weight forward" characteristics.

Beyond the line, extending to the fly itself, is the "leader". And, behind the line, there is also further length provided by "backing", which is really more of the same, but generally not as exotic as the "real" line. As you can see, this is not a simple arrangement of fish-catching elements. It is, at the minimum, a modestly scientific assembly of space age fibers arranged in manner which has proved to confuse the fish, but please the-user thereof.

The fly angler's reel is also an especially interesting device, generally with its roots in the models favored by those British sportsmen who pioneered this variety of taking fish. While not much larger than a doughnut cutter, the reel can store enough line to fight a fish at a distance longer than a football field. Like the rod it is attached to, the reel is of exceptionally light weight, reflecting its manufacture from "aircraft grade aluminum stock". Superior craftsmanship is taken for granted since the usual price tag is two- to three-times the cost of a good quality baitcasting reel.

While most fly fishing is done in rivers and streams, angling for various types of trout and salmon, some of its more adventurous aficionados have moved out into more adventurous waters and have accepted a number of modifications to their standard approach to provide exciting catches of bonefish, tarpon, sailfish and even marlin.

Lee Wulff was one of this country's most noteworthy and successful fly fishermen for over half a century. Jim Chapralis of PanAngling Publishing Company tells of Lee hooking into a monstrous sailfish off Costa Rica and fighting it for over three hours before bringing it to gaff. The fish had taken a dry fly, sounded over and over before finally coming to the surface for a final ceremonial leap, slashing all over the surface, and then surrendering.

Lee was 86 years old at the time!

So it is not fair to say that fly fishing is only for the timid. Its demands for prodigious skill and a comprehensive understanding of the performance parameters of the equipment are exactly what make it so challenging and satisfying. Try convincing a dyed-in-the-wool fly fisherman that it takes more skill to land a 30-pound muskie on spinning gear than it does to land a four-pound rainbow trout on a wet fly!

Some seasoned buff of fly fishing may find the foregoing description inadequate and not altogether complimentary, but I have tried to be fair and sufficiently expository to present the reader with at least a bird's eye view of the sport. We still have two other methods to explore, and we will return now to the "baitcasting," "spincasting, " "spinning" versions.

At least 80% of those who fish today are using casting equipment (other than fly casting) to present their lures to the fish they seek, and the bulk of these are still using the standard "baitcasting" rod and reel. It has proven to be the easiest method to learn, and offers a full range of performance characteristics to attract and land fish. I have been one of its modest vocal supporters as long as I have been at this sport.

The baitcasting rod and reel are generally pretty simple tools, no more complex than an eggbeater or mechanical potato peeler. The rods are the most stalwart of all of those used in fishing, of modest length, easy to transport and care for. The reels are quite simple to understand, generously forgiving, and as easy to maintain as a food processor.

While manufacturers have complicated the line picture by introducing monofilament materials as alternates to the old standard braided nylon lines, these are no mystery for a woman who has darned her share of socks and sewn buttons on everything from a dress shirt to a mackinaw jacket. The knots required to attach leaders and baits will pose no problem for a mother who has tied her kids shoes through all those pre-school years, and has at least a preliminary exposure to crocheting behind her.

Another consideration to support baitcasting as your starting point in fishing is that these tools can be had at more comfortable cost levels. And for those who prefer to make their opening effort with more sophisticated, more feature-loaded versions, these can be had for only a few dollars more than the "standard" models.

Perhaps the most important advantage of baitcasting is that while it is easy to learn, it is best taught by a companion. This is where the fun comes in. Playing (being!) dumb about the whole thing, and asking your significant other to teach you the ropes, can engender more tenderness than you have experienced since your first date. He will probably take you in his arms, grasp your wrist in his, hold you close, and then whisper something like "Just relax. Everything will be all right." And that ought to take you back quite few years!

There was a temptation to include in this chapter a literate description of the casting process. But then I read the material in the accompanying box ("Caster, Know Thy Weapon,") and I realized how futile and confusing that would be. So put yourself in the care of others for this educational experience. Even if it is another lady angler, it will come easier than learning to drive a Harley.

In deference to my many friends who find "spinning" and "spincasting" more to their taste, I will now call your attention to some of the qualities which have made it attractive to them. Most important

Caster, Know Thy Weapon

Casting is accomplished by disengaging the pinion gear flats from the spindle flats. This can be accomplished by using a pushbutton on the side plate; by pressing a quick-casting lever-release on the inside of the side plate; or by using a thumb-bar release that's centered on the rear pillar of the reel. When any of these devices is activated, the pinion is lifted up off of the flats area of the spindle: the spool turns because the pinion hub no longer meshes with the flats on the spindle.

The preparation for a cast involves levers, ramps, cams and yokes—all spring-loaded, so they can be kicked back into position when the handle is turned to pick up the spool and retrieve line.

Casting is controlled in several ways. Most reels have small end-caps (or, more typically, an end-cap on the right side plate), which adjusts pressure on the ends of the spindle to control freedom of rotation. These end-caps, often called cast-control knobs in the reel manuals, are screw-mounted and exert pressure on small spring-loaded beryllium-copper shims, which in turn exert pressure on the stainless-steel spool shaft. Proper adjustment dictates just

enough pressure to allow a lure to drop slowly to the ground when the rod is held horizontally.

While this cast control adjusts play-and-tension on the spindle, control while casting is achieved through centrifugal or magnetic systems.

Centrifugal systems, once very popular (though less so now), incorporate small brake blocks that freely slide on a small bar, which is at right angles to the spool spindle.

These brake blocks spin out as the reel is cast, riding against a rim that surrounds the side of the spool flange. Increased spool speed creates increased centrifugal pressure—therefore braking—during the cast.

Magnetic cast-control systems operate on a basic law of physics: a magnetic field creates magnetic "eddy currents" that slow the spool. The spool does not have to be iron or steel for this to take place. Most work on aluminum spools or parts.

Most such systems use several or more rare-earth magnets of cobalt. These magnets are controlled as to force by adjusting the position of the magnets—thus affecting the force of the electromagnetic field. Most reels have a small dial or slide bar on the left wide plate for this adjustment. ■

Baitcasting is nowhere near as complicated as many of the boys make it out to be. But, if you are the least bit mechanically inclined, this treatise will tell you what exactly goes on inside a reel when you toss your line out to the fish.

of all is the structural arrangement of the line spool which makes it absolutely back-lash free and so simple to maintain.

Both types of reels "spin" the line off a fixed reel which cannot overspin to the degree that congestion develops, thus creating the "bird's nest" problem of a backlash. To many anglers this is advantage enough to choose this method. Baitcasters who tried it, however, found it more difficult to make longer, more accurate casts, and have gone back to their old ways.

Yet the spinning reels have taken over a large share of the market, even with anglers who pursue such more combative fish such as the largemouth bass and even the cantankerous muskie. The benefits which have brought them to spincasting, they will tell you, include these: The reel sits on an offset in the rod handle so that it is easy to reel in with your right hand (and "lefties" are also available). They also come in a variety of sizes, from "ultralight" to heavy duty, and they will work well with monfilament lines of 2-pound test weight up to 50-pound test and above. Now, with 50 years of research and development behind them, these "mono" lines are taking fish of all kinds, and registering many national awards.

Experts like Homer Circle of SPORTS AFIELD believe that further advances will broaden the acceptance of spinning equipment within the next few years, possibly taking over more than half of the total market.

In the meantime, the ease of use, and even lower cost than baitcasting equipment, make the spin cast alternatives worth your examination. For youngsters it is an obvious choice, and many manufacturers today offer beginning "kits" (rod, reel and line) pre-packaged for teaching kids to fish.

To conclude this essay on fundamentals and fishing methods, we turn now to ice fishing for a few fleeting observations and comments.

Which is really all it deserves.

I rush to make it clear that I have nothing against ice fishing. But since this book is written for, and about, female anglers, and their need to get out and enjoy God's great outdoors, I can find nothing to say for it.

Packing your body in every available layer of wool, cotton and nylon clothing available, stuffing your feet in the clumsiest, heaviest boots ever made by mankind, and shrouding your head in scarfs, knit caps and parkas just to go out and sit on the ice does not, in my studied opinion, qualify as true recreation. If you are into self-flagellation, and feeling the need to go out into the bitter cold and suffer at the side of your mate, I cannot save you.

But think about it. Grown men go out onto those frozen lakes and rivers, often deep in heavy snow, hauling sleds overloaded with motorized augers, portable shelters, buckets, baits, floats, rods and beer. And what for?

To catch a few small scaly fish they will bring home, expecting you to eviscerate and de-scale them, and convert them into meaningful nourishing and boneless meals, that's what.

Those folks who are paid to keep score tell us that there are about 2 1/2 million ice fishermen in this land of ours, which is somewhere near the population of Mongolia. I don't know what that signifies, but those cold-weather anglers are just the type who might be comfortable in that rugged and barren land.

Ice fishing, of course, is limited to those areas where ice forms over the surface of existing lakes and rivers. That puts the national arena for

If you have wondered what attracts men to ice fishing you might find an answer in this photo, which appeared in an ad for the "Pop'n'Fish" portable ice fishing shelter. The advertiser, FOF Products of Delavan, Wisconsin, says it's all just in fun...but men do need something to keep them warm.

this sport somewhere north of the Mason-Dixon line, stretched across the continent. As of this date, no practicing psychologist has come up with the true reason why men go ice fishing. My friend Phyllis says that an active ice fisherman is a sign of an unhappy husband. "Who else," she asks, "would forsake a warm connubial bed on a Sunday afternoon to venture out in the freezing cold, just to look down a hole at a bunch of fish?"

The season for ice fishing begins just as soon as the leaves have fallen off the trees, and a glossy film begins to form over the surface of the nearest pond. The addicted ice fishermen then begin to edge their pick-ups, vans, half-tracks and snowmobiles to the water's edge. The instant the surface clouds up, indicating additional ice depth, they light off their engines and head for last year's most productive area.

All of this happens without the benefit of any rational thought, and a few pick-ups, vans and snowmobiles are lost every year because the ice was not as thick as they assumed it to be. And a few fishermen go down with their vehicles, leaving widows and children behind. Nothing so disastrous happens during the summer season, when the True Fishermen return to those waters.

Anthony Accerrano of SPORTS AFIELD has written that "Ice fishing is the only way I know to keep in touch with gamefish during the long winter months. Because, yes, all those pike, bass, trout, walleyes and assorted others are out there, swimming in the depths, somehow surviving in spite of the implausible bitterness of snow and cold...moving and feeding down in the dark world below the ice."

That's all probably true, but don't those fish deserve some quiet time to themselves, to be left-alone from all of us who will be out to play tug-of-war with them when the "real" season opens? The "implausible bitterness" of those winter months beneath the ice is suffering enough, it seems to me.

But the ice anglers will have none of that. They load up with their strange, specialized gear, pack their bodies in long johns, eskimo socks and boots, balaclava facemasks and thermal body suits. Out on the ice, they point their power augers into the snow and chew out a network of eight- or ten-inch holes, confident that they have established direct access to some of the largest, hungriest fish in that particular body of water.

Next they will set up their odd rods ("tip-ups"), baited with lead-headed jigs and miniature minnows, and then wait for the action to begin. This is usually done sitting on an upturned large plastic bucket, eyes directed down into the hole, and feet beginning to numb up as the wind whips across the surface.

This excitement can last for hours, interrupted only by lifting the line, dropping the line, lifting the line, dropping the line, ad nauseum. Keith McCafferty of FIELD & STREAM has it figured out as well as any author on the subject. "Ice fishing," he says, "is nothing more than praying over a hole."

There is another strata of the society of ice anglers which, in the fairness characteristic of this volume, deserves attention. This is the class of these cold-weather boys which does its fishing in small portable structures loosely defined as "ice houses". These enclosures vary from permanent shanties, built on shore, and "sledded" out onto the ice when the season opens, all the way down to light-weight tents, carried into position in canvas bags and assembled on the spot.

Within these enclosures, the angler carries on his "wait-and watch" game, but protected from the wind. In some of the more elegant versions of these shanties there are also heaters, cots, compact stoves, card tables and even television sets! This is the preferred method for pursuing winter fishing, and many resorts or outfitters offer such accommodations on a rental basis, cater hot meals and generous supplies of beer.

Beer is the ceremonial draught of winter fishermen, moreso than with the summer clan. Cold beer is consumed to keep one's self "warm" It is drunk to pass the time while watching TV or the open hole, and it is relished in toasts to triumphant catches. It is sometimes accompanied by stronger stuff, to add to its "warming" properties. There was also a story in THE WALL STREET JOURNAL, a few years back, of a 33-year-old female bill collector in central Wisconsin who plopped a minnow "into her beer and starts drinking. The minnow vainly swims against the flow and vanishes." All in celebration of a trophy winter catch.

It also needs to be reported that many large fish are actually caught by these boys of the winter. Big northern pike are quite common in some areas. Jim Fisher's 1990 catch of a 15-pound, 2-ounce walleye at

Atlas Pits, Wisconsin, earned a spot in the record books of the National Fresh Water Fishing Hall Of Fame. Waters of the Great Lakes area also produce catches of large trout and salmon, but most of those are taken by seasoned practitioners who work the same areas year after year.

Whatever they catch, of course, they richly deserve. Their long hours out in the winter elements qualify them for some type of compensation for stubborn persistence in the face of snow, winds and heavy odds. If there is one type of fishing which should be reserved exclusively for men, this is it.

It has been covered here at this length only to suggest that if you are ever invited to join a male companion on an ice fishing trip you should have a plausible excuse ready. There is absolutely no need to be polite or overly-creative in your response. You want none of it. Fifteen minutes after you got out on the ice you would be praying for sundown or a hot bath. Just don't do it.

Winters in the north country are meant to be spent in quiet contemplation of last summer's successes, and in planning the adventures of the coming season. Read the magazines. Inventory your equipment. Plan your new purchases. Check out exciting itineraries. Go through the catalogues, order new clothes. Just don't go ice fishing.

We have come to the end of our review of three of the most publicized methods of fishing, but there are some folks who will consider it incomplete since it fails to include "trolling" and "deep-sea" fishing. But trolling is really only a subsection of the baitcasting universe, and will be attended to in later chapters as it applies to the pursuit of certain species.

"Deep-sea" fishing has been excluded because the general purpose of this chapter is to establish a starting point for freshwater fishing, that type which is universally available to us in our home areas. It will, however, be discussed in picturesque detail in the chapter relating to "saltwater" fishing...which "deep-sea" fishing certainly is.

That all being explained, we move now to the exciting experience of seeking out, and purchasing, the minimal (but adequate) equipment for your primordial step into the world of angling.

THE JOY OF SHOPPING

"What can you do to become a better-educated tackle shopper? How can you buy tackle that's right for you? Chat. That's it, just learn to chat with the right people and you'll be amazed at the improvement in your buying skills and the resulting quality of tackle you'll be using....Remember, fishing is still a friendly sport, where everyone is willing to share information and to chat about experiences both out of the water and in the tackle store."
- "Solving Tackle-Buying Problems," James Rudnick.
ANGLER & HUNTER, May 1988

Most women making their first visit to a tackle shop, or "sports" store will find it an energizing and emotional experience. Here they are, at last, right smack in the middle of a domain which they had long surrendered for the exclusive travel of men. But there are women's items displayed throughout many of those stores, and there are even women clerks serving customers.

In the most spartan varieties, the visible inventory will be limited to the more obvious hunting and fishing paraphernalia, with attention to women's needs evidenced in minor stocking of rain gear or the ubiquitous T-shirt. Yet their counter personnel may be richer in knowledge of the products they sell than those in the more elaborate establishments.

Your first sortie into either type of emporium should be planned as a reconnaissance mission, to survey the general range of the merchandise available, and to sense the courteous and interested nature of its personnel. You will want to feel the merchandise, examine the labels and check the prices, just as though you were out shopping for a new Spring wardrobe. If your activity provokes the classic "Can I help you?" from an observing clerk, you can reply, "Not today. I'm just looking."

Safe in your car, or back home, you can make some notes on what you saw, review the prices, and then call a friend. If the friend has any credentials in tackle buying, you can review your notes together, and then develop a strategic plan for your return several days later to get down to the serious business of spending money...the first sign of your commitment to the sport of fishing.

Your strategic plan should contain a basic shopping list, enumerating those essential items such as rod, reel, line, a few lures, and some minor associated hardware. It is not necessary that you buy all of it, or any of it, for that matter, on this second visit. If the clerk with whom you become paired does not communicate clear knowledge of his products, and how they can be used effectively, you can thank him, put your credit cards back in your purse, and go to the diner next door for a cup of coffee.

That should be your signal to seek out another similar establishment, and repeat the same process. There, with good luck, you will encounter a caring and understanding soul who (even though male) will win your confidence and deserve your undivided attention. He will ask questions about your fishing expertise, or lack thereof, your areas of interest, and general objectives.

If you like the cut of his jib, and feel that he can be safely entrusted with the truth, this would be a good time to tell him that you do not consider the catching of fish to be a life-or-death matter, and that you are seeking to acquire nothing more than a respectable collection of such tools which will properly equip you without identifying you as a raw apprentice.

That declaration will be direction enough, and you can now expect to be shown a sequence of rods, reels, lines and other related miscellany in the moderate price ranges. The features of each item will be carefully detailed, and, perhaps, with some reference as to how they will assure your success.

If your initial pre-shopping expedition produced a fair understanding of the price ranges for those products, you will quickly know if those which are proposed truly fit the mid-range price level, and you are not being asked to buy more than you need. As you accept each recommendation, your clerk-adviser will become increasingly attentive to your total needs, and a warm relationship will develop.

Should the rod-reel-line purchasing adventure leave you excited and exhausted, the business of buying lures and other miscellany can be left to another day. Withdraw at that point, repair to your fireside, examine your purchases, and possibly expose them to a friend...or even your husband. If, after such review, you remain assured that you were in the right hands, return at a later date, and head for the plastic-and-wood circus which is known as "the bait department".

If the salesperson who served you on your previous visit does not come immediately to your aid, wander in his direction. As your vision spins through his memory, he will recall your earlier encounter and speed to your aid. After you tell him where you plan to fish and what for, he will give you a guided tour down the primrose path of angling folklore and outfit you with at least three tried-and-true fish-catchers. Among them will be a red-and-white spinner (best bet: "Daredevle"), a molded plastic perch-like scooter ("Shad"), and a wooden imitation minnow.

Variations of all three can expand your arsenal, and add to your appearance of inner wisdom within the circle of your early angling

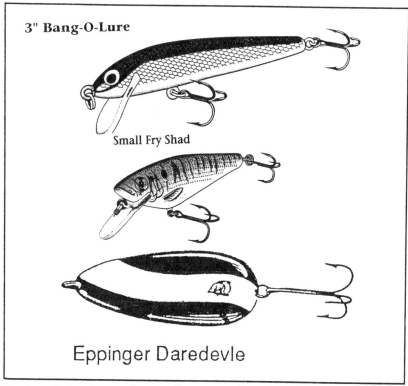

The three baits shown above will get you off to a good start. The "Bang-O-Lure" and "Small Fry Shad" are by Bagley Bait Company, the "Daredevle" has made Eppinger famous, and catches all kinds of fish.

companions. But don't get carried away. You still have leaders, swivels, line and a few minor tools to complete your starting point total package. All of which will be warehoused in a shoe-box size "tackle box," plus a narrow-gauge tubular case in which you will transport your rod to protect it from clumsy companions who rarely watch where they are walking or where they toss their heavy duffle .

Shopping is a sport at which women have always excelled, and the fishing outfitting experience should be no feverish challenge. The unique element of this tackle shop mission is the friendly repartee which takes place between the buyer and seller, which stimulates your purchasing glands as you hear how each of the products presented will assure your competence in the sport and generally add to your well-being.

You are persuaded that the seller has your honest interests at heart, and is not taking advantage of your naivete. He confides in you some

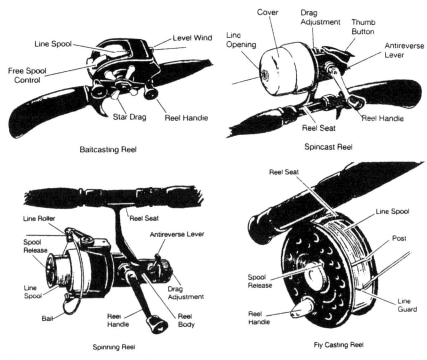

The above illustration will provide a short course in reel identification as well as pointing out the major details of each of the four types shown. (from the student Manual of the A.F.T.M.A. Sport Fishing Foundation).

of his own early fishing travails, and entrusts you with exhilarating knowledge which strengthens your belief that every purchase you have made is the right one.

The reel which he has transferred to your possession is comfortable to your hands, has a convenient thumb-bar release, is equipped with an easy-to-manage star drag, and features a spool with a capacity for at least 200 feet of 12-pound test line, with a 5:1 retrieve ratio. Not over-burdened with expensive gimcracks, and thus not over-priced .

The rod you now own was recommended for its convenient and adequate length (5%- to 6-feet), made with a space-age combination of graphite and fiberglass, mounted with ceramic guides, and offering proper flexibility to perform well with "medium weight" lures. It will serve you well in a wide range of fishing pursuits, and will stand the critical examination of any male angling companions.

That you have come away from this initial investment with a warm feeling of hearty satisfaction is a tribute to the place of your purchases: the classic American tackle shop. Where else in this country of ours can you find an establishment staffed with individuals who have consummate knowledge of their products, and pass it on with such passionate

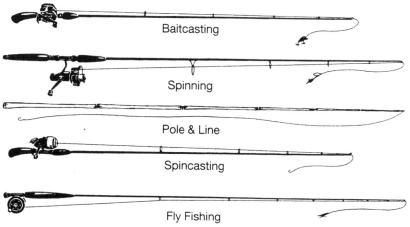

Take a few minutes to study this group of fishing rods before you do your shopping and you will know what to look for as you work your way through the forest of rods which will confront you. Note that the "baitcasting" and "spincasting" rods appear the same but the "spincasting" model will have larger ferrules (holes through which the line passes when you cast).

97

recital of the facts?

Had you gone to one of the large "discount" merchandisers you may have found just as broad an array of items to select from, but they would all have been stacked or hung in long rows on cold display racks, with only a price tag to declare their differences in quality and promise. There would have been no knowledgeable person to spend friendly moments with you, listening to your needs, and translating them into just the right assortment to match your specific requirements.

The major enticement offered by the "mass merchandisers" is that of price, and one of the biggest of those has sought to increase that advantage by advising its suppliers that it would no longer do business with those which continued to sell their goods through sales representatives, or "reps". This power play seeks to eliminate the key contact between manufacturer and retailer: the personal presentation of their products in a manner which will help them communicate their advantages and benefits to the ultimate purchaser.

Food marketers tried that on the women of America when they took the butcher away from their supermarket meat counters, piling their packaged chops, steaks and ribs in plastic-wrapped packages on refrigerated shelves. But those who wanted help and information before we would pay $9.00 a pound for their steaks and $6.00 a pound for their beef roasts would not put up with it. Today the butchers are back where we can see them, talk to them, and tell them to trim our purchases on their meat blocks before we put them in our shopping carts.

In a game as mystical as the sport of fishing, communication is often of more value than knowing that a lure is made of pure cedar or "durable" plastic. What we need to know is what kind of fish it has really caught, how far can we cast it, and what are the most productive retrieve methods. And that's the kind of critical information which works its way through the marketing channels, carried primarily by the manufacturer's reps. Long live the reps, and those friendly tackle shops where we can go to trade fish stories as we spend our money, and as we extend our enjoyment of fishing through the camaraderie of earnest and helpful merchants!

Once you have made a firm commitment to the sport, you will find yourself attracted to off-season journeys to that favorite tackle shop to "see what's new", and then find yourself coming away with new assortments of lures to better prepare you for next year's trips out on the water. This magnetism is sometimes described as "tackle disease" and usually becomes a perennial affliction. After all, spending just a few more dollars on some of those "proven" new "secret" baits really won't bust the family budget, and it could make for a more rewarding season ahead.

The lure manufacturing business is one of the most interesting constituencies of this sport. Many famous names have come and gone over the past several years, and with them those tried-and-true baits which once could catch everything in the water. Today's major survivors include such brands as Mepps, Normark, Bagley and Berkley, all with a challenging variety of contraptions to attract whatever species you choose to pursue.

But alongside those well-respected names you will find many others identifying new approaches to old ideas. They are the product of a number of professional guides and other anglers who have turned this enterprise into something of a cottage industry. Beginning in garages or basements, these novice marketers now offer those lures which they have designed, and which have proved effective for them, and which they are presently pleased to share with you...at competitive prices. There is no sure pedigree of performance to guide you in their purchase, so, once more, you are at the mercy of your selected salesperson.

Educated selection from the multitude of lures on display requires the acquisition of much broader vocabulary than you possessed before you made the decision to become an angler. The English language, which has recently given space to such euphemistic terms as "infra-structure," "networking", "process", and "bonding" has now been augmented by a treasury of self-serving labels for that family of lures which once were satisfactorily identified as "artificial plugs." Today you need to be able to know the difference between "topwater plugs", "poppers", "crankbaits", ""jerk baits" 'and "deep runners".

Add to those such terms as "buzzbaits", "spinnerbaits", "count-downs", "jigs" and just plain "spinnners" and you can sense the learning challenge which confronts you.

Gary Soucie, who published "A Survey Of Freshwater Lures" in the 1985 edition of SPORTS AFIELD FISHING SECRETS described this problem of nomenclature in these terms: "Of all the different kinds of terminal tackle, lures are surely the most varied and the subject of most myth. While the lures themselves have become more 'scientific', the lore about lures has become more like science fiction."

Frank Suick, the Wisconsin muskie angler who invented the famous jerkbait which carries his name, describes it as "a sucker in distress". Which can also describe a bait shopper who comes to the shopping rite without the strength to resist and spend only in moderation.

No contemporary discussion of fishing lures would be complete without at least a cursory review of that odd art form known as the "plastic worm ". As a class, this rather recent arrival in the bait family has been described by notable authorities as follows:

"A lure, or lure type, that can catch nearly any kind of gamefish in nearly any kind of water, deep or shallow, dirty or clear, fast running or calm, fresh or salt."
-Anthony Accerrano, SPORTS AFIELD, April 1987 *

"It's safe to say that no artificial lure produces more fish nation-wide than these colorful pieces of plastic."
-Tim Tucker, BASSMASTER MAGAZINE, August 1987

"Plastic worms are unquestionably the most productive lure for largemouth bass...A novice angler has a chance at hooking a big bass each time he throws a plastic worm."
-Minneapolis STAR TRIBUNE, July 1991

Most of the above exuberance, you will one time discover, belongs within the "science fiction" description offered earlier by Gary Soucie. Nonetheless, it is a fact that anglers everywhere have gone bonkers over this weird creation which has all the charm of a batch of Jello that went bad. When it was still a new item, you could buy them by the dozen for the price of a green pepper, but now that it has proven that it really does catch fish, the packaging has become much more sophisticated, and prices have risen like kites in a Spring breeze.

Yes, this is the third time that I have quoted Mr. Accerano, and that's all because he writes so well about the sport of fishing. I suppose I could have said all of that myself, but most people don't know me from a bale of hay ... and they would rather hear from a real expert (of which Mr. Accerano is certainly one). The same goes for the other many excellent outdoor writers and social scientists which are quoted herein. I have cited them by name so that you might research them further if I have piqued your interest in their discourse on this subject.

Manufacturers have justified all this by creating a whole zoo of new forms with intimidating names, like lizard, crawdad, rattle, "Reeleel", "Crawfrog" and a host of others. Their sales volume grows every year, and I have a clear idea that this "Jellybait" is the best thing to happen to the plastics industry since Tupperware. If bass are one of your early targets, it's safe to say that there is a worm or two in your future. You will have to study the literature to learn how to use it most effectively, choosing between such arrangements as the Texas, Carolina, weedless, slider, spinner, droop and even jig rig. Colors will be a concern, too, because the plastic worm spectrum runs through such exotic hues as "motor oil", "electric black", "smoke pepper", "lemon meringue, "tequila sunrise" and "hot pink".

As if that proliferation of choices is not enough to confuse us, the developers of this plastic menagerie have added the element of "scent" to further enhance its potential for enticing the fish we seek. You can blame it all on those piscatorial researchers who have determined that many species do, in fact, "smell". They can smell the presence of an angler, they tell us, and they can smell a good meal when it comes to their attention. If it smells real good, they clomp their jaws around it,

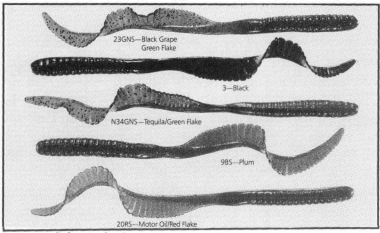

At least one fisheries biologist is on record as saying that bass have never really seen anything like a plastic worm, but they grab at it because "it looks easy to swallow." The specimens illustrated above are modestly referred to by their manufacturer, Mister Twister, as "Thunderworm" lures, especially designed for fishing in heavy cover. Another supplier is now offering half a million dollars to the angler who catches a new I.G.F.A. world record bass on one of its own designs!

and you will soon have another nice bass on your stringer.

At least that is the message which has been conveyed to us in the advertising of their purveyors. Persuasive yet not significantly documented to win the hearts, minds and dollars of anglers everywhere. Outdoor writers, generally, have supported the idea in many magazines and newspapers. But this year, to my surprise, a pair of fishing reporters for one of those major publications set out to conduct a reasonably objective test of the claim.

Their exercise included testing scented and unscented baits, side by side, in an assortment of waters, and for different species. Their conclusion was that the scented baits did not out-perform their naked brothers...but neither did they perform any worse. Another article in the August, 1992, issue of FIELD & STREAM carried a report on baits which were manufactured with the scents applied in the production process, generously lathered on the outer shell, or pumped into the bait structure. Results of a broad exposure of these lures to both fresh water and saltwater species showed somewhat more effectiveness, but was appended with the disclaimer that "None of these scent-enhancers will force a fish to feed if it already isn't interested in food."

I don't know what you want to make of that, but I have yet to be convinced and am sticking to the old-fashioned methods, and keeping those smelly things out of my tackle box. As my mother once told me: "Beware of strangers who come bearing strange potions...".

For centuries we women have demonstrated more understanding in the use of scents than men will ever attain. We have used them vigorously in the attraction and ultimate seduction of the men whom we have chosen. We have used them to bring exciting adventure to a candle-lit dinner, and to re-kindle a marriage fading through too much attention to business, kids or the Chamber of Commerce.

Some years ago, THE WALL STREET JOURNAL described women's cunning use of certain provocative scents to achieve our objectives as "aroma therapy". Avon Products, Charles of the Ritz, Jovan and Revlon were cited as suppliers of fragrances which added to our sexiness, enhanced our self-image and even lowered our blood pressure. The fact that these suppliers wisely decided to direct most of their sales efforts toward women is strong testimony in support of our superior sagacity in the elegant craft of attraction.

That women also have their own "secret" attractant for fish is strongly suggested by one Dr. David Goldsborough of England and further developed by Professor Peter Behan of Glasgow University. Their thesis evolved from the observation that women anglers were catching big male salmon with greater frequency than men who fished the same waters. The reason, it appeared to them, was the chemical message communicated by the pheromones given off by the skin of the female angler.

Salmon are known to be able to detect water-borne chemical "messages" to an astonishing degree. The odors of a man's hand, for example, have repelled and alarmed salmon, whereas those of a woman's hand will not. In 1966 the Goldsborough-Behan theory was given a practical test at the site of the Portlatch Dam on Idaho's Clear Water River. Sure enough, salmon and steelhead trout were sent skittering when a man's hand was placed in the water, but when a woman's hand was put in "the fish continued to swim...with no sign of agitation."

The famous Norwegian biologist, Professor Doving, concludes that "It is quite- possible that salmon can sense the sex hormones of women and become attracted to them even if these come in minute quantities on an angling lure." Salmon today...tomorrow the world! No wonder those men don't want us in their boats!

And speaking of boats, that is the subject we will turn to next.

FINDING TRUE HAPPINESS
IN A BOAT

"With the exception of buying a house, there might not be anything as scary as buying your first boat. Years ago, buying a boat was a relatively simple process....Today, over 2,500 boat manufacturers churn out over 4,000 models, so prospective buyers must do their home-work to ensure that their dream boat doesn't turn into a nightmare they'll pay for long after the monthly payments are finished... By carefully considering exactly what you want in a boat and then spending the time shopping around for the correct craft, you are all but guaranteed you will buy the right boat at the right price and enjoy many years of excellent performance in your first boat."
-"Get It Right The First Time," Mark Thomas,
FISHING SMART, Spring 1992.

I just love boats. I've been in almost every type of watercraft from a 16-foot Old Town canoe to a 700-foot cruise ship, with plenty fishing hull in between. Maybe this affection comes from the enjoyment I experience whenever I am out on the water...any water...and in the company of good friends.Boats are essential to almost every type of angling expedition, excepting only such adventures as stream fishing in waders, or shore fishing from beaches or piers.

For reasons that I have not been able to uncover, there is an abiding association of women with boats. All types of ships are referred to as "her",' and when a proud angler describes his latest bass boat purchase to a friend, he begins by saying, "She's a real beauty...and will get up to flank speed in just ten seconds flat!"

Women have also played an important role in some of the greatest boat rides in recorded history. Take Noah's ark, for one. Without the female of the species aboard that gopherwood craft, sons Ham, Shem and Japheth (to say nothing of the animals thereon) would have had forty dull nights riding out the storm on the way to Mount Ararat. And then there was that legendary ride down the Nile River, in which the cunning Cleopatra is reported to have made the journey exciting for bungling Mark Anthony.

Boat manufacturers and their dealers have helped make the sport of fishing increasingly accessible and invigorating with their interminable proliferation of all types of models to choose from, and in which to pile all of our rods, reels, electronics, lures and other associated tackle. Their marketing efforts resulted in a three-fold increase in our investment in their boats in the ten years between 1975 and 1985, hitting almost six billion dollars in that latter year.

In 1986 there were almost 10 million registered boats on our waterways, with Michigan, California, Minnesota and Florida all listing well over 600,000 in each of those states. Everywhere there is water, there are boats. And the more water, the more boats.

Not too many years ago, the average, run-of-the-mill angler was content with a wooden, fiberglass or aluminum hull with plain wooden-bench seats for three or four, a staunch transom to support the motor, and room for a few tackle boxes, minnow bucket, landing net and assembled rods of the zealots on board. The cost was modest, and the boats were easily trailed on light-weight trailers to the lakes and rivers nearby.

Today it is a much different world. Specialized boats have been built and merchandised to match the waters of specific areas and the comfort needs of the anglers on board. One of the earliest of these versions was the "johnboat" (or just plain "jonboat") which appealed to those folks who patrolled the problem waters of many southern states. Their principal feature was their shallow draft, but they also introduced a number of new creature comforts which have been magnificently enhanced on later models.

Since bass fishing is the most broadly practiced form of this sport, it was only natural that a highly-specialized boat should be developed for that market. Indeed, the "bass boat" is the glittering-jewel of the freshwater fishing industry. While I find very little difference in the physical requirements of bass fishing as against walleye fishing, for example, the purveyors of boats for those good old boys of the bass fishing fraternity have succeeded in selling their dories equipped with everything from a motorized anchor winch to an astrological position finder.

Here, for one illustrious example, are some of the amenities included in a typical moderate-priced bass boat: spacious bow casting deck, built-in aerated live well and tackle tray, extra large rear casting deck, insulated storage compartments, deluxe dash instrumentation panel with built-in fish-finding electronics, tachometer, speedometer, volt meter, water temperature and fuel gauge, plus an over-powered outboard motor with stainless steel propeller, power trim and tilt...and an electric-powered trolling motor mounted on the bow.

All for just $14,000!

For the comfort of the passengers there are even heavily padded swivel "contour" seats that make you feel right at home in your favorite lounger.

Sacrificing a few of those benevolent features can bring the purchase price down to a mere $10,000, give or take a few hundred.

These outfits are what their marketers choose to call "packages", a term which tells you that they have assembled onto the basic hull many of the elements which anglers previously purchased themselves, after selecting the boat of their choice. These include the motors, (outboard and trolling varieties), the electronics, batteries and lights.

This concept was first developed by a large merchandiser specializing in the bass fishing market, and who sensed the sales advantages which could be realized by presenting one complete "unit" which

Bass Pro Shops builds these floating castles for the fresh water angler who insists on everything but a whirlpool bath. Motors fore and aft, automobile-type seats, stereo, electric start, built-in beer cooler, wall-to-wall carpeting, a two-level deck and a control console like a Mercedes. With luck, you could fish with a guide who owns one...and discover the true facts about just how rugged this fishing business really is!

could more easily be financed...and which would incidentally increase his profits more than somewhat. Today there are at least fifteen major boat manufacturers offering this same convenience, and have established their own individual financing resources to help accelerate the purchasing decision.

In tribute to the marketing genius of the boating industry I can tell you that they did not stop their diversification with just the "bass" boat. I have in my files some very persuasive advertising pages from our outdoor magazines which call my attention to "specialized" boats for walleye fishing ... "with all of the essential ingredients" for that pursuit.

Until now, you may not have realized that there was something special about walleye fishing. But I have it on the authority of NORTH AMERICAN FISHERMAN magazine that "today's best walleye anglers use their boats to position their baits. They find structure and fish with sonar equipment, then backtroll across and along the area, bouncing baits on the bottom."

And, of course, no self-respecting walleye hunter would try that in an ordinary runabout.

But millions of us have been catching walleyes for many years with plain old 16-footers that didn't have the "full instrumentation console, built-in ice chest/storage, aerated livewell/baitwell with timer, over-sized rod storage and molded pro pedestal seats" of these babies. Amazing.

There are also other "specialty" boats out there, many of them promoted as "multispecies" varieties, just to convince you that "one size fits all," and they have it.

I have no argument with the industry in its creative sales approach to the pocketbooks of American anglers. Their products have been warmly embraced by the marketplace, and our industrial complex needs all the growth it can generate. If you hanker to take a 17-foot super-powered miniature Queen Mary to your bosom, go ahead.

My own tastes run toward "O.P.B.'s."

That's for Other People's Boats."

Our family has never owned a fishing boat, and there are no plans to acquire one in the future. But we will continue to fish...in "O.P.B.'s".

Our reason for this self-denial is simple. We enjoy fishing in many parts of the country, and in many areas beyond America's own borders.

We do not have a lake cabin. We are mobile anglers. We fish in our home state, in a number of neighboring states, in Canada, and (when we can afford it) in the waters off our east and west coasts, off Mexico, Hawaii and Central America. Fishing has helped enrich our lives by taking us to pleasant camps and lodges in interesting countries and areas where we have met and enjoyed the rewarding fellowship of other anglers with interesting stories to exchange and lingering memories to cherish.

Everywhere we have fished there have been sturdy, sea-worthy boats for our use, well-maintained and of sufficient comfort for a day on the water. We have had no trailers to pull, no extra worries in our travels, and the boats which we haven't owned, insured and maintained have provided the funds to take us to those destinations we have read about and wanted to experience.

There is an old saw, or adage, among the family of many boat-owners that goes like this: "The happiest day of my life was the day that bought my boat. The second-happiest day was the day that I sold it."

Many fishing families will disagree with that position, and will tell you that their dandy little 16-foot rig is the greatest thing that has happened to their marriage since microwave cooking. They make

These Lund aluminum boats are typical of many found at wilderness fly-in camps. They are roomy and sturdy, and will carry three to four passengers.

many one-day trips to a variety of nearby waters, and the boat is their quickest way in and out, and saves them the money and time consumed by rentals. Furthermore, the joint agreement which led to its purchase has assured the wife's inclusion on all, or most, of the angling excursions on which it is used. As the lady cited in chapter two-exclaimed, "We now have a boat, motor, trailer and trolling motor. Carpeting and curtains can wait!"

Some years ago, when my husband slipped mysteriously out of the house to make a number of clandestine visits to a local boat merchant, I sensed what he was up to, and decided to take some damage control action. I sat down and drew up the following declaration and posted it on the refrigerator door, right where he couldn't miss it:

NOTICE TO ASPIRING BOAT CAPTAIN

1 - Any of those boats you are looking at will require a down payment in the same neighborhood as the one we paid on this house.

2 - That is not a good neighborhood to be in, since those "convenient" monthly payments will still be due when the kids are starting off to college.

3 - And don't forget the insurance. Tom Jensen will let you off easy, but it will still cost money.

4 - There is no place in our yard to store it during those long winter months, so you will have to pony up at the marina for storage.

5 - Boat maintenance is something you have never studied, and I am not sure that you have a keen appetite for it today. And what do you really know about trailers?

6 - Having lived with you all these years, I know that you will not be satisfied with the boat as it comes. You will be out every month buying new baubles to "personalize" it. And there goes the bread money.

7 - The arrival of the boat will be quickly followed by the arrival of one of your brothers, and two of mine, all begging to borrow it, like every other week-end. That deal was not in our marriage contract.

8 - Do you really want to tow a boat all the way to Canada, and, if so, does that mean that we will no longer be going to those wonderful "fly-in" camps?

9 - Don't forget that the boat comes with a motor, and when you had that Harley-Davidson back in college you proved conclusively that you had no mechanical skills of merit. And the lawn mower still needs fixing.

10 - Check the classified ads this week-end and see what used boats are selling for. We could take a horrific knock when you get ready to sell it off...like next year.

He did not buy the boat.

But I do not mean to impose those caveats on you. Your plans may call for you to get heavily into the sport, and boat ownership may be just the ticket for strengthening your companionship with your better half, plus the kids, the neighbors kids and their parents. You could become the true epicenter of all community activity, and lead to more social gatherings than the garden club.

One of my favorite boats belongs to my brother. Big, comfortable, powerful and impressive to all of the neighbors of his north country lake home. We fish from it, water ski from it, and just cruise around the lake in it. He knows that the reason I have such affection for it is because it is his. The upkeep, storage and depreciation are his burden, not mine.

His current boat is not his first. He has had several, continuing to upgrade with new models which promise to more completely match his need for a stronger "image" of himself. It's sort of like what Duncan

This is my brother Glenn's latest boat. He doesn't wear them out. He just reads the outdoor magazines and gets hooked on new models every few years. The boat dealers love him!

110

Spencer and Reed Phillips wrote about in THE WALL STREET JOURNAL back in July of 1989: "One of the most fascinating developments is that men are now bombarded by advertisers who tell them how to express their masculinity by buying things rather than doing things...Men are discovering new compensations for changes in their lives. If you can't climb a mountain, buy climbing boots for the winter. You don't have to do something to identify with it. So men buy sailing jackets for the street, jungle hats for the rain. They wear diving watches, flannel shirts with ties, leather flight jackets, rugby shirts, safari shirts, polo shirts—all to say something...One of the things they want, as is shown daily in societies all over the world, is to spend time with other men apart from women."

Nowhere in the Free World is this desire for "image" satisfaction more visible than among those water cowboys who disguise themselves as "fishing pros" or practicing bass fishermen. They are the true "power figures" of our age, screaming across our lakes and rivers at highway speeds in their super-powered comfort creatures. They aren't satisfied unless their rig can hit the high 5O's within moments after they have put them in gear. They zip from fishing hole to fishing hole at Mach 3 speeds, throw a few casts, light off the after-burners and tear on to the next spot. Getting there for them is more than half the fun, it's almost all of it.

They are, indeed, a "unique breed," as Larry Colombo wrote in the February 1987 issue of FISHING FACTS. "They often justify to themselves or to the family a boat which is slightly beyond their means—one that, although they can't really afford, usually finds its way into their life one way or another."

The research to satisfy this power-hungry market goes doggedly on, and writers in all of our outdoor periodicals envisage the "ultimate" bass boat, or its other specialized cousins. "Stick steering" is coming on strong, along with oil injection, high performance propellers and exotic trim controls, just to keep the boat from flipping over on its operator as it sends out a rooster tail ten feet tall and creates havoc for all other boaters in the area.

My advice to any woman who finds herself in a matrimonial arrangement with a man whose tastes run those kinds of toys is to seek a change of venue. I remember the tears that came to my eyes when I read that letter written to Ann Landers by that wife who had spent 43 years with an "avid fishing nut" who spent the household funds on his hobby. "I could have gone around the world first class, ten times, on what this man spent," she wrote.

Ann had it right when she responded with "Marriages work best when both parties share mutual interests. Playing together is the joyous part of any relationship. And it brings lovers closer together."

The message of the preceding intensive discussion for a novice woman angler is simply this: buying a boat today is often as significant a purchase as that of a new car, and calls for a clear understanding of the type which will meet your needs, fit into your budget and give you the satisfaction which you expect. It is the kind, of commitment which is best deferred until you have a few fishing trips under your belt and are firmly convinced that you really need it.

Fishing in the boats of friends, at camps you will visit, and in those of guides you engage will all help you decide which type to shop for. So don't rush into it. Spend the money on those new kinds of clothes, quality equipment, and an exciting new quiver of cosmetics to charm your male companions into inviting you back real often.

If you must have some kind of craft to take you out on the water, you might want to consider a canoe. For just $500 or $600 you can put yourself in a neat little 16-footer which will accommodate you and your friend, and serve as a reasonably safe base for the more modest fishing pursuits, such as panfish and walleyes. It will be easy to transport, and even two women can handle it quite easily.

Whether you elect to buy your own boat or not, there will always be boats for you to fish from, wherever you go. And the more of us women who get out on the water, the bigger the market for the boat builders of America will be. All of which should make those folks delightfully happy, even though you won't see many of us pictured in their colorful advertising...which keeps the editors of our outdoor journals in pencils and morning coffee.

Now let's turn our attention to the subject of electronics, and what they have done to convince men anglers that they will always catch fish, even if they can't tell a lead-head jig from a down-rigger.

SONAR, RADAR AND WHERE
THE FISH ARE

"Today's boater can turn a few dials or press some buttons and have a fantastic amount of information-available instantly. A flip of a switch can provide such things as water depth and temperature, a detailed look at the bottom, boat speed, distance traveled from the dock, and even when color lure you should use to catch the most fish."

- *"Seeing Is Believing",*
FINS AND FEATHERS magazine, 1987.

"Don't yield to peer pressure and buy a Flying Gizmo unit just because Joe Lunchbucket, the resident pro, has one."

-*"Facts about Fishfinders,"*
NORTH AMERICAN FISHERMAN magazine.

When God invented radar, he didn't intend for it to be used against fish. My husband (who was there at the time) claims that radar was invented to help the Good Guys beat the Bad Guys in World War II. Which they certainly did, in everything except economics. But that's another story.

What we are concerned about in this chapter is the manner in which the manufacturers of electronic devices are rushing pell mell toward the day when they will have destroyed the sport of fishing. And I mean completely—destroyed it. The villains in this piece are those mad scientists of California's "Silicone Valley" and their co-conspirators within the laboratories of those companies which litter our tackle shops with their "fish finders", "depth finders "flashers", "LCD" and "GPS" technological gadgets.

These are the merchandisers of devices which are sold on the promise of taking all the chance out of fishing. They have seized upon those heretofore harmless domains of loran, sonar and radar to create frightening "black boxes" which threaten every fish that swims beneath the surface of our lakes, rivers and oceans.

As a beginning point in this discussion you need to understand that "loran" is an acronym for "long range navigation". "Sonar" is a term which similarly is derived from "sound navigation and ranging", and "radar" has its roots in "radio direction and ranging". Under normal conditions, none of these three inventions would have as much impact on our lives as "Nylon", "Orlon" and "Teflon".

But we live in a different world today, and there are just as many angling zealots out there clamoring for these devices as there are merchants who purvey them. They are those fisherfolk who feel they <u>deserve</u> to catch fish every time they go after them, and they will buy anything in sight which promises to fulfill that interest.

The first of these products to come on the scene were those "flashers", rather large and heavy contraptions which recorded the depth of water over which a boat was traveling, and reported it on a dim screen on its console. If the user had exceptional eyesight, and the sun was not too bright, there was an odd chance that he might spy small blips on the screen which were alleged to be fish. In the thirty years since this product arrived on the market many much more sophisticated

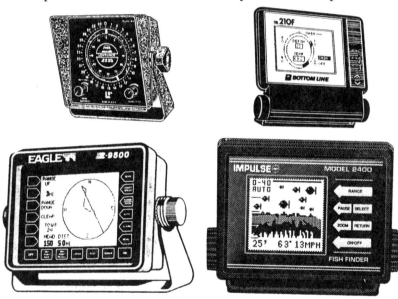

Here are four of the most popular electronic devices used by anglers today. I have not included the fancy new GPS (Global Positioning System) since you wouldn't find much use for it on Little Twin Lake...but many of those war horse bass fishermen wouldn't leave home without one.

versions have come out of the workshops of Tulsa and Catoosa Oklahoma; Eufala; Alabama; Santa Cruz, California; Fort Worth, Texas and other noted centers of the advanced sciences.

Chart paper recorders came along in the 1970's, bringing with them our need to understand what a "pixel" really is, and why the more of them there were, the merrier time we would have viewing them. A "pixel", you see, is a picture element, represented by a tiny dot or square on the screen. If the pixels arranged themselves in orderly fashion, an angler was supposed to be able to separate the targets below and receive clear representation of the bottom surface.

Liquid crystal display units, nicely known as "LCD" came next and remain the most popular models at this writing. More than 30 manu-facturers offer these today, employing sonar technology to generate more clearly-defined images, some even in color. Constant digital bottom depth readings, surface temperatures gauges, speedometers and trip logs were other features which they brought to the earnest angler. In addition, they had become more compact, easier to transport and install.

A fourth version is the video unit which uses a cathode ray tube, much like your home television set, with pictures in six and eight colors, or in two shades of amber. With their bright colors and high resolution they attracted a great deal of attention, and were the favorite of those high-flying boys who could afford the $700 to $2,000 price tags.

Each of these electronic wonders offered an angler more informa-tion about the body of water in which he chose to fish than he could garner from a typical lake map or depth chart. But most of all, they conveyed the promise of taking him to "where the fish are". Then, if he had a reasonable assortment of fishing skills, he would certainly catch more fish.

As a beginning angler, you might properly conclude that such an aid is exactly what you need to register early success. The jury is still out, however, and there will be many boats out on the same water on which you fish that are splendidly equipped with these instruments...and catching no more fish than you are.

Outdoor writer Terry Madewell confesses to the advantages of these electronic "bird dogs" but warns that some of the more complex models "can clutter the mind with unnecessary details, which often distracts from the job at hand: catching fish." Before you buy any, he counsels, "determine your present status as a fisherman and what you hope to do in the future." A good place to begin such evaluation is in the boat of another angler who uses it regularly.

Another important consideration comes from whether you will be fishing with other untutored companions, in the company of someone who "knows" the water you are working, or with a professional guide. It's sort of like the "O.P.B." ("other people's boats") factor: if the others with whom you fish already own one, don't spend your money on one just to have it when you might need it. The going price for any of these gizmos runs between $125 and $400, which is more than just small change. On top of all that, some of them require a special video to learn how to install and operate them, at an extra $12 or $13.

I do not consider myself an expert on electronics, and have enough troubles of my own in fine-tuning our TV or selecting the settings on our dishwasher, so I have distanced myself from all of these devices through all of the years of my fishing. I can't tell "liquid crystal" from genuine Waterford, and don't have the slightest desire to read it. And when it comes to pixels and cone angles, I am about ready to turn in my tackle box.

The real danger which I perceive in all the shenanigans of the manufacturers of these electronic "peeping toms" is that one day they will actually be able to pin-point every fish in any body of water and keep it in focus as those sonar echos bounce back between them and the boat, and finally twitch the fish into snapping at the hook lowered down to it. Fool-proof fishing it may be, but it will also empty our lakes and rivers of their fish faster than they can be replaced. And what about the real "sport" of fishing?

You begin to understand what they meant when the word merchants cooked up that term: "poor fish".

There are some who would argue that it is genetically impossible for a woman to be married for over twenty-five years and still be a warm and caring person. But I have been, and I am. I care for those fish, and the future of fishing. We aren't giving the fish a fighting chance when we hunt them down with all of this silicon chip wizardry.

The scientists tell us that most of the fish we seek rely on a brain

116

somewhere in size between a California raisin and a prune to find their own food, and to avoid becoming the meal of another hungry predator. FISH BEHAVIOR, an extraordinary book by professor Helmut E. Adler, tells us that the life of a fish is not an easy one. Their modest nervous system is heavily taxed in just keeping the creature out of harm's way, sensing the attacks of others, and knowing when and how to partake in the mating game.

"Communication by sound signals is more widespread than is presently apparent," he believes. "Mating calls, territorial defense and warning cries have been identified." And a readiness to engage in courtship is often signaled by a wagging of the tail. But nowhere is there any evidence of any species being equipped with counterintelligence mechanisms to protect them against today's pixel-lated probers. That there are so many fish still around is probably due to so many anglers failing to read and understand the instructions.

I personally take some comfort in the knowledge that George Perry's world record 22 1/2-pound bass was taken when Perry was but a 20-year-old farmboy and didn't know a transducer from a boll weevil. The same for Howard "Rip" Collins and the new world record brown trout of 40-plus pounds caught during some "spur-of-the-moment" angling on Arkansas' Little Red River in May of 1992. Many other prize catches have been made by anglers who were strengthened with no more than the conventional wisdom which tells them where fish go to feed, and what they like to feed on.

Bait manufacturers are hungry to get in on the electronic bonanza, too. I have read reports of some "Electronic Fish Caller" models which use miniature batteries to power sound-making devices in an assort-ment of lures. At this point, however, I am persuaded to believe that like so many other gadgets before them, they will catch more fishermen than fish. But don't discount the possibility of some mad scientist ultimately developing a bait with flashing lights, whirring sounds and erotic scent that no fish can refuse. When that happens, we can all go back to bowling.

In the meantime we can all continue to fish in the manner which satisfies our own individual concept of what the sport is all about; stalking those lunker bass in their natural holding spots, teasing fighting northerns out of their favorite weed-beds, surprising those

117

scrappy panfish under our docks and bridges, and having the time of our lives.

I have talked about "bush" airplanes, but you deserve more information than just the mention. The top photo shows a Cessna single-engine plane, which flies at about 120 miles per hour. The twin-engine Beechcraft shown below has an air speed of 140 miles per hour. The popular DeHavilland "Beaver" is larger than the Cessna, carries four passengers, but has a speed of only 100 miles per hour. No hostesses, and no in-flight meals, but they make for interesting traveling.

BASS, B.A.S.S. AND THE G.N.P.

"If you've never been bass fishing, I'd like to help you pop-the cork on a lifetime of fun awaiting you. It's a great sport! And from the moment you get started, you'll have tens of thousands of bassing pals around the nation, ready to big brother you at a glance."
  -Homer Circle, "Getting Started," SPORTS AFIELD, April 1986.

Bass fishing is Big!

As a fledgling member of the family of anglers who fish for bass you will soon be amazed by the sheer size of that multitude, the time they devote to the sport, and the vast sums of money they spend on its pursuit. I haven't counted them all personally, but I have it on good authority that there are over 16 million bass anglers among us on an average summer day. And that's just those who chase after the smallmouth and largemouth varieties. Throw in all those who prefer white bass and "stripers" and you have another 6 million plus. Altogether they probably number more than all of the practicing Methodists in the 48 contiguous states.

Bass fishermen (and they <u>are</u> mostly men) are also the most intense anglers to ever hold rod and reel. They are possessed with an appetite for information about the sport which is much more than just insatiable. It is absolutely ravenous, bordering on gluttonous. And like the Gospel, the scriptures of bass fishing are preached from the editorial pulpits of scores of outdoor magazines and hundreds of family newspapers throughout the land, week after endless week. The modern apostles of the game create new and more enthralling tales of success and excitement in their lavishly illustrated books, articles, lectures and fireside tales.

Their disciples hang tenaciously on every word, picture themselves in every tantalizing photograph of the author and his "prize fish" Listening to the typical steadfast bass angler talk you come away convinced that it has brought more joy to his life than the innerspring mattress.

As a class, they engage in the sport on almost 350 million days per year, and spend more money on the relentless quest of their favorite fish than our government spends on public health services...and almost as much as we spend on our elementary and secondary schools. How much exactly? About 16.3 billion dollars, which totes up to about 3.8% of our Gross National Product!

Nothing really wrong with that. It's better than spending the money on dog racing or stamp collecting. On top of that, the sport provides employment for hundreds of thousands of people, probably more than such large industrial giants as Boeing or IBM. Consider the number of writers, alone, who keep body and soul together by just composing those endlessly repetitive articles about how it is done, where and with which baits, Add to that number those folks who manufacture all of those mystical lures, specialized rods, reels, boats and electronic gear which are considered by many as essential to even a modest degree of success. Then, too, there are all of those sales people, in the field and in the stores to bring all of that merchandise to our undivided attention.

Finally, there is that legion of showmen who create, promote and produce that seemingly nonstop series of bass fishing tournaments (which we will speak to more definitively later).

Put them all together and you can fill St. Peter's Square in the Vatican City seven days a week. Which would probably be to their liking, since they could then seek the rich blessing which their pursuit often needs.

With all, or most, of the economics of bass fishing now covered, it is time to examine the specific species which has generated such consumptive attention. We begin with the smallmouth variety, since this was the fish that first captured the attention of the freshwater angler. It carries the name of "smallmouth" because its jaws are neither as threatening as those of its now more famous brother. It is also distinguished by a somewhat shallower dorsal fin. Its major attraction was its fighting spirit, demonstrated by an exciting, leaping performance when hooked. But almost as important was its excellent eating qualities, rated by many of its enthusiasts as the finest of all fish taken from our lakes and streams.

The smallmouth bass is also found in both northern and southern angling waters and provides exciting sport when taken on conventional casting (or spinning) gear, as well as by fly fishing. Indeed, much of the enchantment which this fish has for the fly angler is the similarity of methods used to subdue it, in comparison to those used for trout and salmon. Both the floating and sinking types of "bugs" will bring a scrappy smallmouth to the surface and provide an exciting challenge before coming to the net.

Smallmouth bass will take a broad range of artificial baits, from tiny spinners to plastic worms, but have also demonstrated a voracious appetite for minnows, frogs, crayfish, and even dead bugs. I can clearly remember dropping a dead grasshopper down alongside a camp dock and pulling in two whoppers that totaled over ten pounds of bass. Both

THE BASS FAMILY

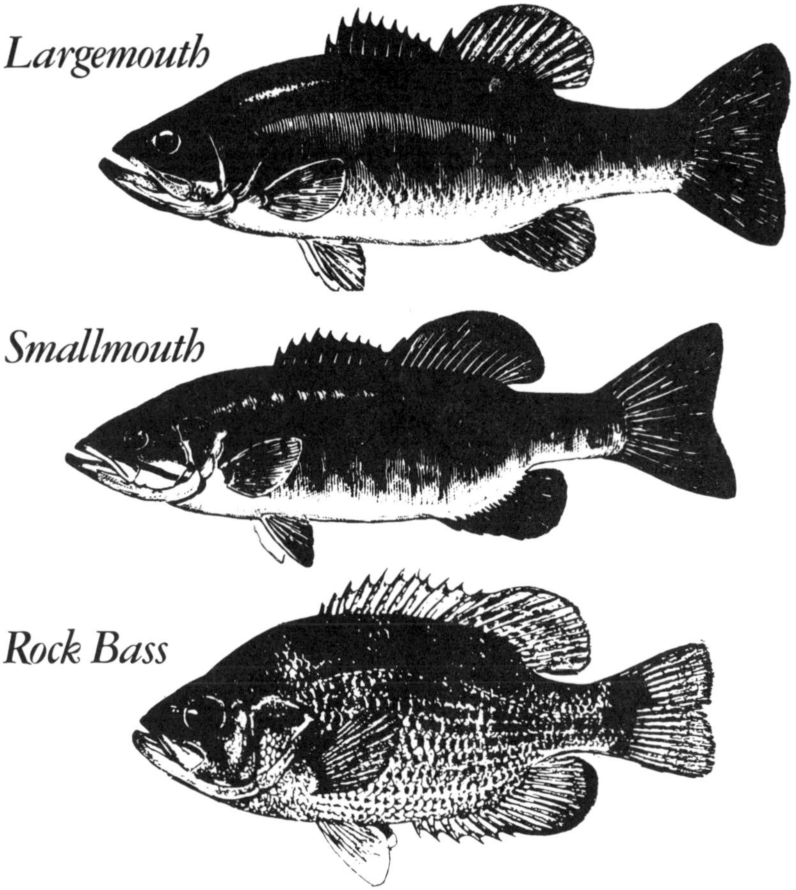

Largemouth

Smallmouth

Rock Bass

Illustrations supplied by the Minnesota Office of Tourism.

took the same grasshopper, the second one smashing it so badly that it ended my fishing for the evening.

Seasoned anglers like to refer to the smallmouth bass as "old bronzeback", and the name has also been passed along by some to the largemouth variety. But the smallmouth still receives praise as the top trophy of the bass family. It is a fancy jumper, and I have always thought that it worked harder to entertain me than any other fish I have ever caught.

The Dale Hollow Reservoir bordering Kentucky and Tennessee has long been one of the most prolific producers of trophy smallmouth, and the current world's record fish of 11 pounds, 15 ounces was taken there in 1955, without benefit of any electronics or "secret" methods. Many "line class" record smallmouth have also come from other southern lakes and rivers, but one 14-pounder was taken from the Wisconsin side of the Mississippi River in 1988. We have caught many in the

Here's a nice stringer of bass, caught in Ontario's Lake Of The Woods. For the "secret" baits used, see the next page.

waters of Ontario, trolling, casting and just "still" fishing with frogs.

These fish prefer quiet waters and can be found under blankets of lilypads, around large boulders, ledges and even river banks. Whenever you find one, you will generally come up with more. They stick together like families in a shopping mall and are every bit as aggressive. Their distinguishing characteristics include their brownish, bronze coloration, with darker colored vertical stripes, tiger-like.

This is a fish which you should seek out early in your fishing career. It will reward you with excitement, as well as some of the tastiest meals you will have over a shore lunch fire.

But the bass that is getting most of the headlines today is Mister Largemouth. The chief reason for this attention is its broader geographical distribution, aided and abetted by its generally larger size and heavier weight. In coloring, it is not a great deal different from the smallmouth, but it does run heavily toward black along its sides, with a darker green cast overall.

The largest catch of this variety is the 22-pound 4-ounce fish referred to in chapter thirteen taken by George Perry down in Georgia back in 1932. Since that time, the greatest excitement in the largemouth bass world was created by a 21-pound, 12-ounce monster taken out of

No "crankbaits", "deep divers" or "jerk baits" were used in catching the nice bass shown on the previous page. Just a few frisky frogs and a couple of deceased grasshoppers. When all else fails, give them a try.

California's Lake Castaic 1990. The lucky angler was Mike Arujo who, along with thousands of other wild bass-chasers, is convinced that there are even bigger ones to be had in that lake.

Almost every outdoor publication has publicized Arujo's catch, along with that of Bob Crupi's lunker that went five ounces heavier but was not verified by a California Department Of Fish and Game biologist. The lake is really a reservoir, less than an hour's drive from downtown Los Angeles with great stores of rainbow trout for forage. That's high living for bass, and they grow rapidly on that menu. But there are many more smaller fish caught in Castaic than those twenty-pound lunkers, just as in other waters around the country.

Nonetheless, the whole wide bass world is watching Lake Castaic, breathlessly awaiting news of the new world's record which sporting journalists tell us will surely come from there. During the course of my study for this chapter I talked with the folks who run the crossroads minimart which is the social and outfitting headquarters for anxious anglers now churning up the lake. In our phone conversation, the resident lady-in-charge told me that there are literally hordes of fishermen and women arriving weekly, from all over the country, to seek fame and fortune in this new "honey hole". She concluded our conversation by promising to call me when that record largemouth was brought to her scales for weighing.

As we go to press, the phone has not yet rung.

But you don't have to go to California to enjoy the fun of landing a husky largemouth. They are to be found in almost as many states as Campbell's soup, or the common dandelion. This general abundance is the fundamental reason for the editors of our outdoor journals to give them such widespread and continuing attention. Over the past several months I have read every joyous word of exactly 337 articles on the subject of where and how to catch "monster" largemouth bass, many of them eloquently advertised to be the "true secrets" of the teller.

The authors include the revered Homer Circle and Buck Perry, plus many latter day saints described as "bass pros" or just plain "fishing pros". Note that I keep enclosing the word "pro" in quotation marks, which I do because I don't rightly know exactly what makes a "pro" a "pro". That term is generally accepted as an abbreviation for the word "professional ", which Webster defines as "one who pursues as a business some vocation or occupation," or "A person who engages for money to compete in sports: opposed to amateur."

My own examination of the credentials of these writers convinces me, however, that many of them are more professional tale-spinners than anglers. I do not denigrate the success which several seem to have achieved, but I am not ready to accept as fact that they pay their rent and other household expenses solely from their skills with rod, reel, and plastic worm, or whatever.

Since no legal limits have been placed their disclosure, I will present for you here all of the unvarnished facts which I have distilled from their reportage:

1 - You have to <u>find</u> the fish before you can catch them.
2 - You have to be at that precise spot <u>when</u> the fish is ready for, or in want of, something to tide it over until-breakfast.
3 - You must <u>present</u> the fish with an object which it perceives by sight, smell, or sound as something akin to its normal diet.
4 - You must <u>hook</u> the fish securely and maintain the upper hand in the conflict which follows if you are going to bring it to your boat.

All of the above you can learn in just four hours in the company of any angler of average experience and communication skills out on the water. But that doesn't mean that you should not read those often breathless adventure stories. In the quiet of your home, they will take you out where the action is, and you can fish right along with the teller and share in his enjoyment of the moment. It beats the editorial pages for sheer joy and contentment in the scale of things in the world today.

Out on the water you will learn by doing and seeing, by making the mistakes every novice makes, and then rejoicing in your ability to overcome those errors and capture the wily largemouth as well as any angler in the immediate vicinity. You will broaden your bait presentation skills by learning how to "flip" or "skip" just the right bait to the precise spot where your dinner is waiting. You will acquire the patience required for success, but also develop the knowledge of when to move on to another spot, plus when and why to switch your appetizer from a plastic worm to a No.3 Mepps Anglia.

None of the above will be accomplished, you must remember, until you get out where the fish are. You have to formulate and execute your own plan to get there, by invitation from your house-husband, a male

HOW TO TIE AN IMPROVED CLINCH KNOT

This is the best knot for attaching monofilament to a lure, swivel or hook.

1. Put line through eye.

2. Make five turns around the standing line, but don't tighten.

3. Thread line through loop above the eye, then through the large loop.

4. Pull coils tight against the eye so that they don't overlap. Trim.

HOW TO TIE THE PALOMAR KNOT

Another great knot for attaching monofilament to a lure, swivel or hook.

1. Pass loop through eye of hook or swivel.

2. Tie overhand knot in double line. Don't twist lines.

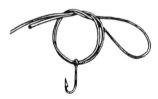

3. Pull loop out far enough to pass over hook.

4. Tighten and trim.

HOW TO TIE THE UNI-KNOT

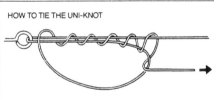

Attach hook, swivel or lure to line.

Run the line through the eye for at least 6". Fold it back to form a double line and make a circle back toward the hook or lure with tag end.

Make 6 turns with the tag end around double line and through the circle. Holding the double line at the point where it passes through eye, pull tag end, as indicated by arrow, until the turns are snugged into a tight barrel.

Pull standing part of line to slide knot up against eye.

CORTLAND LINE COMPANY, INC.

To save yourself the embarrassment of having to be taught how to tie some of the basic fishing knots (by a man), study these illustrations and practice at home. You'll perform like a true veteran!

fishing friend, or a group of other women who have expressed an interest in the sport. For some women (but mostly men), the congenial route to bass fishing has come through joining up with a fishing club. Many such clubs are the local affiliated chapters of B.A.S.S., which is a convenient acronym for "Bass Anglers Sportman Society" (of America).

This is the organization which has been referred to earlier in connection with the heavily-promoted tournaments which it espouses and promotes. Founder Ray Scott tells us that there are over 1,600 such chapters sprinkled over America's bass country, and that their 30,000 members enjoy the experience of teaching new members the tricks of the game, and often invite them in for potluck suppers. While I confess no affection for its corporate chairman because of her apparent inability to understand the compatibility of male and female anglers in the same boat, Ray sounds like a decent sort of a fellow. He conceived the idea for the organization down in Montgomery, Alabama, back in 1967.

With all of the expanding interest being generated in bass fishing, he figured that the time was right to bring all those bassin' (his word) folks together. That he had the right idea at the right time is abundantly demonstrated by its membership, reportedly standing at over half a million on any given day. Many anglers look on B.A.S.S. as the Y.M.C.A. of fishing, sort of a rallying force within which they can gather, share their joys and woes, and generally pray for better fishing tomorrow.

Some of those who came into the fold clung to the naive idea that Ray was just doing this to be a good old boy, and that it was some sort of a non-profit venture. That, they have learned, is not the case. Ray approached the project in a sound business-like manner, and developed it to a profit-making level which attracted a purchase offer from a Birmingham investment company, and which now controls it.

That corporate affiliation has not greatly changed its character. It is-still considered the largest and most successful fishing organization with a subscriber/membership contingent anywhere. Its indentured members gain that status by subscribing to BASSMASTER magazine, its "official" publication, and which has to be the most aggressively advertised house organ ever to pass through the mails. It is the true

Koran of the bass society, and its arrival is eagerly awaited by thousands of aficionados who relish the spirit of brotherhood it brings into their lives, and the faith that it will lead them into the promised land of becoming a true "bass pro"..

If the bass is at the top of your fishing agenda, and there is no one in your family or circle of friends to lead you on your way, by all means send Ray Scott a check for $15.00 and join his bassin' family. Address: P. O. Box 17057, Montgomery, Alabama 36141-0057. Tell him Marge sent you.

Along with the magazine you will receive your own personal jacket patch, auto decal, member's handbook, membership card, plus an opportunity to purchase your very own B.A.S.S. fishing cap at a bargain basement price. And if you can spare the $300 for a lifetime membership Ray will send you a "Lifetime Membership Ring, Life Member belt buckle, Life Member embroidered patch, Life Member cap, and a genuine Life Member license plate." No voting privileges go with all of the above, but you can probably call Ray by his first name when you meet him at your first tournament.

Tournaments are the most visible activities of B.A.S.S. and attract large groups of competing anglers, vying for all kinds of prizes: complete fishing rigs, generous cash purses, and glittering trophies of almost obscene dimension. They bring together vast audiences of spectators and manufacturers' representatives, all cheering for their favorite gladiator. In sheer display and banner-hanging, any one of them will put the Iowa State Fair to shame. And in noise generated, their starting-gun send-off rivals the Indianapolis 500.

As a social event, a typical B.A.S.S. tournament will leave a Boy Scout Jamboree in the dust, and will sell more beer and hot dogs than the Super Bowl. The teams of competing anglers arrive in their colorful jackets and caps emblazoned with the name patches of manufacturers who produce everything from barbless hooks to piston rings. It is sort of a "Miss America" contest in fishing clothes.

The history of bass tournaments is not a pretty one, and the near-gargantuan cash awards have led to shady tricks with huge fish slipped aboard competing boats under the cover of night. Attending officials quickly got onto those shenanigans, and today's events are more closely policed than a presidential inauguration. But critics of those

128

tournaments contend that they are abusive to the ecology and contribute little or nothing to the advance of the sport.

In my view, they are the Sodom and Gomorrah of the sport of fishing, and have done nothing to improve and extend our freshwater fisheries...which should be the true thrust of any organization which claims to be concerned with the future of angling in America. B.A.S.S. and many of the competing anglers protest this evaluation and claim that their activities assist the rest of us by identifying new methods and new lures which will ultimately improve our individual ability to catch more and bigger fish.

To which I reply, "Fiddle-de-dee!"

Tournaments are held every year for every kind of species from crappies to blue marlin...thousands of them. One of the reasons for their popularity is the galaxy of prizes offered, everything from trophies to checks with Very Large Numbers on them. Bass tournaments outnumber them all, and the above ad illustrates the heavy level of promotion with which they are supported.

In one tournament which the organization sponsored recently the winner had a three-day catch of eleven bass, with a total weight of 18 pounds 13 ounces.

Shoot, I have caught more bass than that in a single afternoon with few frisky frogs and a $15 rig while sitting in a 14-foot wooden scow with a 10-horse eggbeater on the stern!

Modest catches like the one reported above might one day embarrass the promoters sufficiently to lay off the hoopla, and turn their attention to those issues which matter most to the majority of us who like to fish, and who would like to preserve it for families yet to come.

In the meantime the tournament drums continue to beat, and now have worked their way into other facets of the sport. There are now panfish tournaments, walleye tournaments, and even "Crappiethons!"

But I digress again. The challenge of this chapter is to convince you that there is fun and fellowship to be had in a fishing boat trying to bring a nifty bronzeback to boat. Trust me, and get out on the water!

NO PIKERS, THESE WALLEYE, NORTHERNS AND MUSKIES

"The walleyes don't possess superb fighting power like a northern pike or salmon. Nor are they especially pretty; with their huge milky eyes and mouthful of wicked-looking teeth, theirs is a face only a mother could love."
-Michael Pearce, WALL STREET JOURNAL,
September 22, 1986

"A northern pike can wolf down a baitfish half its length with a strike of such flashing speed that the human eye cannot follow its progress. ...If you're a newcomer, you'll find that getting started in northern pike fishing is not difficult."
-"Getting Started," Gerald Almy, SPORTS AFIELD,
April 1987.

"As the top predator in any lake in which it lives, the musky literally fear nothing. Not even man."
—"Muskellunge" Jim Rudnick, ANGLER & HUNTER,
September 1986.

We begin this study of the walleye, the northern and the muskie by recognizing right at the outset that the walleye is <u>not</u> a true pike. But, over the years, it has been so identified by many of its fondest admirers and pursuers. It has also been called such things as a pickerel, yellow pike, perch-pike and even a jackfish.

But by whatever name it may be called at your local tackle dispensary, it ranks second among the most popular freshwater game fish today. While it rarely puts up the fight of a bass of the same size, the walleye is famous wherever it is found for its savory eating qualities, and is even featured on the menu of many fine restaurants in cities well beyond its range.

You will find it in the lakes of more than states as well as throughout the provinces of Canada. There will be no trouble recognizing it because its strange, almost opalescent eyes will be a dead giveaway. More rounded out in body than the bass, it runs to greater length measurements, and is generally olive-green along its sides and back, with a white under-belly.

The largest walleye catch on record is a 25-pounder taken by Mabry Harper out of Old Hickory Lake way back in 1960. Lady angler Erma Windorff holds the world record for walleyes caught on 6-pound test line with the 19-pound, 5-ounce lunker she caught on Arkansas' Greer's Ferry Lake in March of 1982. Good on you, Erma!

But the ordinary stringer of walleyes will hold more fish in the 2- to 3-pound range, which is a good range for any family meal. It is the excellent flavor and texture of the fish which have made it so popular, and most anglers are content with modest-size fish, just so they get enough to take home to feed the family. This unique attraction as food has made the walleye the one fish which is almost always kept by the angler, although many states now enforce "catch and release" practices for larger fish which need to be returned to the fishery to assure continuing large hatches to meet the needs of future seasons.

As a novice angler you will also appreciate the relative ease with

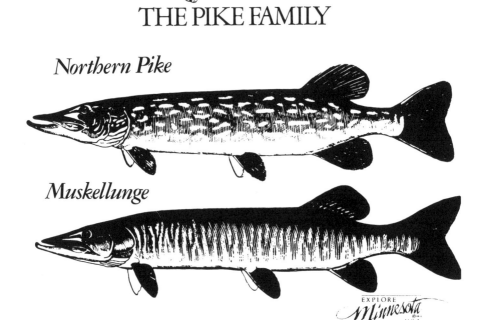

Walleye

THE PIKE FAMILY

Northern Pike

Muskellunge

EXPLORE
Minnesota
USA

132

which they can be caught, and the limited variety of lures you will need to get their attention. They normally travel in schools and prefer to maneuver along shallow bottoms as they search out their meals. Minnows are high on their list of preferred delicacies, and live minnow fishing is both economical and easy to master. A minnow rigged on a spinner or jig is your best bait selection once you have located them.

Slow trolling is the preferred method of many anglers and is the best route to find where they are hiding. Once you get the first one, you can troll back and forth over the same area and come up with more catches. Charter boats in many of our larger lakes use this method exclusively since it produces the largest numbers and greatly pleases fishermen and women on board.

The indelicate leech and nightcrawler (worm!) are also popular alternatives to the minnow and are used on the same type of spinner or jig outfit. The "Lindy" rig is one of the most widely-used arrangements of spinner-and hook to which the live bait is attached. Any tackle shop in a walleye-fishing area will carry them or other just as effective copies. When you do your buying, ask the salesperson how to attach the bait and they will take you through all of the genteel steps.

While the biologists will tell you that the eye structure of the walleye makes it most effective for feeding around dusk, the fish is also taken throughout an average day, once it is located and presented with an irresistible meal. We have had the good fortune of taking them mornings and afternoons, and with small casting spinners and crankbaits over shallow water. Your tackle merchant will readily acquaint you with some of these, but don't buy more than two or three at this point.

One day, after you've learned the tricks of the game, you may hook into a fancy heavyweight, from six to eight pounds or more, and that will greatly increase your appreciation of this rather humble species. It won't leap and run like a big bass, but it will provide an exciting struggle, one that you can tell stories about for years!

Before leaving the subject of walleyes, you should be advised that a sister-species exists which is known as the sauger. This fish is very similar in appearance, but not as dark in color, runs to smaller sizes, and is not the tasty morsel that the walleye is. Its range is also much more limited. It is not a fish to put at the head of your list, but I didn't want you to be surprised if you pulled one in.

There is no other more maligned freshwater fish than the long, lean and testy northern pike. To many calloused old anglers the northern is as unwelcome as a snake in the boat. And, in point of fact, many of those old codgers refer to the northern as a "snake" or a "snake pickerel". The fish does not meet their specifications as a true "game" fish, and it often gets in the way of them catching other, more pleasant species.

One reason for this dislike among some of the old warriors of the water is that northerns are generally so abundant and often show up when they are least expected. The smaller ones are dubbed as "hammerhandles", and the larger ones are very slippery and hard to unhook in the boat. Unless there is an angler in the boat who has expressed a firm desire to keep it, many a guide will return every northern back into the water, unceremoniously, and with dispatch.

But the northern pike has many redeeming qualities to make it a prime target for your early fishing adventures. Among those traits is its ability to propel you instantly into a memorable fighting struggle, wrestling with rod and reel to retain control, prevent his escape, and bring him into your boat. His slick, lengthy body is all muscle, and his fierce, toothy jaws are mean-looking enough to frighten a Marine.

When you ultimately win the battle you will have a keen sense of triumph and proud satisfaction. You are ready for your combat medal and eager for more action.

You will recognize it as a northern by its dark green shading, sprinkled with yellow spots, the size of a kernel of corn, along its sides. The big flat head is accentuated by two mean and piercing eyes. And those long, sharp teeth will tell you that it is a true eating machine. If you have a man in the boat when the fish comes over the side, let him do the handling and unhooking until you have taken a lesson or two.

Northern pike probably acquired that name because they were originally found in our more northern states and most of Canada. They have found their way into such states as Nebraska, Iowa and Missouri, but are more plentiful in those areas with cooler lakes and rivers. While a 5- to 6-pound northern is considered a respectable catch by most anglers, it is the hunt for those 15- to 25-pounders that really turns on the veteran angler. These show up in local newspapers almost every season, but most of them reported by those who venture up into Manitoba or Ontario for their trophies.

Another advantage of fishing for the northern pike is its consuming interest in almost everything that it sees. The object doesn't have to look like a typical forage fish, or even another smaller northern. It will snap at anything which seems to be zipping past it, daring it to strike. The best example of this lack of discrimination is its unabashed attention to simple spinner baits which do nothing more than wobble and twist in the water, and look nothing at all like something to eat.

The Eppinger "Daredevle" was one of the earliest baits developed exclusively for northerns, and it is still the most reliable producer when everything else fails. The "Daredevle" is a rather heavy spoon (because it is shaped like the bowl of a spoon), chrome-plated on its concave side, and striped with red and white paint on its outer surface. It creates a bright flashing action in the water and can attract the vicious attention of a northern quite some distance away.

In later years the marketing minds at Eppinger's responded to the anglers' interest in a wide variety of sizes, plus a smash of other colors. But you will do handsomely with just the original "pike" size in the red-and-white arrangement. Leave the other stuff until later. There are a number of other types of spoons and spinners to consider when you have more money to spend. That will be the time to add a Blue Fox or Mepps spinner, plus a bucktail or two. You will also want to invest in some wire leaders of 8 to 10 inches in length to attach your bait to your line. Those sharp northern teeth are tough on lines (and leaders, too) and can chew them up like cotton candy when trying to escape.

While you will find most northern pike in shallow water ledges and weed beds, you will also discover that you have to go deeper for them when the weather warms up. If your spoon won't take your line down below 10 feet, you will want to hook on one of those crankbaits with a long lip which will scoot it down and out of sight. The Shad Rap is one you can rely on for that type of casting or trolling.

As Gerald Almy says, "If you're a newcomer, you'll find that getting started in northern pike fishing is not difficult." But you will have to steel yourself for the surprise when that husky fish you are pulling in gets its first sight of you and your boat, That's usually when the real action begins and you have show it exactly who is in charge. Keep your line tight, your rod tip up, grit your teeth and hold on. The women of America are counting on you!

The final fish to be discussed in this chapter is the irascible, cantankerous muskie, a true pike, but the most elusive of all. Known more formally as the "muskellunge" in the United States and "maskinonge" in Canada, it is also frequently described in rather profane terms by those who seek it most zealously. It is now found in 31 states, from Utah on the west to New York on the east, from Missouri on the south to all of the Canadian border states from North Dakota all the way to New York. The province of Ontario provides almost all of the muskie action in Canada and has many wilderness lakes and rivers which continue to produce mammoth-size trophies.

A monstrous muskie catch of almost seventy pounds still holds the world record, but there have been 20 others caught weighing over 60 pounds and measuring around five feet in length. Five of those, you will be pleased to learn, were caught and landed by women anglers. But muskie fishing is not for the faint of heart, and I don't recommend it as your opening exercise in the sport of angling.

First of all, the fish is mean looking. It is longer, tougher to land and scrappier in the boat than any other freshwater fish. Its brown-to-green colored body has a huge heavy-swinging tail on one end and a pernicious duck's bill sort of a head on the other...along with jaws that would startle a vampire. Those needle-sharp teeth can cut up a fish of almost its same size in just seconds, and can chop up an unprotected ankle without warning.

Long before "catch and release" practices were adopted by muskie anglers it was usually eaten by its captors, or sold to others, even restaurateurs. Today it is almost universally sought only for the excitement of the catch, and quickly returned to the water to provide sport for other anglers another day or another year. Catches of 40 pounds or more will often find their way to a taxidermist, and will provide fireside conversation for the catcher for the rest of his or her lifetime.

The cadre of anglers who take vigorously to muskie fishing is a unique lot. Most of them will confess that their initial attraction to the fish came after an unexpected catch, or encounter. The muskie took after a bait which was trolled or cast in search of just a bass, walleye or a friendly northern. A good example of such an experience lies in the tale of the young Ontario fisherman who was out on the waters of the

Georgian Bay-Moon River area in October of 1988. He was trolling a small deep-water artificial bait, hoping "for anything," and certainly not expecting a muskie.

But that's exactly what he caught. And not just your ordinary run-of-the-mill muskie. It weighed out at 65 pounds and was the largest catch of its kind in almost thirty years!

It doesn't take a true catch of a muskie to convert a bass or northern angler to the muskie persuasion. It can be just the cold fright of seeing one of these large fish charge after the bait on a normal retrieve. Typically, the muskie will surge up behind the running bait liking a stalking torpedo, nose to the trailing hook, and scaring the daylights out of everyone in sight. If the fish doesn't chomp onto the bait, it will make an explosive, instantaneous turn right at the side of the boat, leaving all on board in a state of shock.

This is the overpowering excitement which ignites the flame of determination within the soul of the angler. He becomes helplessly determined to catch that fish...or another just like it. He has, unfortunately, contracted "muskie fever". For this there is no known cure.

All of those medical and psychological clinicians who have saved so many from drugs, alcohol and nicotine have yet to come up with any treatment, balm, potion or other palliative to return the affected to his or her senses. This, of course, is not all bad news for the tackle industry. While the number of muskie zealots remains at a relatively low level, their sordid search for exactly the right arsenal and tools to attract and capture the muskie has spawned almost a whole new industry within the field of fishing tackle manufacturing.

Baits, rods, reels, lines, nets, tackle boxes and other assorted gear to match the tastes of the true muskellunge hunter run into real money, much more so than the scanty budget which provides for other freshwater quarry. If your husband or significant other gets into muskie fishing, your pin money will soon disappear and your mortgage payments will be in peril.

I can tell you all of this with absolute authenticity, having lived with such a man for more years than I care to remember. Furthermore, I have spent long hours and days in the same boat with him as he flailed wildly and intemperately at the water around us, all the while changing baits, rods and direction of attack. It is not a pretty sight.

Why, then, should any woman of sound mind and body be drawn to muskie fishing? I asked that of Margaret Steiner, a pleasant retired Wisconsin schoolmarm who has become something of a legend within the membership of Muskies, Inc., an international family of some 6,000 feverish followers of the species. Now 72, Margaret is the family boat captain when she and her husband, Duane, head out onto the waters of Ontario or Wisconsin in pursuit of her favorite game fish. "I love the scenery, ducks flying, and even the snow," she told me. "My greatest thrill was the one that got away...over forty pounds. I had her up to the boat twice, but she got off both times. To add insult to injury, she followed my bait again the next day."

Spoken like a true muskie addict.

There are other women like Margaret in the Muskies, Inc. organization, many of them from Wisconsin, Illinois and Kentucky, where men and women gather together in monthly club meetings to moan over their most recent disappointments and to discuss tactics which will assure victory the next time around. You might want to consider visiting such an assemblage to see how your spirits compare with those

I have fished in the rain, in the cold, in tropical heat...and even on the ice. But I take my fishing cap off to Margaret Steiner. She loves to fish so much that "neither rain, nor sleet, nor snow" can keep her off the water. And she loves those fighting Wisconsin muskies!

around you, and if you are really ready for the challenge.

Rose Gibson, Helen Johnson, Nancy McCann and Mary Hoerncke are also among the leading women muskie anglers of Wisconsin. In Illinois, Kathy Noerenberg and Leah Rosset keep pace with most of the men in their state. Ohio's Lynn Hunter, Barb Clemente, Lucinda Zeiher and Connie Bedocs have shown superior skills in catching muskies. Patricia Martinson of Minnesota and Pennsylvania's Rhoda Satonica and Tammy Veltri can also hold their own among the "muskie fever" crowd.

My observation is that these women don't go in for quite as heavy gear as most men are wont to do. They have discovered that lighter rods make the long periods of casting more bearable, and will also sustain them over most trolling action. All this is to their credit. Even male psychologists will admit today that women are more rational than men in most buying decisions. When it comes to fishing tackle, they can sift the fact out of fiction more clearly than their male counterparts. But if you think there are any husbands out there who would willingly let their wives do their muskie gear shopping for them, you're not singing

Jayne Wilde of Rifle, Colorado, was fishing out of Green Island Lodge up on Ontario's Upper Manitou Lake in June of 1992. All over the lake were dozens of eager-beaver muskie maniacs from Wisconsin and Kentucky but Jayne pulled in the prize catch of the month with this 50-inch, 38-pound Canadian muskellunge. That her father, John Noffke, smiling as if he knew she was going to do it all the time.

139

out of the same book as the rest of us.

If I were to take another job, I would love to be a clerk in a tackle store specializing in outfitting muskie fishermen. I would appeal to their chauvinistic interest in acquiring the heaviest rigs in town and sell them the biggest, most expensive rods, reels and lures that we had in the place. I would fill them with so much muskie lore that they wouldn't want to leave until they had cleaned out their checkbooks. The commissions would be luxurious!

But I would also probably break up some marriages, so I will resist the temptation. I leave the moderation to you, recognizing that if you decide to join in the muskie chase, you will proceed at an economic level which will still provide for the regular Sunday offering and new curtains for the kitchen.

SALMON AND TROUT
... LIKE NEVER BEFORE!

"The plain fact of the matter is that dry-fly fishing is <u>not</u> a super-sophisticated or esoteric pursuit! unless you choose to make it so... All flyfishermen are <u>not</u> exceptional, gifted or fluent in Latin, nor are their reflexes any quicker or more sensitive than anyone else's. A completely balanced flyfishing outfit is <u>not</u> a great deal more expensive than the same quality used for spinning or baitcasting. It is all a gigantic hoax."
- "Try A Dry Fly," Jim McCue, OUTDOOR LIFE, May 1991.

America hasn't really had many miracles since the zipper was invented back in 1891. But what has happened to our Great Lakes in the past thirty years just has to be nominated for the Congressional Medal Of Honor.

Back in the 1960's there wasn't much talk of sportfishing around those lakes. The heavily-polluted waters had brought angling to an all-time low, and if you hankered for salmon in your hot-dish, you headed for the local supermarket: pink, in the 14 3/4-ounce can - $1.50; and red sockeye at three times that price.

But back in the research centers of Michigan State University fishery scientist Dr. Howard Tanner came up with an idea which captivated the interest of the state Department Of Natural Resources. Coho salmon, he figured, could find love, happiness and a generous supply of forage fish in Lake Michigan, if someone would just come up with the money to bring them there for a trial marriage.

The amazing success which that proposal has now experienced has cash registers ringing all along the shores of the lake today, and anglers are going home with heavy loads of chinook salmon, Cohos, pink (humpbacked) salmon, and even Atlantic salmon. The charter boats and all of the other associated businesses in this revived industry are reported to be bringing billions of dollars to the area, and making many fishermen and women happier than the day they burned their mortgage.

Jim Chapralis, referred to in earlier pages, and who makes it his business to keep up with salmon and trout happenings around the world, describes the introduction of these fish into Lake Michigan as a "bold stroke of genius because the coho and King salmon are Pacific Ocean fish and only ascend freshwater rivers to spawn."

But there they are today, and folks are catching 20-pounders "right in the shadows of Chicago skyscrapers." And just so they don't tire of that action, Dr. Tanner is now teaming up with Dr. Don Garling to produce a genetically-superior "triploid" chinook that could grow to a monstrous 60 pounds!

Charter boats gather like taxis at an airport in every harbor along both east and west shores. In between, there are piers and jetties from which to cast for passing schools or strays. Chinook catches weigh an average of 15 to 20 pounds, cohos are caught in the six to 10 pound range, but both varieties produce many of larger weight.

What makes all of this so important to you as a fishing novice is that those charter boats supply you with all of the gear and bait that you will need, and the boat captains are generally as comforting and supportive as your kindergarten teacher. All you have to do is sit and wait for one of the fish to take a bait, then take the rod from the captain and put your cranking arm to work. You will bring in fish that will astound your husband, the kids, and even your carpool.

If you are within driving range of any of those shores, you should take the trip, sign on with a charter for a half- or whole-day cruise and live it up with all of the other happy anglers on board. The fish you catch can be filleted for you and you will take home Friday night dinners for weeks to come.

Brown trout and steelhead or rainbow trout that run from four to 15 pounds are also caught in the lake, as they are in Lake Ontario. About the only other places in our country to catch those beauties are up in the streams of Alaska, and that's a far drive for a day of fishing. The tasty lake trout is also found in Lake Michigan, with the ports on the south end, on both the Michigan and Wisconsin shores, hosting the boats that provide the best catches.

These Great Lakes fish are guaranteed to provide unforgettable excitement in the struggle of boating them and the gushing ebullience in the telling about them to all who will listen. Which is much of what fishing is all about.

While lake trout are often discussed in the same society as chinook and cohos, they are not quite as demanding in the catch. When caught early in the season, on or near the surface, they can give you a lively run for your money; but when they head into their deep pools in the heat of the summer they are almost as easy to haul in as a hand-size crappie. Not because they enjoy the ride up to the surface, but because the change in pressure takes the fight out of them.

Ontario's many deep, cool, clear water lakes provide most of the heavy action in lake trout fishing, and many anglers who prefer this fish will seek to be on their trail just as soon as the ice is out (sufficiently for the float planes to get in) in early- to mid-May. That's a sure-fire time for heavy action and will reward you with more fish-per-hour than many other trips you will take But that is also a time that calls for warm clothing and plenty of hot coffee stored in Thermos bottles to keep your blood from congealing.

THE SALMON FAMILY

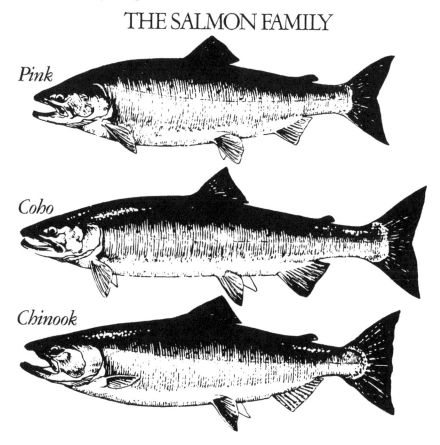

Pink

Coho

Chinook

Some purists will tell you that the lake trout is really a "char", which is really a salmon, but don't let that discourage or confuse you. While these folks will also hold the lake trout in considerably less esteem than the true "stream" trout varieties, it will prove a tough adversary on the end of your line. Trimmed of their higher fat content, they will also make an excellent meal, and it is a favorite fish to smoke for hors d'oeuvres.

Before leaving the subject of salmon it is appropriate to shout one more loud "hurrah" for those fisheries scientists and their Department Of Natural Resources associates who have done so much to bring the sport of salmon fishing into the heartland of America. The Great Lakes contain one-fifth of all of the world's fresh surface water, and this amazing success story has inspired authorities in many other areas to intensify their own efforts to re-condition and re-stock their own waters to provide more rewarding fishing for those of us who look to sportfishing for release and relaxation.

Any attempt to provide a brief yet comprehensive description of trout stream fishing is, at most, hazardous for a woman who has had only a limited experience with it. There are so many eloquent books on the subject, with most of the authors describing the sport in at least semi-religious terms that any true trout fisherman who reads these words will surely claim that I haven't done it justice, nor paid proper tribute to the honorable dedication with which it is practiced.

I will confess to all of that, but also state that I strongly feel that you deserve some insulation from all of that adulation as you contemplate the initial direction which you will take within the broad universe of fishing. Our family library of books on angling contains fully as many on the subject of fly-fishing as it does on every other aspect or species of the sport. There are volumes by Nick Lyons, Lee Wulff, Charlie Waterman, A. J. McClane, Roderick L. Haig-Brown, David James Duncan, John Waller Hills and many others, all of which have taken me into their heart of hearts as they relate the rapturous ecstasy which they have reveled in out on the Beaver Kill or Au Sable as their waders fill with cold water and a seven-inch trout gives them the fight of their lives.

They have taken me into their homes where they hunch over their cozy work-tables to assemble delicate flies out of hackle, fur, tinsel, cork and nylon thread. Articulate in detail, they have patiently described the discrete difference between a "dry" fly and a "wet" fly, and even a "nymph". Their generosity in sharing these precious details with me is almost beyond belief. Each onrushing year they up-date all of this information through pleasant articles in the outdoor magazines. And, if you examine the lists of new books on fishing that are published every year, you will find that they equal or excel the total number of volumes written on even walleye, bass and catfish.

This situation obtains because fly-fishermen are addicted readers on their favorite sport. Their demographics indicate that they enjoy a higher status with their bankers than most followers of other, more abundant fish. They seem to live in a blissful reverie as they read of the triumph and despair of their peers, and would gladly pay the current resident license fee just for the joy of contemplation.

I can say this with reasonable authority since I have a son of mature age who strayed from the more humble quarry of his father in favor of trout fishing. As of this writing, his rate of participation runs this way: reading, talking and thinking about it-92%; time on the water-8%. This will not do for a woman who wants to get out and enjoy the great outdoors. It has not satisfied me. But maybe, after all, as my friend Phyllis says, "Fly-fishing is like love-making for many men. They spend too much time reading about it, and too little time in improving their performance."

On the odd chance that you might have a friend or a husband who is truly into fly-fishing I will attempt to invest you with enough basic information to converse competently on the subject, and possibly provoke an invitation to join him in his next endeavor. We begin with the basics; the fish being pursued.

The trout family includes over a dozen varieties, but it is the brook trout, the rainbow trout and the brown trout which get the heavy attention of the fly anglers. These fish are commonly pursued in our streams and rivers, and especially those that are cold and fast running. The rainbow trout lives a double life, and its migratory version is referred to as a "steelhead", which has a personality all its own. While its maximum weight (in the 30 pound range) runs less than the true rainbow (up to 50 pounds), the steelhead is the fighter whose jumping antics are legendary.

THE TROUT FAMILY

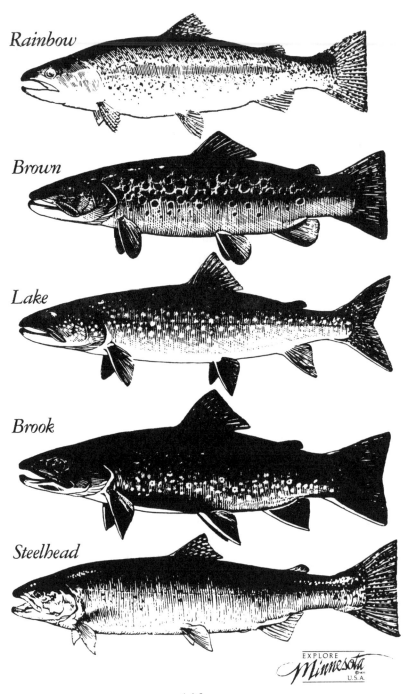

Rainbow

Brown

Lake

Brook

Steelhead

EXPLORE
Minnesota
U.S.A.

During the years in which we lived in Oregon I had the opportunity to share in the early-season fishing for steelhead on the Willamette River. Boats were everywhere, most of them tied up side-by-side in mid stream in what locals called a "hog-line". Baits drifted downstream to attract the steelies as they came in and, when one hit, the boat with the lucky angler disengaged itself from the group to handle the fight and the ultimate landing. The leaping fish made it one of the most exciting days I have had on the water.

The true rainbow is best described as a fastwater fish and is sought in the riffles and pools where they lay in wait for the hatching insects which make up most of their meals along the route. The fly-fisherman responds to the rainbow's interest in such food by presenting it with imitations of those insects with their home-spun "flies" If they have done their homework, and recognize the insects hovering over the surface, the rainbow will snatch the "hatch" and the fight begins. Normal catches of stream rainbows will average 2 to 3 pounds but still provide enough action to thrill the angler.

Brown trout like their water even colder and are more difficult to catch, which helps them survive to an older age. Their name comes from the golden brown coloring, spotted with black and darker brown blotches along its sides and top. A catch of a 10-pounder is considered exceptional, although the current record is now over 40 pounds. Their menu is somewhat broader than that of the rainbow and runs to such other delicacies as crayfish, other fish and even frogs.

To fly-fishermen the brown trout is a special challenge and is the most difficult of all trout to bring to the hook. Proper presentation of the fly is critical and requires pinpoint casting in quarters which are often very restricted. The narrow limits of many streams, surrounded by all types of foliage, require complete line control, the sort which comes only after years of practice. Then, when the fly hits the water, the picky fish may only give it a rush and then turn away as it detects the artificiality of it all. This is the sort of contempt which drives many fly-fishermen to strong drink and occasional wife-beating.

The brook trout is reported to have been the earliest member of the trout family to attract attention among anglers, particularly in the New England states. Maine has a reputation for producing some of the largest catches, as large as 10 pounds, but in many other regions much smaller fish are most frequently brought to net. The persistence of the brook trout as a fishing favorite today is due to continuing research and constant re-stocking from hatcheries in those states where water temperatures support their survival.

As detailed earlier, the fly-angler's gear is highly-specialized and unique to his particular trade. The lines alone are almost surgical in construction and require attentive study and a reasonable knowledge of physics and chemistry. Reels are deceptive in their egg beater appearance, drilled full of holes and shaped like the lid of a Mason jar. The more exotic models are made of space-age, super-light metals with spools controlled by gears and drags that rival a Swiss watch. While not as pricey as a Rolex, they can cost you as much as a cashmere sweater.

It was the fly-fishing fraternity which first brought into use the phrase, "the rites of spring", to describe the early migration of their members out onto the snow-banked streams in pursuit of their prey. This activity comes after months of nervous pacing in front of the fireplace at home, hours of tedious fly-tying, long nights of reading up on the latest product developments, and a visceral uneasiness often mistaken for indigestion.

Those who prefer to buy their own flies will find tackle stores which specialize in them located in many communities located in trout fishing areas. Orvis, the largest supplier to fly fishermen, has them in New York City, Roanoke, Philadelphia, San Francisco, Houston, and Jackson Hole, Wyoming, all well-stocked with the local varieties. It was the in one of these that I had delight of observing a lady of my age outfit herself for the coming season with an entire new assortment of gear, including rod, reel, lines and a good nest of flies, all the time matching the sales clerk, one on one, in the finite details of her needs for certain success. She almost inspired me to try to do the same.

Orvis also operates three-day fly-fishing schools at its headquarters in Manchester, Vermont, (plus eight locations in California and Oregon). For just $385 you will be taken through the total encyclopedia of the sport, and enjoy graduation exercises on privately-owned stretches of the hallowed Battenkill. Lunch, of course, is included.

With the many intricacies of learning to distinguish between a caddis, a cahill, a Hendrickson nymph and a gold-ribbed hare's ear, it is easy to understand why a novice would be attracted to the point of

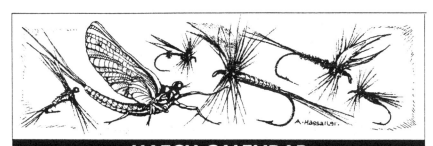

HATCH CALENDAR

Common Name	Hook	Emergence	Species	Hatch	Spinner	Value
Early Grey Stonefly	10	4/1 - 5/15	Multiple species	midday	early afternoon	2
Blue-Winged Olive	18-22	4/15 - 5/11	Baetis vagans	midday	afternoon	2
Hendrickson	14-16	4/27 - 5/5	Ephemerella subvaria	afternoon	evening	3
Lt. Grey/Green Caddis	12-14	5/9 - 5/22	Brachycentrus	afternoon	evening	2
Black Quill	10	5/19 - 6/10	Ritogenia	late afternoon	dusk	3
Pale Evening Dun	18	5/24 - 6/14	Ephermerella	early evening	dusk	3
Grey Drake	10	5/24 - 6/24	Siphlonorus	sporadic	dusk	3
Black Caddis	18	5/26 - 6/8	Taeniptery	morning	late evening	2
Yellow Stonefly	12	5/26 - 6/8	Perlidae	sporadic	late evening	2
Sulphur Dun	16	5/26 - 6/10	Ephemerella	Late afternoon	late evening	3
Green Drake	8	5/27 - 6/14	Ephemerella gutulatta	dusk	after dark	4
Lt. Brown Caddis	12-14	5/29 - 6/4	Multiple species	evening	after dark	1
Brown Drake	8-10	5/31 - 6/12	Ephemera	evening	dusk	2
Mottled Brown Caddis	14-16	6/3 - 6/26	Multiple species	sporadic	late evening	1
Giant Drake	4-6	6/4 - 7/7	Hexagenia	dusk	after dark	4
Mahogany Dun	10	6/8 - 9/29	Isonychia	dull day	sunset	3
Olive/Orange Stonefly	8	6/9 - 6/21	Multiple Species	evening	after dark	2
Lt. Cahill	14	6/12 - 9/20	Stenacron	evening	dusk	2
Damsel Fly	6	6/14 - 9/6	Multiple species	all day	n/a	2

HATCH VALUE: Important 2
Very Important 3
Super Important 4 *ONTARIO OUT OF DOORS*

When fly fishermen head out onto the stream their major concern is to "match the hatch" of those insects flying above the surface. Here is a short list of some of the flies which they carry to fool the fish which are feeding on the real thing.

matriculating and learning from the masters. If you are interested in additional details, you can write to them at 10 River Road, Manchester, VT 05254-0798. And don't forget to request a copy of their "Spring Fishing And Outdoor" catalogue.

Some time ago, hoping to be able to advise you on whether or not this instruction was co-educational, and what the success rate was among its women graduates, I wrote to the president of this school function. To my dismay, he never replied, which can lead one to all sorts of conclusions. I clearly told him what I was up to, and that may be what scared him off. It had the same effect on a few others.

But the testimonials to the therapeutic effect of a day on the stream are every bit as eloquent and persuasive as any of those for bait casting. The exhilaration of landing a small trout or a scrappy salmon is as heavily documented in our literature the feverish joy of taking a three-pound bass or a much larger northern. In addition, stream anglers find a delicious degree of solitude in their special sport. It is an escape into God's great outdoors enhanced by the silken peace which surrounds them.

Their's is a satisfaction which cannot rightfully be overlooked. It may be just the ticket for you, and I charge you not to overlook it. Still another advantage of trout fishing is the specificity of the equipment required, plus the limited areas in which it is practiced. Both augur against this field becoming as overcrowded as the other avenues of freshwater fishing. On top of all that is the attention to the requirements for the support of trout and salmon fishing being given it by our natural resources specialists. With all of that help, fly fishing is in for a good long run, and richly deserved.

SOME ROUGH FACTS
ABOUT CATFISH

"Now that catfish has become an "in" food, you will find it in the most elegant grill houses. This recipe contains nothing fancy, but putting the fish on a charcoal grill is just wonderful. Easy and quick, and very flavorful.
    Catfish fillets
    Olive oil
    Freshly squeezed lemon juice
    Salt and freshly ground black pepper to taste.
"Mix a bit of olive oil, lemon juice, salt and pepper together and whip to the consistency of a salad dressing. Marinate the fish in this mixture for 1/2 hour before grilling. Grill over charcoal for about 5 minutes on a side, or until the fish is lightly browned and begins to flake a bit. Do not overcook."
-Jeff Smith, THE FRUGAL GOURMET COOKS AMERICAN

During the early years of my fishing adventures I seem to remember catfish referred to in the same class as carp ...and regarded as "rough" fish which were not prized by most anglers. All of that has changed over the last ten or twenty years and now the once-lowly catfish is ardently sought after in many states for its sporting character as well as its superior tasting quality. It is this last characteristic which has made it an important food crop in several states, where it is reared in ponds for sale to restaurants.

The total catfish family includes the blue, channel, flathead and white varieties...and even the much-maligned bullhead. It is the channel and flathead catfish which get most of the attention from anglers today, principally because of their broader distribution. The blues run into the heaviest numbers (the current record is a 109-pound, 4-ounce monster taken in Kentucky in 1986), while the whites are the runts of the family, with the largest catch on record was just seven ounces over seventeen pounds.

I confess no affection for the sport of chasing these strange creatures, but they do make for some of the finest fresh water fish dinners anywhere. I made this discovery during our years of living in Florida, where there are large colonies of "Fried Catfish" eateries. Folksy spots, good old American blue collar, oilcloth table covers, and beer in plastic pitchers. The prices are tourist/coach, but the fare is First Class. And you can wipe your plate with the hushpuppies.

What keeps so many anglers from taking catfish to their bosom is not so much their personality as their downright ugly appearance. They are the true Frankenstein monsters of freshwater fish. Weird barbels hang from their chin and sharp spines hide in their dorsal fins. It's not the kind of fish that you want to handle carelessly. My files contain a story about an Indiana fisherman who was stabbed in the chest by a catfish which was being tossed about in his boat. A 5-inch bony fin went through his lung and into his shoulder blade. He wound up in surgery to stabilize his collapsed right lung. Adding insult to injury, the toxic slime on the fish caused an infection that required antibiotics and a respirator to bring his swelling under control.

THE CATFISH FAMILY

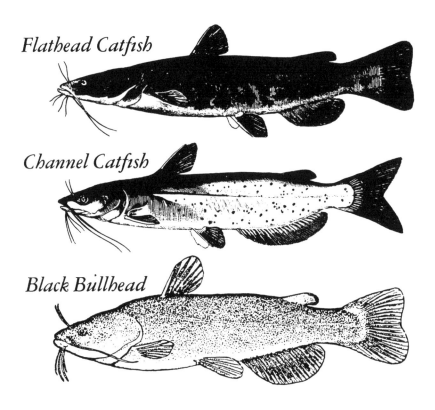

Flathead Catfish

Channel Catfish

Black Bullhead

You will want to select a male fishing partner of cool dexterity when and if you make your first sortie in search of the wily catfish.

While industry statistics show that almost one-third of all freshwater anglers (over 14 million!) now pursue one type of catfish or another, there are just as many who persist in demeaning them because of their lack of gentility and their general abundance. Indeed, there is no "Trout Unlimited", "B.A.S.S." : "Walleye Anglers Of America" or "Muskies, Inc." sort of sewing circle for catfish anglers to gather into and share their joys together. Nonetheless, those who appreciate the economy of the simple tackle required to take them find rich reward in the tasty meals they provide.

As a rather indiscriminate bottom feeder, the fish can rather easily be taken on a variety of very humble baits, many of them so vulgar that they are referred to as "stink baits", These are concoctions of soft cheese, garlic, fish entrails and other similar delights, packed neatly into small mesh bags that are tied directly to bare treble hooks. Other effective attractions include minnows, leeches and small spinners sopped with fish oil or other nauseous scents.

It may not be statistically correct to say that most of the really heavy action takes place in our southern states, but that's where the boys seem to talk most about it. The flathead is often referred to as a "supercat" down there, and catches of 60 to 80 pounds are frequently reported. Marianne E. Willaby is in the I.G.F.A record book with a 64-pounder taken in Texas' Lake Tawakoni in 1989, and she probably didn't even get her picture in the Dallas TIMES HERALD.

There are other lady record-holders for catfish catches, too, like Heather Jo Cunning who landed a 41-pound, 8-ounce channel cat in Nebraska's Snake River in 1986 on 30-pound test line. Cathy Shannon Bookhart also received a "world record" pin from I.G.F.A. for the near-62-pound lunker she caught in South Carolina's Lake Marian in 1987 on 50-pound line.

I am not sure that I would have wanted to be in the immediate vicinity of any of these ladies when they landed those award winning catches, but I have an idea that they may have brought some looks of disbelief to any male anglers who witnessed their capture. You can also bet that none of them offered to take pictures of the event.

Our sporting journals sometimes carry stories of men who have gone to great extremes to land bigger catfish, up to and including dragging them up on the shore when they couldn't handle them at boat-side. But down in Oklahoma there is now alleged to be a cadre of "about 6,000" men who take after catfish in a most extraordinary manner, yet which is considered "traditional" in the area. It is called "noodling" and consists of going after larger specimens with their bare hands. These "noodlers" stalk their prey where they hide in underwater recesses, reaching in and pulling the astonished fish to the surface. Some of them have gone to wearing gloves, which indicates a higher level of intelligence, considering the natural armor of the catfish. Local fishery officials are not at all sure that this practice is good for the resource. It certainly isn't good for the catfish. One day soon we may hear that this sort of piscatorial nonsense doesn't truly meet the standards of sportfishing and will be outlawed. [*]

All varieties of cats have a white under-belly, and most of them are grey-to-black on their top side, but the flathead can be distinguished by its general brown coloration, mottled with darker brown. And, of course, they all look like they haven't shaved for two or three months.

This review of opportunities to enlarge your fishing experience with catches of average-size catfish and bullheads is presented strictly as a service in telling you that they do exist, that they can be as enjoyable watching your tulips come up, and at modest cost in equipment and travel. You should also be advised that converting your catch of any of these fish into dinner is at least moderately more challenging than the simple task of filleting a freshly-caught walleye.

This is because all catfish and bullheads have a distinctive outer skin, instead of those scales which are common to most other fresh water game fish. Furthermore, that skin is as slippery as a handful of oysters. To prepare any of these fish for your barbecue grill or frying pan you first must remove this skin.

This feat is usually accomplished by nailing the fish to a "cleaning board," cutting the skin around the head, then down the back and belly. The skin is then pulled down toward the tail, the meat cut away from

---

Note: A Missouri judge has now fined two locals $600 each for "noodling" catfish in the Fall of 1991, the largest weighing 35 pounds. Missouri officials believe the time has come to call a halt to the practice of grabbing these fish by hand since much of it is being done when the larger fish are spawning.

the bones and cut up into fillets for cooking.

And don't forget Chef Smith's (The Frugal Gourmet) marinade.

I shouldn't have to remind you that the above operation is one which you can rightfully assign to your husband or other male companion, If you have caught the critter, the least he can do is undress it!

PANFISH...AND
OTHER SIMPLE PLEASURES

"I suspect that the reason sunfish, perch, rock bass and crappies are called panfish is that they're at their best in the skillet or frying pan. They're all tasty, if tiny by most standards. What they lack in size, however, they often make up in fast action, a nice change from trophy hunting. And they're fun."
- "Panfish, Please!", Bev Clark, ANGLER & HUNTER, July 1988.

There are many good things to say about panfishing. The fish just seem to be everywhere, bite on almost any kind of bait, and they make a pretty good meal.

But there is also one thing that is terribly wrong about panfishing: most men seem to think that is the only kind of fishing a woman can handle.

I won't debate the argument that panfishing is a fair training ground for a novice angler. What I do protest is the conviction held by so many of our male counterparts that women are neither physically or mentally capable of expanding into more challenging arenas.

When you suggest to any veteran fisherman that you would like to join him on his next trip he is quite apt to reply, "But I'm going after bass...not sunfish!" And if you suggest to the same person that the time has come for you to be invested with some of the tools of the trade he will most likely head for the nearest discount count store and come home with one of those plastic-wrapped rod-and-reel rigs packaged for kids.

He may even buy you a small bobber, a couple of tiny jigs and give you a short soliloquy on how to attach a wiggly worm. He will then pack his duffle, toss his gear into the pick-up and head out to join the boys on Lake Wapagasset.

At this point you have one of two choices to make, depending on your determination and who has the higher-paying job in the family. You can elect to take the proffered gift and go out and do as bidden, catch yourself a mess of perch or crappies, and feed the kids a fish dinner. Or you can take the fishing kit back to the store from whence it came, get a full refund, and head out to a tackle shop and talk to the nice man behind the counter about your fantasies...and what he can do to help you fulfill them.

I refuse to make a recommendation for either direction. In favor of the first choice, however, I can promise that you will experience a modicum of delight in proving to yourself than you can catch a fish and are properly preparing yourself for another confrontation on the same subject as your credentials become more apparent. You will also have the comfortable satisfaction of having learned how to tell one end of the rod from the other and which way to turn the crank on the reel when you see your bobber slip below the water's surface.

Taking the second choice could provoke a confrontation resulting in you sleeping alone for a few nights. On the other hand, if your husband is the true sport that he told you he was during your courtship, he might yield and take you along for the whole shot. You really can't figure men out. If your mate runs to the stubborn category, choice Number One could be the best way to preserve your chances for that new stereo system you've been looking at.

Assuming that you subscribe to the theory that discretion is the better part of valor, we will direct the next few paragraphs toward a discussion of panfish, what they are, where they are, how you can catch them...and why you shouldn't have to clean them for dinner.

While there are reported to be almost 50 species which fall within the total family of panfish, the ones which you are most likely to come cheek-to-jowl with are the yellow perch, the bluegill, black crappie and rock bass. Together, they provide the greatest percentage of all fishing in the United States because they are found in almost every type of lake, river and stream. Even in city parks and farm ponds. They favor shallow water, and in clear water you can even watch them as they toy with your offering, and when they ;actually take it in. This is in itself a learning experience which will have some value as you graduate into the chase for more contentious species.

Panfish are most often caught on small hooks bearing worms (or pieces thereof), tiny minnows, grasshoppers and other dead insects. The line is dropped into the water where the fish are suspected to be, and a small bobber is fastened to the line at a point which will keep the bait just above the bottom. If you can't see the fish below, the bobber will tell you when they come calling and when they have made the decision to trust you as a kind benefactor. When the bobber goes down, the end of your rod should go up. Voila! You have caught a fish.

It isn't always that simple. You may have to bring in the bait, set it at a different depth, replace the bait, and maybe even move to a new location. But if you catch one, there is a good chance that more will follow. Panfish usually hang out in groups, like kids around an ice cream truck. The loss of one of their members doesn't seem to bother them, and they even seem to express a curiosity toward taking the same ride as the dear, departed brother. Or sister.

THE PANFISH FAMILY

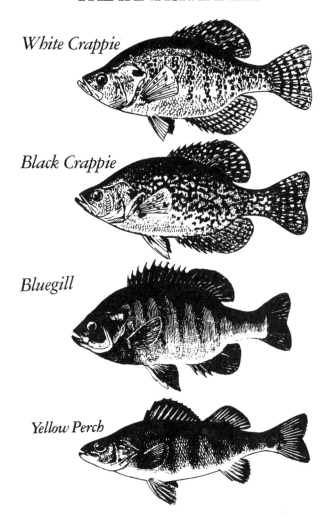

White Crappie

Black Crappie

Bluegill

Yellow Perch

Since these fish are so abundant, daily limits are usually very generous and you can continue your catching to your heart's content. But you also need to acquire the skill to unhook and release those that you cannot accommodate in your evening's menu. There will be other days to fish, and other anglers just as anxious as you to have a good day on the water.

The bluegill (sunfish or "sunnie") is the most commonly caught panfish and can be recognized by its almost round (sunshaped) configuration and the dark spot along its gill plates. The pumpkinseed is another variety of this fish which is best identified by its brighter colors, powder blue stripes and orange spots. The bluegill's body runs more to yellow and orange hues. Down south, these fish are known as "bream" for reason yet to be explained.

Crappies are the second most popular panfish and are found in almost all of the same types of waters. They have a silvery-green or olive-drab appearance and will grow much larger than the "sunnie" They are also somewhat more demanding to catch, and will often respond better to a minnow on some sort of jig. They like to gather around submerged objects or bushes and can reward you with several catches when you have found that hide-out.

The perch is considered by many to be the most preferable of all panfish because it can provide larger fillets, is easier to prepare for the pan, and will deliver more fighting action on the end of the line. They have a taste for live minnows, but attack them rather gingerly before making the fatal bite. In appearance the perch has the look of a small walleye, but has a lighter, yellow color with a few olive green bands running vertically along its sides (which is why its proper name is "yellow perch") .

When you come upon a gathering of perch you will be in for a run of fun catches, mostly under a pound each. As with all other panfish, they will excite young anglers and even other novice anglers of a more advanced age. They can be caught from docks, shore, or underway in a boat trolling a minnow on a small jig.

One final species of panfish we will also discuss in this lesson is the rock bass, which carries that name because of its proclivity for abiding in the area of stone rubble or larger rocks. The more rubble, the more rock bass you are apt to find. It has much of the same appearance as a sunfish, with dark olive coloring on its sides. Its red eyes and the dark splotch on its gill flap are other identifying clues.

In addition to its inclination to take baits dropped to near-bottom, it can also be taken at the surface with miniature "popping" type artificial lures. Solid muscle from stem to stern, it is capable of putting up a vigorous struggle considering its small size. Average catches run well under a pound and the current record is only 1-pound, 13 ounces.

Like other fish of this category, its most redeeming value is its function of serving as a surrogate catch for anglers still acquiring skills and the taste for more stirring adventures. Many conservationists concerned with the proliferation of larger sporting species will appreciate all of the rock bass you remove from our fisheries. The rock bass has a nasty habit of glomming onto the same smaller fish and other prey which are important to the rest of the fish community.

Many families which retreat to lake cottages for the summer will rely on panfish for many of their meals, which is just fine and dandy. It helps them rationalize the cost of the outpost and cuts down on the hamburger inventory. The unhappy pitfall of this arrangement, however, is that the house-mother on the premises usually winds up as the official fish cleaner. This is not as it should be.

While our family has never experienced the mixed joys of owning a lake retreat, we have been guests at many. Over and over I have witnessed excited youngsters and beaming fathers parading proudly into a kitchen with their stringers or buckets of miniature panfish, then thrusting them at the already harried mother to disembowel, de-scale and generally immerse them in cracker crumbs, egg batter, margarine, cream, and transform them into the evening meal.

If God had meant for women to be cleaners of panfish he would have equipped us with magnifying lenses for our eyes and the skill of a surgeon with a scalpel.

Throughout the total span of human history women have carried their share of the household chores, from shoveling snow to ironing undershorts. But enough is enough. The husband who affects the role of an outdoorsman to his spouse and offspring can jolly well draw his trusty filleting knife from its scabbard and splatter the mess on his own khakis.

I am all for panfish, and I commend them to you heartily for the learning exercises which they will provide. They can also offer delight to your children when all of the "Star Trek" videos have been exhausted. They can save money from food shopping that-needs to be spent on new sneakers. But write it down and post it on the refrigerator door: "I don't clean panfish."

ADD A DASH OF
SALTWATER ACTION

"After fifteen or so minutes more of trolling the baits across the blue water, the reel toward the port quarter of the stern lets out its rapid, machine gun protest as the hook is hit. I leap out of the chair, grabbing for the rod to set the hook, a rather useless effort by the human holding the rod since the beast hooked against the pressure of the speeding boat either sets the hook itself, or it doesn't. Reeling as fast as I can and gulping for more air than my lungs want to take in, I try to focus my eyes into the gulf about where the end of the line should be. The reeling becomes suddenly too easy... suspiciously easy....I frantically crank the spool. Then a hundred—two hundred—a thousand, million yards before me, above the dream sea of the bill-seeker, waters are lifted by a blue-silver sailfish, arched with its sail fanning and its tail hidden just beneath the sea. Scream? My Lord, I scream my delight at seeing my first-ever sail on."

- "Salt Water Won't Let you Lose," Billie Phillips,
GRAY'S SPORTING JOURNAL, Spring 1989.

I have a feeling that many fishing families pick their summer vacation destinations the same way they select their food market: it should be rather close at hand, have good products, pleasant people and affordable prices.

And that's an acceptable formula for keeping the grocery budget under control, but if you apply it to angling adventures it is not going to show you much of the world. It will also deprive you of the possibility of experiencing some of the most electric thrills which sportsfishing has to offer.

Up and down our Atlantic and Pacific coasts and that of the Gulf of Mexico millions of American anglers get their kicks out of fishing for an entirely different group of species. And you can add to those numbers those folks who take advantage of a trip to Hawaii to venture onto the deep waters off the coasts of its major islands for some of the most challenging encounters with bigger fish than they ever dreamed they could bring to boatside.

Striped bass, bluefish, sailfish, blue marlin and white marlin, dolphin, grouper, bonefish, tarpon and permit are waiting out in those waters to broaden your total fishing experience, and to provide you with unforgettable memories...plus some delicious meals. Anglers who are lucky enough to live on or near those coastal areas have been enjoying this heavy-hitting action all the while that those of us who live in the inland states have been content with our annual expeditions to our local lakes and rivers for bass, trout, walleyes, northerns, muskies and assorted panfish.

The mission of this chapter is not to disparage the freshwater fishing which has its own satisfactions and rewards but, rather, to encourage you to consider a further amplification of your "Out On The Water" adventures by sharing in the rich bounty offered by our saltwater fishing grounds. All that it requires is a little advance planning, and budgeting, to make it happen. When you have done the necessary research and studied all of the travel folders you may be happily surprised at how little more it will cost.

You can begin by writing to the state fishing authorities listed on later pages, reading the extensive literature which they will send you. You will find lists of docks, dockmasters and even charter boat captains from which you can solicit more specific details. Then you can total up the dollars and decide when and where you will go and after what kind of fish.

Along our eastern and northeastern coast you can tangle with the amazing bluefish which form an almost endless parade from Florida to New England from March through May, and head back south again in late autumn months. These savage feeders provide some of the most exciting action of all saltwater fishing. They travel in monstrous schools, sending fleets of smaller baitfish jumping at the surface to get away. Drifting or trolling with artificial or natural baits will produce catches in the 8- to 10-pound range with fighting excitement of much larger freshwater fish. Often described as the "wolf of the sea" the bluefish is extremely popular with east coast anglers who await its arrival off their particular shore during the periods of its migration.

In protected bays along the coats the bluefish can be fished from smaller boats, but charter boats, or party boats, are a much better bet in offshore waters which can get choppy and otherwise hoary. Surf casters take their share of bluefish each year but they have to wait for

Saltwater Fish

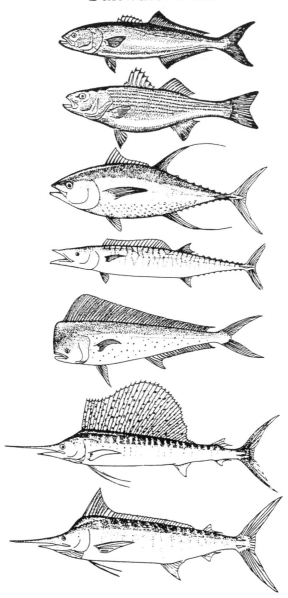

Here are some of the most popular saltwater fish sought by anglers working the waters off our coasts. From top to bottom: bluefish, striped bass, California yellowtail, wahoo, dolphin, sailfish and blue marlin. For sheer excitement you can't beat the struggle any of them will give you on your first deep water adventure.

the fish to come within the range of their lines to get their attention. But when a bluefish is hooked it provides a relentless struggle which can only be won by maintaining complete, tight-line control at all times.

The striped bass, or "striper", is another favorite of east coast anglers and has been for over three hundred years since our first settlers relied on it for food. While its annual migrations are similar to those of the bluefish, the striper is much more heavily pursued in the northeastern areas off New Jersey, New York and the New England states. Its immense popularity for both sport and food have contributed to the growth of a massive fleet of charter boats working out of Montauk Point on the far eastern tip of Long Island.

With average catches running well over 20 pounds, the striper is a tough adversary and calls for heavy work whether landed on a boat or from shore. When October rolls around, the striper joins the bluefish in providing some of the greatest angling excitement of the year in the Montauk area. Because of the overwhelming numbers and size of the fish abounding there at that time, the action which takes place is considered by many to be the greatest concentration of fishing activity anywhere, at any season.

Over one hundred years ago some enthusiastic striper fishermen placed large numbers of the fish in tanks, loaded them on a train and shipped them all the way to the west coast. Surprisingly, many males and females survived and began the reproduction cycle which ultimately resulted in the striper becoming a major player in the sportsfishing activities in the northern California and Oregon coastal waters. With all of the other excellent fishing in those areas, the striper does not get the same attention as it does back east, one reason being that is does not swarm in such great schools.

I confess at this point that I have never fished for either the bluefish or the striper but have read enough about them in books by John Hersey and John N. Cole to know that I would enjoy the action. A lady angler who has landed an 8-pound bonefish is much more apt to attract the attention and admiration of the fishing society than one who has captured a bluefish of equal size. And even a small sailfish catch will provide for more community envy than that of a 30-pound striper.

And that's what we ladies need most today: recognition and envy. So let's now focus our attention on those other ocean waters where more glamorous fish are to be found. We can begin with Florida.

Most of the charter boat action in the Sunshine State takes place from the Palm Beach area all the way down to Key West. As you will discover when you write to the Florida Game and Fresh Water Commission, there are flotillas of sea-worthy craft available at almost every city marina along the route. There you can arrange for a half-day or a full-day charter for your group (or join a group of other unattached anglers) and be out in the famous Gulf Stream in just a matter of minutes.

As you leave the bay or channel leading out to the deep water your boat captain will be up on the flying bridge keeping the boat within the marked passage and all the while searching the sky above for flights of feeding birds. It's that way with most saltwater fishing: the hovering birds announce the presence of small fish on the surface, and those same small fish attract larger fish from below. Dolphin, cero mackerel, sailfish and even marlin will soon find the smaller fish and drop by for a tasty lunch.

That's when the mate on the boat will lower the outriggers, place firmly-harnessed bait fish on the lines and drop them off to the stern as the boat trolls over the center of action. All you have to do is sit in one of the deck chairs, keep your eyes on the baits fluttering on the wave tops behind the transom, and wait. This is comfortable fishing. There are cool beverages on board, and maybe you brought along a sandwich or two. You are completely relaxed, enchanted by the sweep of the birds overhead and the gentle roll of the waves.

Then it happens. If you were paying attention, you saw the tip of a bill or a fin come out of the water, then disappear below the surface. You hear the snap of the retaining clip as the line pops off the outrigger. The mate jumps in front of you, pulls a rod out its holder, jerks it sharply up as he cranks on the reel and shouts, "Fish on!"

And then you are in the fighting chair with that heavy rod in your two hands. The reel sings, the line speeds out, and the captain yells, "Hang on!"

Is that exciting? Almost as exciting as your wedding night, and a lot more demanding on your motor skills.

The good news is that you are in the company of a seasoned captain and crew who know how to make even your first major fish encounter a successful one. The boat speed and direction will be carefully choreographed to give you the upper hand over whatever is on the other end of your line. The mate will tell you when to exert effort on the reel, to raise and lower the rod, and when to just sit still and wait for the fish to become less obstreporous.

As all of this takes place, the fish will run, dive and perhaps even leap. You will be frightened, exhilarated and challenged all at the same time. You will become stubborn and determined to win the battle, and do just what you are asked by the mate and the captain, even though they may not both ask for the same action. You came on this boat ride to catch a fish, and, by golly, you are going to do it!

When the fish is finally beaten, by your persistence and the captain's maneuvering, you begin the heavy cranking on that monster reel. The line comes in, slowly but surely. The mate watches for the steel leader, grabs it with a gloved hand as it comes over the transom, drives a sharp gaff into the side of the fish and swings it on board.

The battle is over, you can't believe what you have just done. But

Much of the enjoyment of a deep sea fishing trip comes from the heady experience of riding in one of those beautiful, well-equipped yachts built especially for the sport. The two Rybovich cruisers shown above are some of the finest you will find at fishing piers anywhere .

there it is. A fish you can talk about with pride and exuberance in the presence of the most reserved circle of male anglers.

"I caught a _____ -pound _____!" you exclaim.

It could have been a 20-pound bull dolphin, a seven-foot sailfish, a 60-pound white marlin, a 30-pound kingfish...or even a 150-pound blue marlin. Or maybe an even bigger one. Whatever it was, it will make a great picture, cram your mind with thronging, aching memories, and make you happy that you had the courage to try.

The dolphin is the most colorful of saltwater game fish; a bright yellow, green and blue sliver of all muscle. It travels in large schools which provide catch-after-catch action until they are spooked and move on. Most will be small, 5 to 10 pounds, but the bulls and cows are often in the same group and put up spectacular leaping fights as they try to throw the hook. On top of all that, it is a delicious dinner fish and featured at many oceanside restaurants.

While the largest dolphin ever caught weighed 87 pounds, Barbara Kibbee Jayne holds the record for 30-pound test line with a 73-pound, 11-ounce catch, and Mrs. Eugene Wooten holds the world title for 20-

This 22-foot "center console" boat by Mako Marine is a favorite with many guides working offshore waters of the east coast. The canvas top keeps the operator and anglers out of the sun when not fighting a fish. Small but seaworthy, it will take you many places you couldn't reach in a larger craft.

pound line with an 83-pound, 6-ounce dolphin! Not bad for a couple of anglers in skirts!

Or maybe it was a sailfish that took your bait. The Atlantic sailfish is probably the most photographed catch along the Florida coast, and quite likely hangs over more fireplaces than all other saltwater game fish combined. It is colorful, flamboyant and majestic. It generates more action per fighting minute than anything you will hook into on inland waters. Its enormous dorsal fin, taller than the entire width of its body, makes it particularly picturesque and adds to its maneuvering ability. The steely blue color of its sides and its silvery underbelly also accents its beauty and memorability as an exciting catch.

While sailfish will measure up to eight feet in length, their narrow body limits their weight to much less than might be expected for such a long fish. Average catches will weigh around forty pounds but provide thrills equal to other fish of much heavier weight. They are caught almost year around off the Florida coast and are generally in abundance during the winter vacation months, In February of 1980 charter boats operating out of Palm Beach took part in what is perhaps the greatest sailfish catch in recorded history. Within a period of less than five hours several hundred sails were brought to boat during a spectacular feeding frenzy. All boats in the area raced toward the action and caught and released fish almost as fast as they could handle them. One boat landed 83!

For a novice woman angler the sailfish offers a rewarding introduction to deep-sea fishing. The tackle is relatively light. Once hooked, the fish is not really difficult to control in spite of all of the tail-walking gymnastics which it will perform, and the seasoned coaching of the boat crew almost guarantees a successful catch worth every dollar the experience will cost you.

Deborah Maddux, Gloria Applegate, Helene Tournier, Mrs. Pamela Jean Durkin and Mrs. Ellen Botha all hold world line class records with catches up to 108 pounds, so you needn't shy away from a sailfish expedition.

Marlin caught off the Florida coast are Atlantic "blues" and "whites". The blue marlin is the heavier of the two, but catches in these waters rarely run over 250 pounds, which is still a true monster for those of us more accustomed to a four-pound bass or a six-pound walleye. They are usually found much further off shore, require heavier tackle with live bait producing the most catches. Watching a mate lash a live blue runner or goggle-eye bait to a large stainless steel hook is exciting in

Deborah Maddux, a legal secretary, began attracting the attention of the fishing world in 1986 when she set two swordfish records in just five days while angling off Panama. The 303-pound Pacific blue marlin that she is smiling over in the above photo was caught on 12-pound test line in August of 1990 off Costa Rica. Twelve pound test line! Described in THE INTERNATIONAL ANGLER as a "five-foot human dynamo", she now holds world line class records for eight classes of billfish, including swordfish, white marlin, blue marlin, striped marlin and black marlin. In six years of fishing she has accomplished what no other angler has done in a lifetime of fishing! Oh yes, that 303-pound blue in the photo took five hours of struggle before being brought to boat. Not bad for a lady angler!

itself, but when one of those big fish takes it in and heads for deep water you are in for a much more demanding struggle than that put up by a sailfish or a husky bull dolphin. But don't let that keep you from trying. My collection of photographs of blue marlin catches in the Florida area include those of Glenna Johnson-Voller of Wauwatosa, Wisconsin, with a 203-pounder, and local angler Margie Brown with one that went 168 pounds. Margie's catch took 53 minutes to bring to the boat and she will never forget fireworks of that encounter.

Another clipping that I enjoy re-reading is the story of Irene and James Woods of Oswego, New York, who both caught blues on a January day in 1985. Irene's was a respectable 110-pounder while husband Jim had the prize of the day with one that weighed 235 pounds. What interests me most about this story is that if Irene was the one who suggested the trip to her husband, he will be in her debt forever! Which ought to suggest something to you.

There are many other stirring catches to be made in these same waters, such as the scrappy wahoo, the husky yellowfin grouper, the stubborn bonito and the dogged amberjack. The time of year in which you fish, the condition of the sea and other weather factors will pretty much determine the ones your captain will go after. But the most important thing to remember is that the boat crew will do everything possible to help you catch the fish of your choice. The tips they receive from happy anglers are important to them, as well as the reputation they earn from being one of the top boats of their marina.

Another fish popular with Florida vacationers is the heavy-hitting, monstrous tarpon which is fished in the shallow lagoons and backwaters just off the coast. This silver-blue fighter is famous for its acrobatics on the end of a line and its ability to control the fight for long periods of time. Fishing for tarpon is done from smaller charter boats, many of them skiffs which are poled through the water by the guide standing in the bow. When fish are sighted the guide will direct the angler where to cast. If the fish is properly hooked in its tough jaws the fight will be on, and so will the ride to follow him as he tries to escape.

The tarpon chase is pretty much of a "bare bones" experience. There is no fighting chair in the humble skiff and the guide cannot maneuver the boat to shorten the battle as a deep-sea charter captain can. Constant line control is essential and any slack can cause the loss of the fish.

While I classify the tarpon as more likely quarry for men anglers there are ten women listed among the current twenty-two world line class record holders, one with a catch of over 218 pounds!

Light-tackle enthusiasts consider the bonefish as the scrappiest fighter for its size anywhere and approach it with the same dedication and commitment as the freshwater muskie hunter. Somewhat like the muskie, the bonefish must be stalked and is every bit as fierce a combatant as the much bigger muskie. It is found in backwaters similar to those frequented by the tarpon. Guides with small skiffs operate all down the Florida Keys, beginning at Key Biscayne, within view of the Miami skyline.

A silver-blue torpedo of a fish, it will often travel in groups which can be sighted by the guide as they stir up the muddy bottom in their search for food. When they detect danger they scatter with lightning speed and require consummate stealth in any successful approach. From what I have been able to learn, the true bonefish angler is a paragon of patience and bullseye-sharp in his casting ability.

A typical Florida bonefish catch may go only four or five pounds and an eight-pounder is a genuine Holy Grail catch for its captor. In spite of all the skill and persistence required for successful bonefishing there are still six women anglers holding world line class records, just two less than all of the men listed with similar honors. Harriet Masinter holds the 8-pound line record with a 14-pound, 4-ounce bonefish caught near Islamorada in October of 1988. There are probably thousands of male bonefish hunters who would give their late model Mercedes convertible for that catch!

If you have a yen to add a bit more color to your next visit to the east coast of Florida you should also consider adding a trip to one of the Bahama islands to your itinerary. Most American travelers know very little about the Bahamas and that they begin just fifty-four miles off Fort Pierce and extend some 700 miles to the southeast. Along this strand of atolls and islands are many famous fishing grounds offering all of the fishing action of the Florida coast plus a delightful Caribbean atmosphere. There are big game fishing clubs and marinas sprinkled throughout the islands, and all easily accessible from Miami and Fort Lauderdale. Just mention Bimini or Walker's Cay to your friendly travel agent and she will spill out a whole file of colorful folders telling you where they are and the price of admission. The few dollars it takes to get there can be regained through some of the lower accommodations costs and the charter boat rates will be no more than those in the Palm Beach or Miami areas.

There is a lot of fun to be had eating, shopping and sight-seeing on the Bahamas, plus plenty of night life to make the trip a romantic interlude for you and your partner. And a group of adventurous young women would find it especially memorable. It will provide more commanding conversation for the future than equal time spent up at Bill & Jane's While away Camp on Rigorous Lake.

There's even more international flavor to be enjoyed in the country of Belize, less than a two-hour flight out of Miami, at the east end of Mexico's Yucatan peninsula. Until 1981 this subtropical paradise was British Honduras, and you probably had never heard of it. But take a look at your map and you will find it, just beyond the western tip of Cuba, south of Cozumel. At last count there were at least two regularly-scheduled airlines flying there from Miami with exotic beverages served on board during the flight.

Albacore	Halibut	Mako Shark
Amberjack	Jack Crevalle	Thresher Shark
Barracuda	Horse-Eye Jack	Tiger Shark
Black Sea Bass	Jewfish	Cubera Snapper
Giant Sea Bass	Lingcod	Mutton Snapper
Striped Bass	King Mackerel	Snook
White Sea Bass	Spanish Mackerel	Tarpon
Bluefish	Blue Marlin	Tautog
Bonefish	White Marlin	Big-Eye Tuna
Bonito	Permit	Blackfin Tuna
Cobia	Pollock	Bluefin Tuna
Atlantic Cod	Pompano	Little Tunny
Pacific Cod	Runner Rainbow	Wahoo
Dolphin	Sailfish	Weakfish
Black Drum	Spotted Sea Trout	California
Flounder	Hammerhead Shark	Yellowtail

Anglers along our Atlantic, Pacific and Gulf coasts have the good fortune of being able to pursue an almost endless variety of saltwater species, 48 of which are listed above. If you've been hung up on bass and crappies, the time has come to taste the excitement of hooking into one of these.

For your fishing adventure you will want to check in at one of the tropical resorts on Ambergis Cay, a narrow spit of land that sits right at the edge of the barrier reef which is home to some of the finest sportsfishing anywhere. Large and small charter craft will take you back on the flats for tarpon, bonefish, permit and snook or into deeper waters for barracuda, grouper, kingfish cobia and jack crevalle.

Natives of Belize are a pleasant mix of Creole, Carib, Mayan, Mexican and other assorted indigenous varieties, but they all are extremely hospitable and friendly. The weather averages about 84 degrees year round, and the water scenery is entirely unique. In between fishing trips, or at the end of your stay, you can visit Belize City and witness a hard-working people bustling around their modest shops and unpaved streets. A settlement founded by shipwrecked sailors over three hundred years ago, it still has many reminders of its colonial past yet offers comfortable bars and restaurants in which to relax and swap fishing stories.

There are scores of other bases from which to go saltwater fishing along the coast of the Gulf of Mexico, from western Florida all the way over to the eastern shores of Texas. In Mexico, itself, there is great deep-sea angling out of Acapulco and Mazatlan plus the many fishing villages at the southern tip of Baja California. The San Diego area of the Golden State is another center of charter boat activity. If your travels take you to any of these areas you owe it to yourself to inquire about the facilities available to take you out onto the water and hook up with new fishing adventures.

And don't forget Hawaii. Our fiftieth state is famous for the marlin fisheries reached from marinas on Oahu (that's where Honolulu is) and Kailua-Kona on the big island of Hawaii. We have fished the Kona coast on many occasions and have never been disappointed with the action over the deep waters which are so close to the shore. Large dolphin (called "mahi mahi" here), yellowfin tuna, wahoo and marlin are caught every day from well equipped charter boats with excellent crews. Further off shore you can witness the passing of large schools of huge whales as they roll up and over the surface.

Hawaii can be more than just leis and luaus if you take the time to ask for help in lining up a day of fishing, or even just a half-day. The island scenery is magnificent when viewed from a fishing boat and the ocean, alone, is almost awe-inspiring. You may well hook into fish of over 400 pounds which, even if you lose them, will leave an unforgettable memory of grandeur. You can listen to the radio chatter between boat captains as they exchange reports of large fish which show up on their underwater electronics, and then wait in silent anticipation as you watch the trailing lines over the transom. You will be absolutely captivated, and maybe even speechless...at least until you hit the dock.

Skip the pineapple plantation tour, or even the volcano viewing, for just one day of your next trip. With any luck at all you will come up with a few mahi mahi to take to your hotel for your chef to prepare a special meal for your group before you go home once again. It will taste more delicious than Minnesota walleye or Missouri catfish and will be all the more unforgettable because you caught it. Right there in God's great outdoors.

Coming upon a school of dolphin makes for some exciting moments in any charter boat. While most of the "schoolies" run under ten pounds, and two 25-pounders shown above were caught in the same area as the many other smaller fish. The name "dolphin" confuses many people (who think of those performers seen in so many aquariums). The dolphin shown above is also known as the "dorado" in other countries, and as "mahi mahi" in Hawaii. The fish is most brilliant when freshly caught . . . and that's the best time to get your photographs. Of course those biggies were caught by the lady anglers!

TRICKS, TACTICS AND TRIUMPH

*"In poker, you will always be holding some kind of hand when you enter
a pot. It may be strong, weak or merely full of promise. Before you can plan
a winning strategy, you must look first at your cards and assess them. In daily
life, you will always be holding some kind of 'hand' when you enter a
confrontation. It, also, may be strong, weak or merely full of promise. Before
you can plan a winning strategy, you must look at those real-life cards and
assess them."*

*-Mike Caro, "POKER FOR WOMEN...A COURSE FOR
DESTROYING MALE PARTNERS AT POKER, AND BEYOND."*

My memories of my mother and father are still quite clear in my
mind in spite of the many years that they have been gone. They were
both hard-working parents, instilled with the strict Scandinavian work
ethic, and they brought up five kids in one of the most unusual
households in modern family history.

Our home was an upstairs apartment over the morgue of Minnesota's
most populous county. As a deputy coroner, dad was "on call" at all
hours, seven days a week to drive to the scene of any homicide or
mysterious death which took place within a range of about fifty miles.
The morgue spaces on the first floor and our apartment were often
visited by doctors, police officers, F.B.I. personnel and other law
enforcement officials associated with any of the "cases" which had
been retrieved to our building.

With that kind of a work pattern it was easy to understand why dad
like to get away and go fishing. Many of his fishing groups were made
up of the same mix of doctors and lawmen. The trips were usually made
over week-ends to places no more than two hundred miles away. No,
I was never invited along, but it was taken for granted that the nights
at their fishing cabins included the smoking of cigars, the sipping of
good whisky, the playing of cards and the telling of gory stories
associated with their work.

Their fishing was done from small wooden boats with only oars for
power, and with just enough simple tackle to guarantee a family-size
catch as they trolled over their chosen lakes. Dad always seemed to
bring home plenty of filleted walleyes to provide at least one good meal

for the family, plus exciting tales about how and where they were caught.

My mother accepted dad's need to get away for those trips and never expressed any disappointment at not being invited along. But I was fascinated by it all and resolved that, as soon as I was old enough, I was going to go fishing...if not with dad and his pals, with someone, someplace.

It took more years than I thought it would, but I finally did get out there and, once I got into it, I kept enthusiastically at it. I married just a few months short of my twenty-second birthday, an event which my parents considered an act of both justice and mercy. My live-in permit had expired eight months earlier, and there were still three other siblings in the nest.

The man who joined me in that exercise was one that I had picked for the assignment at least five years earlier. He didn't know that, and it was just as well. It made the consummation easier. He tried to get away a few times, but I never let it happen. And he didn't. During the years of our courtship I had managed to meet and become friends with his mother. She figured that I was a good catch, and joined in the effort. The early years of our marriage were tested by tough economic times, separation during his military service, and then four re-locations: from Washington, D.C. to Miami, to Minneapolis and Montreal, and then back to Minneapolis. Over an interval of thirteen years we managed to have two sons, keep them in jeans and sneakers and prepare them for college. Later, we made the decision to start our own business and I assumed the role of CFO (chief financial officer) and kept us on reasonably good terms with our banker.

In addition, I served as PSC (principal supplier contact), which was no great burden since we had only one "principal" supplier. Its representative was a man young enough to be my son, and who visited only when he was in need of lunch or motherly advice. When we made the decision to retire and sell the business it reflected the solid growth of strong management.

I mention all of these experiences to help establish my credentials for commending to you the following proposals on how to get invited to go fishing by your selected companion, how to enjoy and survive it, and how to communicate positively about it with others. Let's begin with the business of getting invited.

If your targeted companion is a male (your husband or significant other), you already know that he comes with an inbred sense of superiority, and a firm conviction that you are invested with inferior motor skills and a vocabulary not seasoned to the rigors of a typical fishing expedition. It is important that you understand and accept that position. But it should not cause you to lose out.

One obvious way to attack that problem is through flirting or flattery. One young woman I know makes a good living out of teaching other women in business how to overcome such stereotyping through a course called "The Art of Seduction," which sounds sexual, but "isn't about how to take your pants off." She talks about people who aren't classically beautiful or extremely intelligent but have so much self-esteem and confidence that they just captivate others, especially men.

Being a good listener is one of her basic teachings, which she pairs with a plan to kill your listener with kindness. A little friendly body language helps, too, she says. You can do all of those things when you broach the subject with your selected partner. Listen attentively, nod willingly, smile gently, tell him how much you admire his experience and prowess in the sport. Moseying close won't hurt either, and a pecky little kiss to underline your admiration will add emphasis to your admiration.

Psychologist Ellen Kreidman also recommends praising your man in front of others, leaving stick-on notes around the house saying things like, "I love you," "Our children are lucky to have a dad like you," and perhaps, "I'd love to go fishing with you." Underline the word "love". And don't overlook the power of a candlelight dinner as the occasion to bring up the subject.

Whatever avenue of attack you choose, you can brighten it up with sparks of conversation in which you use a few proven catchwords to get his attention. You can ask him to define "structure," "presentation," or "terrestrials." Or you can plead with him to, once more, tell you about that lunker bass he caught last summer. Few men can retreat from such an opportunity to express their omniscience, and the odds are now heavily on your side.

Assuming that you have achieved your objective, you will want to direct your attention to the matter of dress, and outfitting yourself in a manner which will make him pleased with his decision to invite you along. We talked about clothing in chapter five, and you will want to review that as you select your wardrobe. But you will also want to consider the added advantage which comes with packing a mild assortment of lingerie for those nights in the cabin, reflecting on the day in front of a warm stove or glowing fireplace.

Reflect also on the positive impact which can be achieved by adding to your costume with a few accepted accessories of the sport. Consider the Leatherman Tool, a pair of long-nose fishing pliers, or even a modest fishing knife. All of those come with handy leather holsters which slip nicely onto your belt. You put one on, and pretend to forget that it is there. While the effect on your partner may be more intimidating than the sight of a pocket "beeper", it will readily communicate a sense of understanding and preparation.

If your trip is to extend over a few days, the chore of packing will involve some restraint over how you might prepare for a business or family trip. A soft-sided duffle bag is a must, and the load must be light. Clothes packed will be rolled up, not folded, and tucked in with such other items as a small toilet kit, a flashlight, small portable radio, sunglasses, rain gear, camera, film and batteries...plus small vials of

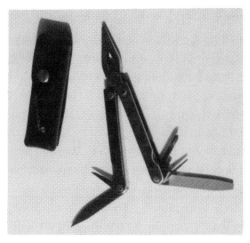

Skilled craftsmen are known by their tools, and many male anglers aspire to the role of outdoorsman by carrying a menacing Bowie knife in a sheath at their belt. The above Leatherman Pocket Multi-Tool will do nicely for you...and kill your male fishing partner with curiosity. Its twelve different blades will do everything but clean the fish...and it's almost as small as a lipstick case. You'll find it in Cabela's catalogue.

cologne or perfume to enhance the evenings.

Packing the rods, reels, lures and other tackle can be left to your partner, whose manifest experience will determine the proper selection. But you might add to his delight in inviting you by slipping a few snack items into your own duffle, or even some olives for the martinis. Everything is fair in love and war!

Once you arrive at your destination and head for the boat which will take you out on the water, a very special deference is called for. This is the moment at which you permit him to demonstrate his profound wisdom by establishing the pecking order of who sits where, how the tackle will be arranged, and who will operate the motor. If you are not fishing with a guide, your male partner will certainly want to play "boat captain". Over the many years that I have been looking at the advertisements of boat manufacturers, from Astro to Quantum, I have yet to see one in which a woman was at the controls. Most of them have showed no women in the boat, at all.

When the fishing actually begins, the level of your aggressiveness should be weighed against the performance of your partner. At the outset, you will want to cast where he tells you to, use those baits which he consigns to you, and nod knowingly when he tells you that, "They're hitting short today," or "The Solunar Tables are against us."

The most challenging problem which you will face will come if and when you catch a fish before your partner...or a bigger fish. Artful womanly modesty is immediately called for. You could try to lose the fish during landing, or you might tell him to release it, because you are certain that he will catch more and bigger ones. Or you could tell him how grateful you are that he brought you along...to share in such a rapturous experience. But don't overdo it. If you continue to out-fish him, just keep score so you can remember the numbers to tell the other girls back home when the trip is over.

If you are fishing with a guide, you can also help your partner sustain his ego by telling the guide what a great fisherman he really is. Repeat some of the stories you've heard from him, embellish a few details...whatever comes to mind to establish his pre-eminence. It won't hurt a bit, and it can help insure a repeat invitation.

At the same time, you should be honing your own skills, concentrating on your casting to improve distance and accuracy, and maintaining control on your retrieves. You will want to learn how and when to set the hook, how to handle a fish in the boat, and how to release it so it will live to fight another day. Watching which baits are attracting the fish, knowing when to switch to others, how to attach and remove them are some of the fundamentals which will make you a welcome companion.

Many fishing trips will also include frequent drinking of coffee, soft drinks or cold beer. Joining in this element of the game is almost compulsory. But if you have a normal bladder, the time will come when you may have to announce, "I need to go to the bathroom." The more urgent the need, the more clearly you will need to communicate that fact. In most instances, this announcement will be met with a sigh of despair, the reluctant reeling in of lines, and heading for the nearest shore.

Poison Ivy
Rhus radicans

Two threats to a pleasant fishing trip are mosquitoes and poison ivy.
Always carry along a can of insect spray to avoid the former. And the best
way to avoid the latter is to look carefully when attending to your needs
back in the brush. You will be happy I warned you.

181

Assuming there is no camp close at hand, you will be heading into the woods, out of sight of the other anglers, and properly attending to your needs. Tucked in a jacket pocket, or in your socks, you will have that packet of tissues which you brought along for the occasion, and you acquit yourself with honor. (It must be assumed at this point that you are able to recognize poison ivy, and have not nestled down into a lush garden of the stuff).

If, on the other hand, you are on a charter or party boat, your problem is less severe. You just find your way to the "head" and follow the flushing instructions so you don't sink the boat.

Since there are so many types of fishing trips which can be taken there is really no one set of rules which will apply to all, but any woman with an average understanding of men's determination to play a leadership role will be able to respond in a manner which will preserve peace and harmony within the boat. We do all of this not just because of a selfish desire to become a continuing partner in these fishing experiences, but because we truly enjoy being with that man in the boat with us. We are there because we are a part of his life, and he is a part of our's. We enjoy being together, and fishing is one special avenue to put us together in the healing atmosphere of the great outdoors,

Jonda McFarlane, writing in an article for NEWSWEEK magazine put it this way: "Throughout history, it has been this union — in which each partner is concerned with the good of the other —which above all other forces has made it possible for men and women to experience their greatest joy. It is this built-in support system that enables them to be the best they can be... A sunset watched in solitude on a foreign shore only increases your loneliness; the same sight shared with a loved one is a special moment."

A day on the water together can provide a replenishment of the love and respect that brought us together in the first place. The number and size of the fish caught play only a minor role in the togetherness which has been achieved. Soaring bald eagles overhead, the heron honking along its flight, or even a young doe at the water's edge help create a special feeling of being alone together. That's what much of fishing is all about.

If you are on a wilderness lake, you may be sharing in the rare pleasure of a shore lunch, with your guide preparing a hearty meal over an open fire, including fillets from the fish caught during the morning. For many anglers, this casual interlude in the day's activities provides many of the most treasured memories of any fishing expedition. For you and your partner it will provide the sensual, quiet luxury of recreating the fun and excitement of the early hours on the water, and pleasant moments to plan the afternoon...and other adventures together.

Here is an introduction to what a "shore lunch" is all about. The above photo shows the guides cooking up a mess of fish and fried potatoes over an open fire. In the bottom photo, three happy anglers relax and enjoy the tasty meal. Including coffee made from the lake water!

The guide who is your host recognizes the chemistry taking place, and goes about the business of cooking and serving the meal which will be an added catalyst to the romance and relaxation of the moment. This is what you have been missing all of those past years, and brings a rare closeness which you will want to share just as often as possible.

But maybe not.

You may have the good fortune to be associated with a group of other women who enjoy doing things together, and who include fishing among their interests. In that case, you can forget all earlier suggestions relating to the chores of catering to a male companion and focus, instead, on just having a great time with your lady friends. The notes regarding dressing and packing for the trip will still apply, but much unfettered fun is to be had just by being yourself while observing the rules of safe boating and engaging the services of a qualified guide to give all of your group more time to fish.

The accompanying essay on "How To Get Along With Your Guide" will be helpful in winning his enthusiastic support of your efforts, including instructions on how to improve your casting, your bait selection, and preventing the loss of any large catches. If a shore lunch is in the day's program, it can be every bit as rewarding and genial...and the guide will probably work a little harder to make it a special treat. A little praise and cajolery does wonders with most of them.

As with any other sport, the recollection of joyful moments thrives on their re-telling and sharing them with others. If a friendly, receptive audience cannot be found in your household, or at your place of work, there are fishing clubs in many communities which offer a generous mixture of interested listeners and fellow sympathizers when needed. These are similar to the "support groups" so many women seek out in their business relationships. An important difference, however, is the benevolent interest which fishing club members grant equally to tales of despair and triumph. This, of course, is a trade-off condition, and each member is obligated to be as radiant a listener as those she seeks to hear her own lamentations or expressions of jubilation. You will find it a hearty exchange which is balm for the soul and feeds the desire for further adventure.

Another bonus of such affiliation is the opportunity to learn from visiting speakers, ask questions and share in some "hands on" instruc-

How To Get Along With Your Guide . . .

Next to favorable weather conditions and your fishing skill, your guide is the most important determining factor to a successful fishing trip. All camp owners and managers realize this and do their best to hire a competent guiding staff, but they realistically point out that it's not a matter of thumbing through the "Yellow Pages" and ordering a half-dozen experienced guides.

Years ago, I spent an entire season at a northwestern Ontario fishing camp as a guide. I shared the same quarters with the guides, so each night we would "gossip" about our parties. This experience certainly provided me with an insight from the guide's point of view. Here are some of the complaints that were often registered:

• The fisherman who comes to the camp for the first time, and immediately tells the guide where and how to fish his waters.
• The fisherman who continually spouts off on how great the fishing was at another lodge. (If it were that good, we'd reason, then why did he change camps?)
• The obnoxious person who bragged about all the money he makes, but at the end of the trip would leave a meager tip.
• The people who use abusive language. "Some guys cuss so much while fishing that you wonder why they bother to fish in the first place."
• The person who can hardly cast, sets hook too late, loses fish and blames the guide, the waters or the resort for his ineptness.

On the positive side, here are some characteristics of a fisherman that are appreciated by guides:
• When weather conditions are unfavorable, he understands that fishing is likely to be poor and doesn't expect miracles.
• An appreciation for the beauty of the land.
• An upbeat temperament, even when fishing is poor.
• Some assistance in chores, especially on portages and shorelunches.
• A "pat on the back" or a couple of words of appreciation, when a guide does a great job of landing a fish, prepares a particularly fine shorelunch in the rain or performs any of his other duties well above the "norm".
• A fisherman who promises to send an item or photos and actually does it.

Some fishermen, realizing the tremendous importance of a guide, occasionally go "overboard" and spoil him. Treat your guide as an important member of your team and chances are that he will produce good fishing for you.

What happens if your guide is uncooperative, surly or totally inefficient? We all have our bad days occasionally (Remember: he may have been guiding every day for many weeks before you arrived), but if his poor attitude continues, mention it to the manager or owner. If possible, a replacement will be made.

"Let us know while you are at camp, when we may be able to do something about it. Some guests tell us that they were dissatisfied with a guide *after* the trip, but then it is too late to do anything about it," many camp managers echo.

Fishing Club News
180 N. Michigan Avenue, Chicago, IL 60601 (312) 263-0328

Jim Chapralis of PanAngling Publishing Company supplied the above guide for winning the love, affection and support of your fishing guide. Read it and you will be a better client than your blowhard male companion.

185

tion. Group trips by club members also can add to your independence from relying on men companions for invitations, and generally increase the amount of time you will be able to get out on the water. Two good ways to locate such clubs in your area include calling your newspaper's outdoor editor, and visiting the outdoor sports shows which are held in your city. Make the effort to find them, and begin enjoying the warmth of their fellowship.

The "shopping guide" pages which follow will also lead you to a number of national organizations which may not have chapters in your community, but publish educational materials which will help satisfy your growing appetite for more information on every aspect of the sport. There are clubs for almost every species of fish, plus a few "umbrella" organizations which direct their attention to the entire spectrum of angling. Check out one or two. You will find yourself among friends, and increase your chances for continuing success.

N.O.W.—and—T.H.E.N.
(A Benediction)

"How did men respond to the challenge posed by the women's movement? With a deafening silence. Only very recently has the male voice been heard in the land on its own behalf—and then not very loudly. Why have men been unwilling or unable to respond effectively to the new woman? One reason certainly is guilt. Men must concede that women were indeed victimized by various forms of discrimination and to some extent still are."
-Bill and Laurie Wishard, "MEN'S RIGHTS".

I am not one of those who marches under the banner of the National Organization For Women, and I don't really have any smoldering animosity toward men. After all, I am married to one. He is a long shot from being perfect but, as I have told him many times, I prefer him to what is in second place.

The "women's movement" is now over one hundred years old. It began back in 1848 at the first Women's Rights convention. That's when Elizabeth Cady Stanton put forth the position that "We hold these rights to be self-evident, that all men and women are created equal." Then activist Betty Friedan added fuel to that postulation when she wrote, in 1963, that "The time is at hand when the voices of the feminine mystique can no longer drown out the inner voice that is driving women to be complete."

Four years later, Betty figured prominently in the establishment of N.O.W. and became its first president. Today the organization is headed by Patricia Ireland who points to its membership of "about 250,000" as evidence that it speaks for the majority of U.S. women. Yet, as strong and vocal as it is, there are large groups of other women who believe that N.O.W. is much too militant, and that the problems we face with the male gender can be solved with fewer parades, demonstrations and oral fireworks.

Sure, women have had a bad rap. And men have been the cause of much of it. We have not always been treated fairly within the family, within the workplace, in government, in athletics, and in the fields of finance and business. Anthropologists have traced this discrimination back to the days of Indian tribes and later periods of history. Even

Aristotle has been cited as accepting women "as subordinate, subrational creatures—not as dumb as oxen but not up there with male citizens."

Throughout the years of the Renaissance of the middle ages, the industrial revolution beginning in the eighteenth century, the discovery and settlement of the western hemisphere women were always treated in the same manner, stereotypically inferior to men. Today, in the mad rush of the twentieth century, the focus of these feminists has been directed more intently on such matters as our right to equal pay for equal work, sexual harassment in work situations and our lack of a fair voice in the making of the laws we live by.

All of this has been useful, and most of us have benefitted by it. We are advancing to higher levels of leadership in most areas of enterprise, and being successfully represented in the courts when discriminated against because of our gender. We have more control over our lives, and we are getting a big kick out of seeing the men run for cover.

It was bound to happen.

That women have always been endowed with more fortitude than their male counterparts has been pointed out by author Marilyn French in her book, "The War Against Women". "Since the beginning of human life, women have taken responsibility for the well-being of the human race, she states. "Men die at a rate greater than women in every decade of life. They are emotionally stunted, unable to provide emotional support, cannot have babies or raise them, or even make their own dinner."

That we continue to exist, continue to marry men and have their babies (some of which turn out to be men), is rich evidence of our superiority in many areas of the human equation. And we will continue our advance within the framework of our families, our communities and our business lives. Recent Gallup polls have reported more and more women finding satisfaction and recognition in their lives, and are content to believe that their condition will continue to improve. Susan Faludi, author of "Backlash", probably says it best: "No one can ever take from the American woman the justness of her cause."

Since this book is about fishing, and our opportunities to share more equitably in its whole-hearted enjoyment, we need to move now to consider how this gradual emancipation will ultimately impact our future, In this contemplation we will relate back to those forces which have yet to wake up to our existence as a viable market, as competent companions, and our impatience with them. These include the total range of suppliers to the sport, its journalists, and those men with whom we would like to fish.

The tackle manufacturers are a totally unpredictable group, many of them too small to develop a sophisticated understanding of marketing, plus those larger ones who think only in terms of huge tournaments to

Many promotions have been sponsored by tackle manufacturers and others to increase participation in the sport. But, up to this point in time, none of them have mentioned us girls. So why not a campaign to "Take Your Wife Fishing"?

carnivalize the sport, their gaudy "pro" field staffs, and their over-concentration on bass fishing. Within this group there are at least two companies who have demonstrated an encouraging breadth of understanding which might, one day soon, lead them to discover us, to welcome us, and to serve us proportionately to our interest. These-two, Berkley and Normark, have shown signs of marketing citizenship far beyond any of the others, and which might one day sufficiently strengthen their courage to at least show a picture of a female angler, rod in hand, having a dandy time on the water. Other manufacturers may follow.

Whether those trade association "councils" and other educational, units will ever acknowledge us is a matter of vague contemplation at this time. They are still confused about the true demographics of the market, and appear to be led in their decision-making by advertising agency personnel who have minimal experience in the sport, and who have never seen a woman angler land a fish bigger than a tiny bluegill. Innovative programs to bring more women actively into angling have been denied their support while they continue to peck away at programs to get current fishermen to get out more often...and to take the kids along. I don't know if anyone in the industry is keeping score, but I will bet a fancy steak-and-potatoes dinner that the retail cash registers have not hit any high notes from that activity.

Once more, I rush to make it clear that I am not opposed to educating kids about fishing. Anything that will take them away from television for a few hours a week will always get my vote, but any marketing executive worth his salt should be aware of what happens to a woman angler when she once tastes the giddy, wild excitement and pleasant triumph of landing her first feisty bass, salmon or sailfish. To coin an expression, the lady is hooked! She will come back for more. She will spend to outfit herself to broaden her arsenal. She will travel to where the fish are, stay in enchanting fishing camps, ride in well-equipped boats, engage the services of knowledgeable guides...and go on having the time of her life. She will become (listen, guys!) a CUSTOMER!

Since those marketing experts cannot find news about such transformations taking place within those major outdoor journals, I strongly recommend an immediate membership in I.G.F.A., and the compulsory reading of its bi-monthly newsletter, "The International Angler."

In a single issue they will find more information, and more photographs, detailing the happy fishing adventures of women from San Diego, California, to Benton, Kentucky...and many other great fishing centers around the whole wide world. These are proud, confirmed lady anglers, using every kind of lure, every type of rod and reel, every type and weight of line, fishing from every type of boat, out of every type of fishing camp or marina, in every state of the Union...and all the way to Fiji and Egypt!

And they spend money, boys.

Some day, when they really open their eyes to the real world, the tackle manufacturers and their marketing consultants will wake up to this reality.

But don't count on the boat or motor manufacturers. Their product, they seem to perceive, is power...raw power. Speed, noise, glitzy packaging, and male ego-satisfaction. A spate of them will tell you that they have recognized us by at least putting one of us in the illustrations

One of the major benefits of an I.G.F.A. membership is receiving its publications: the annual "World Record Game Fishes" book, and the bimonthly newsletter, "The International Angler", which carries more pictures of women anglers in a single issue than you will see in a one-year collection of those mass-circulation outdoor magazines.

191

used in their advertisements. But either sitting there placidly at the side of our master, or longingly admiring that "nice fish" which he has just boated. Men buy those boats and motors, they earnestly believe. But they fail to recognize that those "convenient monthly payments" are coming out of somebody's household budget which must be balanced to pay the rent, buy food for the table, and have Elizabeth's teeth straightened before she turns fifteen.

Expect no change from that quarter. Let's examine the journalists, those publishers of the monthly, bi-monthly, annuals and "special" issues which keep the sport breathing throughout the year in the homes of sportsmen everywhere. Those leading outdoor journals referred to in earlier chapters appear to find themselves in a tough "no-win" situation. While they proffer an occasional article relating to an outstanding catch by a woman, or an angling expedition taken with her husband, none of them have ventured to run a continuing succession of "me and Phyllis" stories, for example. Somehow, a tale of two women in a boat struggling with a monster northern pike catch wouldn't fire up the reader's excitement to the degree that the same piece, with Pete and Mike in the same boat might have.

And any issue with the picture of a woman angler on the cover, regardless how notable her catch might be, would bring an immediate shower of letters to the editor, asking "What goes on here?" Popular fishing writer Charlie Waterman took note of this problem in "Women Of The Wilds", an essay he wrote for GRAY'S SPORTING JOURNAL: "One of the more masculine of outdoor publications has received outraged letters whenever female contours have become too prevalent in the action, and writers and photographers have been warned. Another publication says their readers feel differently...and some authors have named it "Fishing And Tits" magazine." He could say that in GRAY'S SPORTING JOURNAL because that rather comfortable New England-based publication has always been more democratic in its selection of material, providing an almost devil-may-care amount of space to women in the sport (although much of it concerned with the practice of properly cooking fish and game).

A few editors of the other magazines have made modest passes at the kids' market by including a section for "junior readers" in occasional issues. Most of this, it seems to me, is shallow and patronizing to their fathers. There are short articles on such fundamentals as hook sizes, knot-tying, bait nomenclature and fishing regulations. It all appears very tentative, and is not likely to expand or continue.

Don't ever entertain the idea that these hallowed male-oriented journals will ever elect to include a special section for women. Their publishers would not risk irritating the men on their subscription lists with such blather (that's what the boys would call it). Those women outdoor writers cited in our opening chapter may come up with phenomenal stories of sensational catches by women of their communities, but they will quite likely be rejected, ignored, or boiled down into minor notes to be included in those trifling articles which are

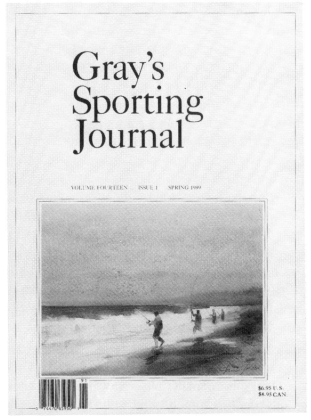

When you have settled comfortably into the sport of fishing, you will want to explore the pages of GRAY'S FISHING JOURNAL, a delightful publication which regularly publishes some of the finest fish stories told anywhere. For subscription information, write to them at P. O. Box 2549, South Hamilton, MA 01982-9986.

sprinkled in the back-of-the-book pages of those publications which accept them. The checks will be small, and the authors will realize that things really haven't changed.

Will we find their stories in GOOD HOUSEKEEPING or GLAMOUR? I don't think so. Maybe, just maybe, one day there will be an outdoor magazine for women. But don't hold your breath. It takes big money, and heavy advertising support. And we already know what the industry manufacturers think about women as a market.

Recognizing the obvious futility of this intransigence among the industry suppliers and its reporters, our only remaining hope for interested support for our need to be invited further into the sport lies with our husbands, fiance, or other selected male companions. I think we can handle them.

We have already discussed certain tactics of persuasion (up to and including seduction) and even some rational approaches. In my most solemn review of the problem, I am convinced that a rational approach offers the greatest chance for success. Let me tell you how I have come to this conclusion.

Every day our newspapers carry stories of relationships being damaged or destroyed by tension among the partners. Indeed, there are countless marriage counselors out there making a fancy living, driving expensive cars and sending their kids to the finest colleges, all off the hefty fees they collect for listening to men and women tell them why and how they can't get along. The Baylor College of Medicine in Houston, Texas, even has a special program called "We Care For You", which concentrates on marital communication and the improvement of partnerships. Psychologists of varying qualifications regularly conduct seminars for troubled couples, and our libraries add new volumes every week from authors who proclaim a high degree of expertise on the subject.

And, when all of that fails, the legal fraternity comes in for the final coup de grace, and a generous share of the spoils. The troubled partners rarely win and the literature gets heavier with every failure. It doesn't have to happen that way.

My consummate recommendation is to hit the problem head on. We begin with recognizing that the person we want to go fishing with is very special to us. We have selected him from the entire universe of males available to us because we care very much about him. We like the cut of his jib. We go well together. We get along in the other things we do. We may even have given birth to his children, learned to love his parents, and perhaps even some children from a previous marriage. We are a team.

We go to church together, to the precinct caucus, the school board levy hearing, and sometimes the movies. What's so different about going fishing together? Nothing very important.

I remember reading somewhere that a man's best friend is usually his wife, and that 85% of those folks who have divorced would remarry their spouse...if they had the opportunity. What I derive from that information is that most couples made the right choice the first time around, but let little problems upset them to the point that they permitted the relationship to fall apart.

The tract which I received from Baylor University repeated a truth that we all know and recognize: "Remember that good marriages are not made in heaven. Like other special things in life, marriages must be nurtured. By practicing effective communication you can add life as well as years to your marriage." (The piece is free, Write to Baylor College Of Medicine, Office of Public Affairs, One Baylor Plaza, Room 176B, Houston, Texas 77030. Ask for "Marital Communication: The Key To A Healthy Partnership") .

Professional speaker and practicing psychologist William Nagler, M.D., hits the problem much more directly in his new book, "The Dirty Half Dozen". His approach is based on his discovery that satisfying long-term relationships are not about abstract concepts like romance, honesty, or intimacy, but about elements which are much more familiar and far more obvious. His "Dirty Half Dozen" simplifies the whole business of compatibility and how to make it work.

"Why" questions, he tells us, are incendiary, potentially explosive, and never solve anything. Asking your selected partner "Why won't you take me fishing?" will only make him feel bad, and that he is being evaluated. And nobody likes to be evaluated. The answer to most "Why" questions, he tells us, "is usually some variation of 'Because I am a terrible person, and I deserve to be shot'."

Resentment sets in immediately, and everything heads downhill from there. (Consider such humdingers as "Why don't you like my brother?" or "Why did you buy that new motor?").

Since your goal is to win an invitation to fish with him, a "What" question offers a much better chance of victory. Try "What can I do to make your next fishing trip more pleasant?" or "What can I do to convince you that I would be fun on your next fishing trip?"

His answers will take time, so be prepared to wait.

You have eliminated the tension, and you have forced him to review his affection for you and the fact that you have been an enjoyable and sympathetic partner on many other types of activities ...and that you just might be pleasant to be with in a boat, out there on the water, someplace. Together.

You can start packing.

The product of all this discussion is a motto, or maxim, for men which I have given the acronym "T.H.E.N."

A deliberate, structured denial of most everything associated with "N.O.W." (which is anathema to all men), "T.H.E.N." simply tells your partner to "Take Her Everywhere, Now."

And, of course, it includes fishing.

Whatever tenderness, patience and planning it takes, we need to bring our man to the understanding that life is short and that each day of our being together is a flower that will not blossom again. He needs to be led to the realization of true fulfillment, the greatest joy, of any relationship is just plain doing things together.

I haven't printed any membership cards, and it isn't required that you get him to sign an affidavit of acceptance of the creed. Just deliver the goods. Be a grateful and enjoyable partner. He will be surprised, delighted, and think it was all his idea.

Men are so dumb!

MARGE'S
HANDY HOUSEHOLD
SHOPPING GUIDE
FOR FISHING ADVENTURES

Figures computed by the Fish and Wildlife Service tell us that only one of every four anglers has fished in waters outside his or her home state. And that's too bad. We are a very mobile society, traveling over the hills and through the woods to grandmother's house, or to Glacier National Park for our vacation, but rarely taking along the fishing gear which could help us discover the angling adventures which are available nearby.

In the next fifty-one pages you will read about the boundless recreational resources of-our continent, all ours for the taking if we but schedule the time to take them in. Going back to the same old places year after year may be the comfortable way to satisfy our fishing interests, but there is so much more to be discovered and enjoyed.

These individual state reports will tell you which fish are most abundant, where they are, and what it will cost for a license to catch them. In some states, special fees or stamps will be required for certain species, and you can check that out when you arrive. Information is also provided to tell you where to write for even more detailed material. I encourage you to write to any and all areas which pique your interest. Within a few days you will receive a surprising packet of literature to help you plan your visit.

With the data provided in this guide, plus what you receive in the mail, you will be the most knowledgeable person in the household on the available species, where to go for them, the most effective baits, clothes to pack, and even some of the interesting sights to see along the way. Make notes, dog-ear the pages, compare costs, consider the time and travel required...and then do it: get out on the water, new water, new wilderness...and open your life to the wholesome enjoyment of the great outdoors!

We dare
defend
our rights.

Cost of individual resident license: $9.50.
Non-resident license: Annual: $16.00. Short-term:$8.00 (7-days).

Where to write for more information:
Alabama Department of Conservation,
64 North Union Street, Montgomery, AL 36130.

Licenses issued in a recent year: 600,000.

Most popular species:
A wide assortment of bass, including largemouth, smallmouth, spotted
and stripers bluegills, all types of catfish, crappies and walleye...plus
tarpon, red snapper, tuna, bluefish and sailfish in the Gulf of Mexico.

Every woman likes to shop in a well-stocked supermarket. It makes for more selective and interesting shopping. Alabama is that kind of a state for anglers of all kinds. Its Department of Conservation and Natural Resources has done a leadership job in maintaining and expanding its fisheries throughout the state and, as a result recreational angling represents over half a billion dollars in business today. Almost 20,000 people are employed in fishing-related jobs, all working to provide memorable and rewarding adventures on its lakes, rivers.

The popular largemouth bass can be found in all regions of the state, and Florida-strain fish have now been added to its fishing menu. The Tennessee River, in the north, has four major reservoirs (Guntersville, Wheeler, Wislon and Pickwick) with first class bass angling. West Point Reservoir on the Chattahoochee River, the Black Warrior river basin, Lake Jordan, and the "Wiregrass" area in the southeast corner will easily fulfill your wish for hefty lunkers.

Walleye are the popular quarry at Lake Tuscaloosa and the scenic Cahaba River. Hybrid striped bass is outstanding on Lake Eufala and the Columbia Reservoir. Lake Martin is famous for the spotted bass which is rather endemic to Alabama. Large catfish are found in the Alabama River and in the Gainesville and Aliceville Reservoirs.

From Mobile Bay on the southwest you can head into the Gulf of Mexico where your charter boat will take you out to where the tuna, bluefish, sailfish and tarpon provide heart-throbbing action. One final note about Alabama: Lady angler Susan Holland holds two state records (for spoonbill catfish and paddlefish) with both fish weighing exactly 52 pounds, 12 ounces. Wow!

ALASKA

North to
the future

Cost of individual resident license: $10.00.
Non-resident license: Annual: $50.00. Short-term: $15.00 (3-day).

Where to write for more information:
  Division of Fish and Game, Subport Building,
  Juneau, AK 99801

Licenses issued in a recent year: 340,000.

Most popular species:
  Ring salmon, Coho salmon, sockeye salmon, burbot, rainbow trout,
  steelhead, cutthroat trout, artcic grayling, Dolly Varden, Artic char,
  lake trout, northern pike. State fish: Ring salmon.

There are 12 sportfishing management areas in Alaska, each with its own bag and possession limits, so you will want to check the fishing regulations booklet which you will receive from the state. In saltwater areas- many salmon and trout varieties, as well as rockfish and halibut are available throughout the season. This southeastern area extends from Ketchikan on the south to Skagway on the north. Turner Lake is a favorite spot for cutthroat trout.

The Yakutat area offers all five species of Pacific salmon in both fresh and salt water, plus a variety of trout in many lakes and streams. Several inlet areas along the southern coast are famous for rainbow trout, but interior waters contain some of the state's true world-class fisheries. The best of these are accessible only by floatplane.

This is an immense recreational fishing area which has attracted many of the world's leading anglers, but requires special planning to assure camp and guide availability services such as those provided by Pan-Angling's Jim Chapralis can provide all the details you need for a memorable, rewarding Alaskan adventure.

Here are some state records for its most-sought species: Artic char-17 pounds, eight ounces; cutthroat trout-8 pounds, 6 ounces; Dolly Varden-17 pounds, 8 ounces; king salmon-97 pounds, 4 ounces; lake trout-47 pounds; rainbow trout-42 pounds, 3 ounces; and steelhead-42 pounds, 3 ounces.

In addition to its fantastic fishing, Alaska offers some of the most majestic scenery in all of North America...another reason to consider it as a future destination.

God
enriches.

Cost of individual resident license: $12.00.
Non-resident license Annual: $38.00. Short-term: $18.50 (5-day).

Where to write for more information:
  Game and Fish Department, 2222 West Greenway,
  Phoenix, AZ 85023

Licenses issued in a recent year: 450,000.

Most popular species:
  Largemouth bass, striped bass, channel and flathead catfish, crappies
  and bluegills plus rainbow, brook and brown trout.

For a state known best for its warm year-round weather, Arizona has a surprising variety of fish species, found in its high mountain trout lakes and streams to its desert lakes and big rivers. Local anglers favor its trout streams and pay an additional $40 for the stamp needed to pursue them. (Trout fishing is included in the short-term non-resident license but requires an additional payment of $40 on an annual permit).

Lake Havasu, which was formed in 1938 with the completion of Parker Dam, provides year-round action for largemouth bass, striped bass, catfish and panfish, But there are also many other lakes throughout the state which offer excellent catches on most of these fish, among them are Lake Mead, Lake Powell, Roosevelt and Apache Lake.

Lakes within the limits of such cities as Phoenix, Scottsdale and Tucson also offer family fishing for bass, catfish and panfish, with rainbow trout stocked in them during winter months. For lunker river catfish, Arizonians head onto the Colorado, Verde, Salt, Black and Gila Rivers. Much of this fishing takes place at night when the bigger fish are cruising around.

The state record for flathead catfish is a whopping 65 pounds, while a 32-pound, 4-ounce catch holds the channel cat record. The top largemouth bass taken in Arizona weighed 14 pounds, 8 ounces, but a 24-pound, 3-ounce northern pike was taken from Upper Lake Mary in 1981. A 16 pound, 7 ounce brown trout caught in 1985 holds the state record for that species. And, somehow, a 12 pound, 12 ounce walleye was caught in Nelson Reservoir in 1989!

The next time you head to Arizona for a little winter rest and recreation, take along your fishing tackle and add to your vacation fun.

ARKANSAS

The people
rule.

Cost of individual resident license: $10.50.
Non-resident license: Annual: $25.00. Short-term: $8.00 (3-day).

Where to write for more information:
Game and-Fish Commission , State Capital Grounds,
Little Rock, AR 72201

Licenses issued in a recent year: 700,000.

Most popular species:
Largemouth bass, channel catfish, crappie, bluegill, rainbow trout,
brown trout, cutthroat trout.

There are probably a lot of people you know who couldn't locate Arkansas on a map of the United States but it is genuinely one worth finding and visiting. It calls itself "The Angler's Paradise" and is working hard to be just that.

Arkansas has over 9,000 miles of streams and over half a million acres of lakes, bayous, ponds and sloughs scattered throughout the state. Among these are many state park lakes and U.S. Forest Service lakes with catfish and largemouth bass awaiting anglers who prefer scrappy fish, and plenty of panfish for those who will settle for less.

Merrisach Lake, off the Lower Arkansas River has produced many 10- to 14-pound largemouth catches, and De Gray Lake near Arkadelphia is known for monster, hybrid striper bass. King-size walleyes have been taken from Greers Ferry Lake, and Ouachita Lake, maintained by the Corps of Engineers, has recorded striper catches up to 40 pounds!

Current state records list an 80-pound channel catfish, a 22-pound walleye, 19-pound rainbow, 16-pound largemouth bass and an enormous- 40-pound, 4-ounce brown trout caught in May of 1992 the largest ever caught on rod and reel in the Little Red River. The Little Red, along with the White River, have long been famous for their trophy trout catches, and attract many followers of these scrappy fish.

There are also, twenty cities with lakes open for public fishing. Wherever you go in the state you will find plenty of challenging action. And there's an information hotline you can call for current data on what fish are biting where. Just call (501) 688-8000, and then press 4252.

CALIFORNIA

I have
found it.

Cost of individual resident license: $21.00.
Non-resident license: Annual: $55.75. Short-term $6.75 (one-day).

Where to write for more information:
Department of Fish and Game, 1416 - 9th Street,
Sacramento, CA 95814

Licenses issued in a recent year: 2,000,000.

Most popular species:
Largemouth bass, striped bass, channel catfish, flathead catfish, blue
catfish, king salmon, coho salmon, brown trout, cutthroat trout, plus
various saltwater species.

California leads the nation in fishing licenses, boat registrations, tackle sales...and
anglers intent on catching the new world record largemouth bass. But the species
which gets the most attention year around are its trout. The state has 30,000 miles
of streams, and 6,000 lakes...plus 1,200 miles of coastline...all producing exciting
action for its multitude of fishermen and women.

Its high Sierra streams are famous for their pristine, protected environment and
are home to some of the most fabled trout on the continent, including the South Fork
and Little Kern golden trout. Coho salmon, along with chinooks and steelhead join
the cutthroat as prime targets for its large cadre of dedicated fly anglers. Rivers and
streams throughout the northern half of the state are excellent fishing grounds for
these exciting catches.

Lake Casitas and Castaic Lake are now world-renown for their monstrous
largemouth bass, and either one is expected to be the site of the new world record
any day now, These same lakes, heavily stocked with hatchery rainbow trout, also
keep the trout anglers enthusiastic, and the bass getting fatter.

Cheryl Duncan registered a new ladies' record for Pacific-bonito with a 11-
pound, 13-ounce catch in 1992, and Sandra "Honey" Beazley broke the women's
record for California yellowtail with her 37-pound, 8-ounce jumbo taken in May of
the same year. Put yourself into one of those charter boats working off the Pacific
coast and you can share in some of that excitement, and even get in some whale
watching while you're doing it.

Among other notable catches in California waters is the 88-pound king salmon
taken in the Sacramento River in 1979.

**Nothing
without
Providence**

**Cost of individual resident license: $20.25.
Non-resident license: Annual: $40.25. Short-term:$18.25 (5-day).**

**Where to write for more information:
Game, Fish and Parks Division, 6060 Broadway,
Denver, CO 80216.**

Licenses issued in a recent year: 700,000.

**Most popular species:
Trout cutthroat, rainbow, brown, brook and lake trout, plus kokanee
salmon, walleye, northern pike and even muskie.**

You will immediately know how proud this state is of its fishing waters when you receive the packet of materials regularly sent out to prospective anglers. The "Colorado Fishing Map" is an exceptional full-color presentation of angling opportunities in 126 lakes and streams plus fifty lakes and ponds of the Denver area alone.

Colorado takes special pride in its eleven lakes, rivers and reservoirs which provide outstanding large trout action. One of these, the South Platte River, produced the state record rainbow catch in 1972, an 18-pound, 5 1/2-ounce whopper. The Spinney Mountain Reservoir, also in this group, recorded a record 6-pound, 13-ounce kokanee salmon in 1986.

Another colorful brochure, "Colorado Fishing Hot Spots", takes you through the state's five wildlife regions, with complete travel directions and detailed data on which fish can be caught where...and even when. Among some of the "Hot Spots" reviewed you will read-about Trapper's Lake which holds the largest population of native Colorado cutthroat trout in the world, and the Cherry Creek Reservation State Recreation Area, famous for having produced more record fish than any single body of water in the state (among them an 18 1/2-pound walleye!).

If you like even bigger fish, there's a 30-pound northern pike catch credited to Vallecito Reservoir and 30 1/2-pound brown trout in the record books for a 1988 catch in Roaring Judy Pond. Get the Colorado fishing packet and put this great state on your itinerary for an unforgettable adventure iñ your future!

CONNECTICUT

**He who
transplanted
still sustains.**

Cost of individual resident license: $9.00.
Non-resident license: Annual: $17.00. Short-term: $8.00 (3-day).

Where to write for more information:
Board of Fisheries and Game, State Office building,
Hartford, CT 06106

Licenses issued in a recent year: 200,000.

Most popular species:
Largemouth and smallmouth bass, northern pike, striped bass, panfish.

For a state as small as Connecticut is, it offers an immense variety of sport fisheries; 175 lakes and ponds, over 100 rivers and streams, plus the exciting off-shore salt water grounds. There are off-shore bass management areas offering top-quality angling for both largemouth and smallmouth.

With a goal of providing exceptional fishing for its residents, the state operates four trout management areas, all employing special stocking and management concepts which have been judged as truly unique for trout habitat. In addition, Connecticut has seven "trophy" trout lakes, but with a limited season. The current record brown trout is a 16-pound, 14-ounce fish taken out of East Twin Lake in 1986. An 11-pound, 10-ounce rainbow set a new record for that species in 1988, taken out of the Salmon River.

One of the largest freshwater fish taken in the state is a 29-pound northern pike landed in Lake Lillinonah in 1980. The biggest largemouth on record is a 12-pound, 14-ouncer caught in 1961 out of Mashapaug Lake.

Offshore fishing in the Atlantic Ocean offers some king-size action in pursuing sharks, white marlin, striped bass and bluefish. A 650-pound mako shark is the largest Connecticut saltwater catch on record, but there is also a 108-pound white marlin catch in the books, which beats mine by quite a few pounds! The top striper is a 75-pound 6-ouncer taken in May of 1992, proving that there are still lots of the big ones around. Bluefish are still very popular with many anglers in this state, and catches up to 20-plus pounds are not uncommon.

DELAWARE

Liberty and independence

Cost of individual resident license: $8.50.
Non-resident license: Annual: $15.00. Short-term: $5.20 (7-day).

Where to write for more information:
  Division of Fish and Wildlife, P.O. Box 1401,
  Dover, DE 19903

Licenses issued in a recent year: 20,000.

Most popular species:
  Rainbow trout, brown trout, largemouth and smallmouth bass, striped bass, panfish...plus a full range of saltwater species in offshore waters.

Compared to some of the larger "supermarket" fishing states, such as Colorado and Arkansas, Delaware is sort of a "minimart" for angling adventures. Its best known fishery is that located off its eastern shore in Delaware Bay and along the Atlantic Ocean. Fishing from both private boats and charters focuses on Atlantic mackerel, bluefish, weakfish and such bigger game as sailfish, white marlin, blue marlin and even shark.

Surf fishing is popular with the state natives who head for Delaware Seashore Park and Fenwick Island State Park to try for passing schools of sea trout, flounder kingfish and bluefish. Those who prefer to head out onto the ocean will find fleets of charter boats at Bowers Beach, Slaughter Beach and Lewes.

For freshwater fishing enthusiasts the state has restored 25 scenic millponds and maintains them with stocks of largemouth bass, catfish, chain pickerel and panfish. Tramp Pond, Bellevue, Killens Pond and Lums Pond are especially popular with family groups, reflecting Delaware's dedication to provide pleasant outdoor recreation for its citizens.

The northern half of the state contains several designated trout streams, among them are Delaware, White Clay Creek, Mill Creek, Pike Creek, Christina Creek, Red Lewes Beaver Run and Wislon Run, all within the Brandywine Creek State Park. White Clay Creek is on record with a 9-pound, 4-ounce trout catch made in 1984. A whopping 2-pound, ll-ounce yellow perch was taken from Red Clay Creek in 1976.

Those who develop a liking for catfish can find plenty of action at Haven Lake near Milford where many are caught over ten pounds.

FLORIDA

In God
we trust.

Cost of individual resident license: $12.00.
Non-resident license: Annual: $30.00. Short-term: $15.00 (7-day).

Where to write for more information:
Division of Game and Freshwater Fish, 620 South Meridian,
Tallahassee, FL 32399-1600

Licenses issued in a recent year: 900,000.

Most popular species:
Largemouth bass, striped bass, channel catfish, white catfish, bluegill,
redear sunfish (shellcracker)...and a full spectrum of saltwater species,
the most popular being sailfish, dolphin, marlin and shark.

With all of the entertainment centers now located in the Orlando area, more and
more families are putting Florida on their travel plans. But beyond those glitzy
hotels and amusement parks there are thousands of inland lakes offering some of
the most challenging fishing in America. While other states receive a great deal of
attention for their largemouth bass catches, it's my guess that Florida produces more
bronzeback lunkers every year than any (or all) of the others. The current state
record of 20 pounds, 2 ounces has stood for almost sixty years, but 10- to 15-pound
catches today are quite commonplace if you plan your trip right and employ the
services of a knowledgeable guide.

You will receive over 100 pages of help in your planning from the five regional
guides provided by your inquiry to the address shown above. Besides landing many
larger fish than you can find around your home waters, you will also experience the
sighting of alligators, alligator gars and some huge catfish. The Everglades, too, are
an amazing sight and will provide for bright conversation among the boys back
home.

And if you want something even more exciting to talk about, head for any one
of the deep sea fishing charter marinas along the east coast...starting up around Palm
Beach and continuing right down to Key West. Get up your own group, or join one
being made up by the boat captain, and then spend either a half-day or a full day
patrolling the Atlantic waters for scrappy dolphin or acrobatic sailfish, or any of the
others which will provide greater fulfillment than you ever believed you could find
in the sport of fishing!

GEORGIA

Wisdom,
justice and
moderation

Cost of individual resident license: $7.50.
Non-resident license: Annual: $20.00. Short-term: $5.50 (5-day).

Where to write for more information:
State Game and Fish Commission, Floyd Towes East,
205 Butler St. S.e.
Atlanta, GA 30334

Licenses issued in a recent year: 700,000.

Most popular species:
Largemouth bass, striped bass, catfish (blue, channel and flathead),
northern pike, rainbow and brown trout, and panfish.

In addition to its many productive lakes and rivers, Georgia maintains 28 reservoirs which provide first class fishing for lunker bass and large catfish. There are also many state park lakes offering large catches of bass and panfish. Channel catfish are also a popular quarry and current records include a 53-pound flathead and a 44-pound, 12-ounce channel catfish.

The Savannah River still holds the world record for largemouth bass with George Perry's 22-pound, 4-ounce catch recorded sixty years ago. Blue Ridge Lake produced a 38-pound muskie landing in 1957 and an 18-pound, 2-ounce northern pike was taken in Lake Rabun in 1982. If you like even bigger numbers, consider the 63-pound striped bass caught in Oconee River in 1967.

Trout fishermen and women-will find rewarding action in streams located throughout the state. A 15-pound rainbow was taken out of a private pond in 1985, but there are many of near size in other public waters. The largest brown trout catch on record is an 18-pounder caught in Rock Creek in 1967. Check the "Guide To Georgia Trout Regulations" for season and possession information.

West Point Lake, a Corps of Engineers project, is a major recreational area stretching east from the Alabama border with fishing piers and commercial marinas from which to fish for largemouth bass, channel catfish and panfish, such as crappie and bream. Lake Seminole, located on the Florida border, is another Corps of Engineers project formed by the Jim Woodruff Lock and Dam. It has excellent habitat for bass, catfish and bream, many of which can be caught directly off a fishing deck adjacent to the tailrace below the dam. All of which helps make Georgia a "peach" of a state for fishing.

HAWAII

The life of
the land is
perpetuated
in
righteousness.

Cost of individual resident license: $3.75.
Non-resident license: Annual: None. Short-term: $3-75 (30-days).

Where to write for more information:
   Division of Fish and Game, 530 South Hotel Street,
   Honolulu, HI 96813

Licenses issued in a recent year: 8,000.

Most popular species:
   Largemouth and smallmouth bass, rainbow trout, channel catfish,
   tucunare and oscar, all from inland waters. From the offshore waters:
   yellowfin tuna, dolphin, wahoo and marlin.

If you've never been there, let me tell you that Hawaii is much more than leis and luaus. It is truly an exotic vacation destination with the most hospitable people to be found anywhere in the fifty states. And while Honolulu is a fun-filled city with a world-class beach, there are many other areas which deserve your attention. There are five other major islands besides Oahu, each just a short flight away, but all adding to a greater appreciation of the native beauty of this Pacific paradise.

There are public freshwater fishing areas on Kauai and the "big" island of Hawaii, as well as Oahu. While there are only five small natural lakes on the islands, there are also over 250 freshwater reservoirs ranging up to 400 acres in size offering high quality angling for bass, catfish and that odd-looking species known as tucunare. The Wahiawa Reservoir (also known as Lake Wilson) is only 30 miles from Honolulu and offers excellent fishing from the shore. A 48 1/2-pound channel catfish was taken from its waters in 1965, but there are also scrappy bass running up to seven pounds.

Trout fishing is quite limited, with Kokee Lake on Kauai providing most of the action in a short summer season.

But the greatest fishing memories of Hawaiian fishing are created on the deepsea charter boats available at marinas on Oahu, Maui, Kauai and Hawaii. Charter rates are quite reasonable, and all of the boats are large, comfortable and seaworthy. The materials available to you from the Division of Fish and Game include a complete roster of boats available, their captains' names, and telephone numbers. Give one of them a call, and have the thrill of a lifetime!

IDAHO

It is perpetual.

Cost of individual resident license: $16.00.
Non-resident license: Annual: $41.00. Short-term: $18.00 (10-days).

Where to write for more information:
   Fish and Game Department Box 25,
   Boise, ID 83707

Licenses issued in a recent year: 430,000.

Most popular species:
   Rainbow, cutthroat, brown, brook, Dolly Varden and lake trout
   kokanee, chinook and coho salmon; largemouth and smallmouth bass.

The few times that I have been to Idaho I have found it to be a place of exceptional scenery. There are over 16,000 miles of fishing streams, over 200,000 acres of lakes and even more acres of reservoirs waiting to be enjoyed-by the visiting angler. Since much of those waters are available only by horseback or hiking, fishing pressure is exceptionally light. But those who find their way to these pristine waters are rewarded by memorable catches of trout, salmon and bass.

Only electric motors are allowed on rafts or boats, and float tube fishing is especially-popular on many of the mountain streams. The Snake River, bordering Washington and Oregon, is famous for its salmon catches, but has also produced catfish over 30 pounds, and even a 394-pound sturgeon!

Salmon migrate from Idaho to the Pacific via the Snake River as well as the Clearwater and Salmon Rivers. A 45-pound chinook still stands as the state record after being caught almost thirty years ago. The Clearwater river produced a 30-pound, 2-ounce steelhead in 1973 which still holds the state record.

To preserve its fisheries for future generations Idaho enforces "catch-and-release" practices in many of its lakes and streams. The Coeur D'Alene Lake and its drainage area is especially popular for its abundant kokanee trout, while Pend Oreille Lake, further north, offers a full variety of brown, Dolly Varden, rainbow and lake trout.

Resources management is heavily emphasized within the state to preserve the wild trout fishing for which it is so famous among fly anglers everywhere. There are even more than one hundred streams stocked with hatchery trout for "put-and-take" fishing in many highly accessible areas.

**State
sovereignty,
national
union**

Cost of individual resident license: $7.50.
Non-resident license: Annual: $15.50. Short-term: $8.50 (10-days).

Where to write for more information:
Department of Conservation, Division of Fisheries;
524 South 2nd Street, Springfield, IL 62701-6424

Licenses issued in a recent year: 800,000.

Most popular species:
Largemouth and smallmouth bass, walleye, northern pike, muskie,
channel and flathead catfish, hybrid striped bass...plus coho and
chinook salmon, rainbow and brown trout.

For a state most widely known for the city of Chicago, the Cubs, White Sox and the Bears, Illinois is an amazing sportsfishing area. Its many natural lakes and rivers offer as varied an assortment of species as any other state, and all in easily accessible waters.

Surprisingly, the Division of Fisheries reports that catfish rate at the very top with. Illinois anglers. And they come big! Alton Lake alone has produced two 65-pound blue catfish, and Lake Warren is in the record books with a 60-pound flathead.

Fishing for muskies has also become popular with residents, and Otter Lake and Somerset Lake have both yielded near-30-pounders. The Kankakee River in the northeast corner of the state produces excellent walleye catches, the largest being a 14-pounder caught in 1961. Northern pike also are found in king-size in the Fox chain of lakes. Bass are found almost everywhere, and a daily bag of 6 fish is in effect throughout the state.

Most of the recent news about Illinois fishing has come from those who have now taken to Lake Michigan for salmon and trout. Charter boats are available at many of the ports from Waukegan to Gary, and there are 13 public piers available for those who prefer that more economical approach. The action on the lake has been especially rewarding over the past few years, and rainbow trout have been caught up to 24 pounds, brown trout to 28 pounds, and even lake trout over 28 pounds. Chinook and coho salmon are also getting a lot of attention with some chinooks going over 30 pounds and coho almost 20 pounds. The top chinook on record in the state is a 37-pounder caught by a lady angler, Marge Landeen, who landed it in 1976. Well, somebody had to do it!

Put Illinois on your list for a superb fishing adventure in the future!

Crossroads
of America

Cost of individual resident license: $8.75.
Non-resident license: Annual: $15.75. Short-term: $8.75 (7-days).

Where to write for more information:
Indiana Department of Natural Resources,
608 State Office Building, Indianapolis, IN 46204.

Licenses issued in a recent year: 650,000.

Most popular species:
Largemouth bass, striped bass, catfish (blue, channel and flathead),
muskie, panfish...plus chinook and coho salmon and brown trout,
steelhead and lake trout.

Wherever you go in Indiana, you are going to be near a place where you can throw out a line and catch a fish worth talking about to the folks back home. There are state parks, natural lakes, reservoirs and rivers to fish in all the way from Gary down to Evansville in the southwestern corner of the state. Lake Wawasee, just northwest of Fort Wayne, is excellent for bass and panfish. Lake James, located to the northeast, is also a favorite for bass, northern pike, walleye and panfish.

The large Monroe Reservoir in southcentral Indiana is best known for lunker bass but also offers many other varieties of catches. It is also interesting to note that three lady anglers hold current state records: Jennifer Schultz for a 14-pound, 12-ounce largemouth, Melissa Grimes for a near-10-pound white catfish, and Joan Draving for a 4-pound, 9-ounce crappie...all great catches!

Indiana anglers are also enjoying the introduction of large trout and salmon in Lake Michigan, and have access to many charter boats out of the Gary-Michigan City area, as well as from four major fishing piers. A 38-pound chinook holds the state record, and a 20-pound, 12-ounce coho is the largest recorded of that species. Steelhead provide most of the trout excitement, along with browns, and rainbows, with catches over 20 pounds not uncommon.

The St. Joseph River, which flows through a northern corner of the state, is expected to provide additional trout and salmon action as fish ladders are installed to help these migrators over the four dams which blocked their passage until recently.

IOWA

 Our liberties
we prize
and our
rights we
will maintain.

Cost of individual resident license: $10.50.
Non-resident license: Annual: $22.00. Short-term: $8.50 (7-days).

Where to write for more information:
Iowa Department of Natural Resources, Fish & Wildlife Division,
Wallace Building, Des Moines, IA 50319-0034

Licenses issued in a recent year: 425,000.

Most popular species:
Largemouth and smallmouth bass; blue, channel and flathead catfish;
northern pike, walleye, muskie, brook, brown and rainbow trout.

It's time to forget all of those old images that you might have had about Iowa. Sure, it is still widely-known for its tall corn, lean beef and fat hogs. But, more than all of that, it is a superb state for great fishing In addition to its more than 200 lakes, Iowa offers easily-accessible angling on 25 rivers. Altogether, this tremendous fishery provides a wider variety of species than a number of the more famous fishing states.

If you have to see it to believe it, then write for the Iowa packet of fishing guide books at the address above. In addition to the beautifully-illustrated "Fish Iowa" folder, you will receive booklets on the best places to fish in each area of the state, special trout fishing information, and even an up-to-date list of Iowa's all-time record fish.

This last piece should be especially refreshing to every woman angler. Right there on the cover is a picture of a happy lady angler, and on page 18 there are some facts that will shock the pants off a lot of men. The state record for largemouth bass is held by Patricia Zaerr with her 10-pound, 12-ounce catch made in 1984. The largest walleye on record fell to the skill of Gloria Eoriatti in 1986. And Mrs. W. Buser's 6-pound, 8-ounce sauger is the tops for that species. Three women! When you get out there on those Iowa waters, we will have even more to brag about.

There's surprising trout fishing in 48 spring-fed streams and two small ponds, with rainbows leading the varieties caught. But the real jewel of Iowa for serious anglers is its "Great Lakes" area in the northwest corner of the state. There you will find Big Spirit, East Okoboji and West Okoboji Lakes, three of the most beautiful blue water lakes in the world, all with BIG fish waiting just for you!

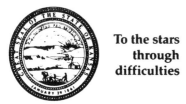

**To the stars
through
difficulties**

Cost of individual resident license: $10.00.
Non-resident license: Annual: $25.00. Short-term:$10.50 (5-days).

Where to write for more information:
  Kansas Forestry, Fish and Game Commission, P. O. 54A, R.R.2, Pratt,
  KS 67124.

Licenses issued in a recent year: 300,000.

Most popular species:
  Bass:-largemouth, smallmouth, striped and white; walleye, channel
  catfish, flathead catfish and crappie.

In addition to the fact that President Eisenhower was born there, you probably don't really know much about Kansas. At least I didn't until I got into fishing.

But Kansas today is like many other middle-America states: responding to the growing national interest in fishing by creating massive reservoirs and maintaining them with large stocks of popular species, and designating many state lakes for fishing only. Its official fishing guide lists 150 lakes of which 44 are major angling attractions. There are also 10,000 miles of fishable streams, including 25 rivers which provide some of the best action throughout the season.

The real monster of the state is the channel catfish, with a current state record of 87-pounds, 5-ounces caught in the Pomona Reservoir in 1990. Today those fish can be found throughout the eastern two-thirds of the state. The striped bass was introduced to Kansas anglers 25 years ago and now generate some of the largest catches of all species. A huge 43-pound, 8-ounce striper was taken from the Wilson Reservoir in 1988 but many other lunkers are caught every year.

Walleye fishing has also prospered in its lakes and reservoirs and a 13-pound, 1-ounce catch is the current state record. Northern pike also thrive in Kansas' reservoirs and a 24-pound, 12-ounce monster is recorded being caught by a husband-and-wife pair in the Council Grove Reservoir in 1971. I wonder which of them really deserves the credit! (I'm betting on the lady).

The most common of all Kansas fish is the white crappie, which Iooks a lot like its black brother but grows a bit bigger and delights the state's panfish anglers.

United we
stand,
divided
we fall.

Cost of individual resident license: $8.50.
Non-resident license: Annual: $20.00. Short-term:$7.50 (3-days).

Where to write for more information:
   Department of Fish & Wildlife Resources, State Office Building Annex, Frankfort, KY 40601

Licenses issued in a recent year: 635,000.

Most popular species:
   Largemouth and smallmouth bass, walleye and sauger, muskie, rainbow, brown and brook trout.

Over the years I have considered myself to be a fair apple pie baker. But I take my hat off-to the women of Kentucky's Casey County who cook up a 3,000-pound apple pie every year to feed the visitors at their annual Apple Festival.

But you can also take your hat off to the state's fisheries administration for stocking and maintaining its water resources to provide a broad range of fishing adventures. Largemouth and smallmouth bass can be found almost throughout the state. Walleyes abound in its clear deep lakes, saugers patrol its rivers, muskies are now being caught in a large number of lakes and creeks, and trout can be successfully fished in almost fifty streams and over two dozen lakes and tailwaters.

Cumberland Lake, located in the southcentral part of the state, offers an amazing smorgasbord of almost everything you could ever want to catch, including walleye, brown trout, largemouth bass as well as sauger, giant rockfish, and even sturgeon. The mighty Tennessee River is famous for its giant catfish, and there is a record of a 100-pound blue caught there in 1970! Imagine, a 100-pound catfish!

Trout enthusiasts can choose from 50 streams-and almost as many tailwaters and lakes to pursue browns brooks and rainbows. You will need a trout stamp, however ($3.50), and "catch-and-release" is encouraged in all waters.

If your tastes have now moved towards more sporting catches you can join the thousands of Kentuckians who fish for muskies in over twenty rivers, streams and lakes, including Dale Hollow, the large reservoir on the Tennessee border. Cave Run Lake is another famous muskie haunt and gets heavy action throughout the year. ✓

LOUISIANA

Union, justice and confidence

Cost of individual resident license: $5.50.
Non-resident license: Annual: 15.50. Short-term: $10.50 (7-days).

Where to write for more information:
Louisiana Department of Wildlife and Fisheries
P. O. Box 98000, Baton Rouge, LA 70898

Licenses issued in a recent year: 550,000.

Most popular species-:
Largemouth bass, striped bass, catfish plus snapper, pompano, cobia and mackerel in its bayous and swamps...and those marlin, dolphin and other saltwater species caught in Gulf of Mexico waters.

You will probably be as surprised as I was to learn that Louisiana has almost four million acres of fresh water lakes, lagoons, rivers and marshes which are rich in the nutrients to support many popular gamefish including the largemouth bass, striped bass, catfish and crappie. These exceptional waters are scattered generously throughout the state and are within easy reach for local anglers.

The 185,000-acre Toledo Bend Reservoir, located on the Texas border, is the state's best-known recreational area (and that includes New Orleans' Bourbon Street), with 46 marinas, landings and lodges from which to fish. Lake Concordia and the False River are true trophy lakes for largemouth bass but there are many more which will give you a day of exciting angling with a daily limit of eight fish.

Striped bass have also been introduced into Louisiana waters including Toledo Bend, the Pearl, Sabine, Calcasieu, Mermentau and Tchefuncte rivers, plus many of the larger lakes. The current weight record for the striper is over 38 pounds, but average catches run in the ten-pound range.

The state also has some 600 miles of coastline along the Gulf of Mexico with a large fleet of charter boats to take you out after the abundant dolphin schools, cruising marlin, sailfish and other challenging saltwater species. The famous Gulf Stream passes close to the Louisiana shore and the action starts early after leaving the docks at Cameron on the west to Grand Isle on the east.

Smaller boats are adequate for many of the coastal bays which provide excellent flounder fishing.

I direct.

Cost of individual resident license: $15.00.
Non-resident license: Annual: $42.00. Short-term: $17.00 (3-days).

Where to write for more information:
  Maine Department Of Inland Fisheries & Wildlife, 284 State Street,
  Station 41, Augusta, ME 04333

Licenses issued in a recent year: 250,000.

Most popular species:
  Largemouth and smallmouth bass, muskie, Atlantic salmon, brook
  trout, brown trout, lake trout, landlocked salmon and the "SBS" trio:
  stripers, blues and sharks, all caught along the 3,500 miles of coastline.

Moosehead Lake is Maine's largest and most popular fishing retreat, famous for its landlocked salmon. Along its shores are many camps with knowledgeable guides to take you where the big fish are and provide a memorable vacation. Sebago Lake, just west of Portland, is another well-known spot for landlocked salmon but also is home to largemouth, smallmouth bass and large brown trout.

In the "downeast" area, East Grand Lake, West Grand Lake and Grand Lake Stream are excellent waters for the landlocked salmon plus trout and smallmouth. Fly fishing enthusiasts flock to the Aroostook River during fly hatches for challenging brook trout and brown trout catches, the latter going as high as six pounds.

The Maine Professional Guides Association has members throughout the state who can take you to lakes, rivers and streams where fiesty fish will make your trip absolutely unforgettable. You will receive a full roster of their membership when you write to the address above.

Offshore, on board a charter boat, you can experience explosive fishing for stripers in the 20- to 50-pound class, plus bluefish, blue sharks, giant bluefin tuna and even-cod. Portland's Commercial Street and Boothbay Harbor's Brown Brothers Wharf are among the many ports where these boats are moored. There are also party boats available at Bar Harbor, Kennebunkport, Rockland, Sedgewick, York Harbor and many other coastal towns.

And, before leaving the state, you will just have to drop in at L. L. Bean's great emporium in Freeport and see what's new in fishing clothes!

**Manly deeds,
womanly
words**

Cost of individual resident license: $8.00.
Non-resident license: Annual: $15.00. Short-term: $7.00 (7-days).

Where to write for more information:
Department of Natural Resources, Tawes State Office Building,
Annapolis, MD 21401

Licenses issued in a recent year: 400,000.

Most popular species:
Brook, brown and rainbow trout; largemouth and smallmouth bass;
catfish, muskie, northern pike and walleye. Saltwater species caught in
Chesapeake Bay and offshore include bluefish, flounder, channel bass
and kingfish.

A look at the map will quickly tell you that Chesapeake Bay is the most prominent
geographic feature of Maryland. It is also one of the greatest fisheries in America!
Containing a great variety of both freshwater and saltwater fish in its ninety-mile
length. And its famous oyster bars provide delicacies for restaurants across the
entire country.

Liberty Reservoir, in the northcentral part of the state, attracts many bass anglers
and produced a whopping 8-pound, 4-ounce smallmouth in 1974. Gunpowder
River, Hunting Creek, Bear Creek, Beaver Creek and the Savage River are among
the finer trout waters of the state.

The Patuxent River holds many northern pike, with a 20-pound, 13-ounce catch
being the current state record. Walleye are also found in Deep Creek Lake, along
with largemouth bass. In 1989 a 23-pound tiger muskie was taken from this same
lake and is the record catch to-date for that species, three pounds heavier than a
record muskellunge taken from Conowingo Dam waters in 1978.

Along its Atlantic Ocean front, Maryland anglers take charter boats out into the
deeper sea for bluefish, flounder, seatrout, channel bass and kingfish. White marlin
are also frequent catches, along with school tuna and dolphin. Surf casters stake their
poles in the sands of Assateague Island as they wait for passing schools of channel
bass, as early as May and until late Fall.

Many designated trout streams provide action for brook, brown and rainbow
trout.

MASSACHUSETTS

By the sword
we seek
peace, but
peace only
under liberty.

Cost of individual resident license: $17.50.
Non-resident license: Annual: $22.00. Short-term: $16.50 (7-days).

Where to write for more information:
Massachusetts Division of Fisheries & Wildlife, 100 Cambridge Street,
Boston, MA 02202

Licenses issued in a recent year: 250,000.

Most popular species:
Brown, brook and rainbow trout; largemouth and smallmouth bass;
channel catfish, lake trout, landlocked salmon northern pike, tiger
muskie and walleye. The winter flounder is the favorite with offshore
anglers.

Boston has always been one of my favorite cities with its rich New England flavor
and so many historical attractions. I never really realized the vast fishing resources
of the rest of the state until I began to study some of the record books. It was then
I discovered that four women anglers now hold top spot for catches of channel
catfish, chain pickerel, sunfish and brown trout.

That really got my attention. Particularly Dana DeBlois whose 19-pound, 10-
ounce record brown trout was caught in 1966; Mrs. James Martin's 9-pound, 5-
ounce chain pickerel taken in 1954, Heather Bulger's 2-pound, 1-ounce bluegill of
1982...and that 26-pound, 8-ounce channel catfish landed by Dana Dodge in 1989!
Massachusetts is good to its lady anglers!

Quabbin Reservoir, located in the central part of the state, is a hot spot for bass,
pickerel, lake trout, and brown and rainbow trout. The record state lake trout, over
22 pounds, was also taken from there, as was the 13-pound record rainbow. There
are also many major rivers and ponds which produce a variety of trout, but most in
smaller sizes.

Small lakes and ponds on Cape Cod are also popular with trout anglers, but bass
and pickerel are also caught on the Cape.

Most of the saltwater fishing off the Atlantic shore is done from small boats, with
flounder, striped bass and bluefish getting most of the attention.

Wherever you go in Massachusetts you can count on good fishing waters
beingclose at hand, so don't spend all of your time in Boston.

MICHIGAN

If you seek
a pleasant
peninsula,
look about
you.

Cost of individual resident license: $9.85.
Non-resident license: Annual: $20.35. Short-term: $5.35 per day.

Where to write for more information:
Michigan Department of Natural Resources, Box 30028,
Lansing, MI 48909

Licenses issued in a recent year: 1,500,000.

Most popular species:
 Largemouth and smallmouth bass; channel and flathead catfish;
 muskie, northern pike, Atlantic, coho, chinook and kokanee salmon;
 brook, brown, rainbow and lake trout; and walleye.

If you are looking for bargains in America's supermarket of fishing areas, you can stop right here in Michigan. This "thumb-shaped" state, sticking up in the middle of our Great Lakes, is an enormous recreational angling area. Fly fishermen know it best for its famous Au Sable River, located in the northeast section of the state's Lower Peninsula, Brook trout have been the most popular quarry there for many years; followed by brown trout and rainbows. But Michigan also has over 150 more streams, creeks and rivers to attract fly enthusiasts.

There is also a liberal supply of inland lakes offering good bass and northern action, but the real action spot for walleyes today is Saginaw Bay where fish as large as ten pounds are becoming commonplace. Once almost completely ruined by over-fishing and pollution, Saginaw Bay's resurgence as a major walleye fishery is considered just short of miraculous.

Lake St. Clair, adjacent to Detroit, is a continuing source of exciting muskie catches, as it has been for over half a century. But it is the 3100-mile shoreline (second only to Florida) that is the focus of much of today's fishing activity in Michigan. With charter boats available all along the lakefront, and something like 150 piers to fish from in Lake Michigan, Superior and Huron, anglers have easy access to the exciting salmon and lake trout now in abundance. Elaine Bender, you will be pleased to know, holds the state record for Atlantic salmon with a 32-pound, 10-ounce catch made in 1981. The top chinook for the state is a 46-pound, 1-ounce monster caught in 1978, and the record coho is listed at 30 pounds, 9 ounces. For lake trout, the record is an even 53 pounds!

MINNESOTA

The star of
the North

Cost of individual resident license: $13.00.
Non-resident license: Annual: $27.00. Short-term: $19.00 (7-days).

Where to write for more information:
Department of Natural Resources, Division of Game and Fish,
500 Lafayette Road, St. Paul, MN 55155

Licenses issued in a recent year: 1,500,000.

Most popular species:
Walleye, northern pike, largemouth and smallmouth bass, muskie, coho
salmon, lake trout, brown, rainbow and brook trout.

Since Minnesota is my home state I will try not to be overgenerous with praise.
But the fact that there are one and a half million licenses sold every year should
convince you that most of our residents consider the $13.00 cost a genuine bargain
in freshwater fishing. There are, after all, 5,483 fishable lakes, 15,000 miles of
angling streams and almost 2,000 miles of trout streams within the state.

Minnesotans spend more time talking about (and eating) walleyes than any other
species. Larger-clear water lakes in the northern half of the state produce most
catches, but they are also plentiful in our many rivers, including the Mississippi.
Northern pike can be had in all areas throughout the year, including those taken by
ice fishing. The state's largest northern was a 45-pounder caught over sixty years
ago, but those being caught today rarely go over twenty pounds.

The muskie is also a heavily-pursued Minnesota species, particularly in the larger
northern lakes, but now the good folks at our D.N.R. has planted them in many urban
area lakes and even the city folks are excited about them today. A 54-pounder taken
in 1957 in Lake Winnibigoshish ("Lake Winnie") is still the state record.

Trout anglers get their kicks in the streams concentrated in the eastern half of the
state, some flowing into Lake Superior on the north. That's where the record 16-
pound, 12-ounce brown was caught in 1989. Largemouth and smallmouth bass are
also immensely popular, although they don't compare in size with those biggies
found in California and Florida. But we have them in large numbers and they
provide excellent sport for anglers of all ages.

Lake Superior catches of chinook and coho salmon are making big news today
in Minnesota as in the other Great Lakes states.

MISSISSIPPI

By valor
and arms

Cost of individual resident license: $4.00.
Non-resident license: Annual: $20.00. Short-term: $6.00 (3-days).

Where to write for more information:
Mississippi Dept. of Wildlife, Fisheries & Parks,
Game & Fish Commission,
P. O. Box 451, Jackson, MS 39205

Licenses issued in a recent year: 450,000.

Most popular species:
Largemouth and smallmouth bass, catfish, crappie, walleye, tarpon and
flounder.

Many southern states are best known for their fishing action in or near their big
reservoirs and Mississippi is no exception. The Grenada Reservoir in the northern
half of the state is a major attraction for those who prefer largemouth bass and
sunfish (bream). Up in the northeastern corner the Pickwick Reservoir offers a wide
variety of species, including sauger. But Pickwick is also famous for its large catfish,
headed by the 65-pound, 8-ounce record flathead taken there in 1987. The state's
record blue catfish weighed over 53 pounds and the top channel cat was just short
of 44 pounds.

The Mississippi River, running the full length of the state's western border, also
provides action on many types of game fish, as do its darkwater streams in the
southern half of Mississippi.

The Tennessee River, which feeds the Pickwick Reservoir, is on record with a
walleye catch of 9-pounds, 10-ounces taken in 1985, which is good-sized walleye
anywhere! Pickwick also produced the state record 7-pound, 15-ounce smallmouth
in 1987. There are 6 fish-producing reservoirs in the state as well as twenty-one
lakes which have been stocked with bass and bream.

On the south, many streams which feed into the Gulf of Mexico offer both
freshwater and saltwater species. Boats and guides available along the 90-mile Gulf
coast can take you to exciting tarpon action as well as out where the flounder,
bluefish and seatrout are caught. There is also surf fishing available from some of
the offshore islands in this area, including the Ship, Horn and Cat Islands.

The welfare
of the
people shall
be the
supreme law.

Cost of individual resident license: $8.00.
Non-resident license: Annual: $25.00. Short-term: $8.00 (3-days).

Where to write for more information:
Missouri Department of Conservation, P. O. Box 180,
Jefferson City, MO 65102-0180

Licenses issued in a-recent year: 1,000,000.

Most popular species:
Largemouth bass, brown and rainbow trout, walleye, muskie and
spoonbill paddlefish.

There may be a more enterprising state in America today than Missouri but I can't think of any. In just the past few years Missouri has transformed its Ozark Mountains area into a sprawling resort and retirement community, built an immense entertainment complex in the little town of Branson, and generated some of the most exciting fishing anywhere in its vast network of lakes streams and rivers. If they were out to "show me"; they have done it in spades!

The guidebooks which you can receive from the address above will give you precise information on where to catch the fish of your dreams, and even when. On top of that, they even have two full-color pictures of women anglers in their regulations booklet. There are almost one hundred public lakes and over eighty streams to pick from, and over 200 species of fish lurking in those waters.

Here are just a few "hot spots" to begin with: Table Rock Lake in the Bull Shoals area on the south is great for bass; Lake Taneycomo provides great rainbows and brown trout action all year round; Lake Stockton is outstanding for walleye fishing Truman Lake has bass that even Republicans can catch; Pomme de Terre Lake has been stocked with muskies since 1966 and holds some real whoppers; and for those who like something really different there are giant paddlefish waiting for you on the Osage River.

And when you visit Missouri you will want to make a special point of visiting Bass Pro Shop's Outdoor World described by many as the "world's greatest out-door store": This is a true fantasy-land, located in Springfield, in the southwestern quarter of the state. Its massive five-tank aquarium is worth the trip alone, and will give you a close-up look of many of America's most popular game fish.

Gold
and
silver

Cost of individual resident license: $9.50.
Non-resident license: Annual: $36.00. Short-term: $8.00 (2-days).

Where to write for more information:
Montana Department of Fish, Wildlife & Parks,
1420 East Sixth, Helena, MT 59620

Licenses issued in a recent year: 375,000.

Most popular species:
Brown, brook, rainbow, golden, bull and lake trout; kokanee, grayling,
northern pike, channel catfish, walleye and largemouth bass.

If yours is one of those families which likes to visit our national parks your travels may one day take you to Montana. There, up on the Canadian border, sits Glacier National Park, with 200 lakes and many trout streams. That would be a good point to begin your fishing adventures in this state, one of the most important trout angling areas in all of the United States.

Every dyed-in-the-wool fly fisherman has a nagging desire to get out onto one of its coldwater streams to try for its great variety of this species. And with good reason. Montana is literally laced with productive waters throughout the state. Here are some interesting numbers representing current state records: lake trout: 29 pounds, bull trout: 25 pounds, l0 ounces, cutthroat: 16 pounds golden: 4 pounds; rainbow: 21 1/2 pounds, rainbow/cutthroat hybrid: 30 pounds, 4 ounces, and lake trout: 42 pounds.

Places like Red Eagle Lake, Flathead Lake, Ashley Lake and Two Medicine Lake are home to many of these records and attract many visiting anglers. Flathead Lake is the largest of these, located near Kalispell, is also the largest natural freshwater lake west of the Mississippi. Trolling for large lake trout is one of the real thrills of fishing this lake, but small cutthroat trout, large northern pike and largemouth bass are also in abundance.

In the eastern part of Montana there are warmer waters which offer angling for channel catfish, walleye, and bass. The Fort Peck Reservoir, located in the northeastern section, has produced the state record catfish, coho and king salmon. The Yellowstone River cuts through the southeast section of the state and has good walleye fishing as well as trout at its southern end. There is no area in Montana which doesn't provide rewarding fishing and glorious scenery. And, oh yes, the state largemouth record is held by a woman angler.

**Equality
before
the law**

Cost of individual resident license: $11.50.
Non-resident license: Annual: $25.00. Short-term: $7.50 (3-days).

Where to write for more information:
  Nebraska Game and Parks Commission, P.O. Box 30370, Lincoln, NE 68503

Licenses issued in a recent year: 250,000.

Most popular species:
  Largemouth, smallmouth and striped bass, bluegill, walleye, northern pike, muskie.

Most notable among Nebraska's wide variety of fishing resources are its 45 reservoirs sprinkled throughout the state. Merritt Reservoir, located just south of Valentine is considered one of the finest all around fishing lakes of the midwest. A crackerjack of a walleye lake, it is also a hot spot for channel catfish, yellow perch, muskie and smallmouth bass.

The McConaughy Reservoir ("Big Mac") runs 22 miles in length, stretches to a width of 4 miles and is over 140 feet deep near the dam. You'll find it some 50 miles west of North Platte...probably covered with Nebraska anglers in search of its famous striped bass, tiger muskies and even coho and kokanee salmon. Five state record fish have come out of "Big Mac" including a 44-pound, 10-ounce striped bass and a 24-pound, 4-ounce tiger muskie.

But there is also the Missouri River running along its eastern edge, plus almost 50 lakes which offer good catches of walleye, perch, northern pike and flathead catfish. The Missouri also is known for its outstanding fishing for sauger, and you will be pleased to learn that the state record for that fish was caught by one of us: Mrs. Betty Tepner, who landed her 8-pound, 5-ounce prize in 1961.

Grove Lake, west of Norfolk, is not a large lake but produces lunker northern pike, largemouth bass and bluegills. The current record northern, a 29-pound, 12-ounce monster, came out of Grove Lake in 1984. Grove also holds the record for the largest bluegill to-date.

When you-write for information you will receive an 80-page "Lake Guide" and "Nebraskaland's Guide To Good Fishing", both of which will help make your Nebraska visit well worth the trip.

And, oh yes. Don't forget Cabela's great fishing and hunting emporium at Sidney, out on the panhandle in the west. As my friend Phyllis says, "Going to Nebraska without visiting Cabela's would be like going to a Polish wedding and not staying for the dancing!"

All for our
country

Cost of individual resident license: $15.50.
Non-resident license: Annual: $35.00. Short-term: not available.

Where to write for more information:
Nevada Department of Wildlife, Department of Fish and Game,
Box 10678, Reno, NV 89520

Licenses issued in a recent year: 150,000.

Most popular species:
Largemouth bass, channel catfish, muskie, chinook and coho salmon,
Brown, brook, rainbow and cutthroat trout.

You probably have a lot of friends who think that the only places in Nevada where they can be winners are Reno and Las Vegas. They couldn't be further wrong...if they have any interest in fishing.

This state has quality fishing waters equal to many of its neighbors and has at least twenty-two species to test your skill and brighten your day. Its seventeen counties contain streams, lakes, reservoirs, rivers and ponds, plus Lake Mead, Lake Mohave and the Colorado River to capture your interest and enthusiasm. There is a "Nevada Stream Classification System" guide awaiting you when you write for more information. This huge fold-out pin-points every one of those resources and identifies the species most frequently caught in them.

Lake Tahoe, just west of Carson City, produced a gigantic 37-pound, 6-ounce mackinaw trout in 1974, and Cave Lake in White Pine county was the site of the record brown trout catch in 1984, a 27-pound, 5-ouncer!

Walleyes were introduced into Rye Patch and Chimney reservoirs in the early 1970's and have become very popular with Nevada anglers. The state record of 13-pounds, 14-ounces came out of Rye Patch. Lahontan Reservoir has now been added to this list and is already producing catches of over 10 pounds.

Lake Mead, an easy ride from Las Vegas, is the center of salmon and largemouth bass action, and Lake Mohave, nearby, is known for its excellent rainbow angling. A state record rainbow catch of 16 pounds, 4 ounces was taken there in 1971, plus a 11 pound largemouth landed in 1972.

Just north of Reno lies the great Pyramid Lake (in the center of the Pyramid Lake Indian Reservation), offering trophy cutthroat trout fishing, and lays claim to the record 23 1/2-pounder caught there in 1977.

NEW HAMPSHIRE

**Live free
or die.**

Cost of individual resident license: $23.25.
Non-resident license: Annual: $35.00. Short-term: $18.50 (3-days).

Where to write for more information:
 New Hampshire Fish and Game Department,
 2 Hazen Drive, Concord, NH 03301

Licenses issued in a recent year: 160,000.

Most popular species:
 Largemouth and smallmouth bass, northern pike, lake trout, chinook
 salmon, walleye, brown and rainbow trout.

This is a state of picturesque natural beauty, well-known for its White-Mountain range and national forest. Mount Washington, over 6,000 feet high, attracts large groups of tourists every year. Lake Winnipesaukee, to the south, is a vast cold water fishery surrounded by many outstanding New England resorts. Its deep holes produce many large lake trout, and smallmouth bass can be caught around many of its islands and bays.

Throughout the state there are hundreds of trout streams, ponds and brooks which offer rewarding fishing for brown, brook and rainbow trout. Running down through the middle of New Hampshire is the Connecticut River which attracts many fly fishermen in search of larger brown and rainbow trout. The state's top rainbow, a 14-pound, 3-ounce fish, was caught there in 1978. The river also produced the top walleye on record in the state, a 12 1/2-pounder caught in 1981.

Over 150 warmwater ponds, streams, lakes and reservoirs also feature quantity catches of largemouth and smallmouth bass, northern pike and walleye...and yellow perch are almost everywhere.

There are many high-quality resorts and hotels along its scenic highways and byways which can serve as your base of operations as you explore nearby waters for your favorite species, and go sight-seeing among its 182 high mountains. Be sure to take your camera!

At its southeast corner there are 18 miles of Atlantic Ocean coastline with sandy beaches and charter boat ports to take you out into deep waters for bluefish and stripers, plus other saltwater species common to this New England area.

In your spare time you can stroll through local shops and enjoy the rare luxury of tax-free shopping.

Liberty and
prosperity

Cost of individual resident license: $15.00 ($25.00 family).
Non-resident license: Annual: $23.00. Short-term: $15.00 (7-days).

Where to write for more information:
New Jersey Division of Fish, Game & Wildlife,
CN 400, Trenton, NJ 08625-0400

Licenses issued in a recent year: 250,000.

Most popular species:
Largemouth and smallmouth bass, muskie, northern pike, walleye,
channel catfish, brown, brook and rainbow trout.

New Jersey is another state which provides a comprehensive guide to help its anglers reap the maximum reward for their time on the water. A "Places To Fish" booklet is available with lists of hundreds of lakes, ponds, rivers, creeks and brooks with accompanying information on the exact species to be found in them.

One of the earliest states to implement progressive resource management practices, New Jersey stocks over 600,000 trout in its waters every year and has introduced many new species to provide a wide variety of fishing excitement for resident and non-resident anglers.

There are also more than thirty wild trout streams to provide a special challenge to those fly fishermen who prefer the extra fighting action of those fish. The Delaware River, running along the western border of the state has long been a popular smallmouth bass fishery but has also added muskie fishing excitement for its anglers in recent years. A 37 1/2-pound muskie, a true wall-hanger in many states, was taken from there in 1982.

Lake Hopatcong, located in the northern quarter of the state, is home to the state channel catfish record of 33 pounds, 3 ounces, but also produced a 13-pound rainbow trout catch in 1988, and a 6 1/2-pound brook trout record over thirty years ago.

New Jersey also has 130-miles of Atlantic Ocean coastline from which charter boats operate during the summer months, taking groups out for tuna, white marlin and other saltwater lunkers.

I probably don't have to remind you that Atlantic City is also located in New Jersey, but I will because you may sometime think of visiting it...without considering adding the sport of fishing to your trip. It is close at hand and requires nothing more than just a little advance planning.

NEW MEXICO

**It grows
as it goes.**

Cost of individual resident license: $8.50.
Non-resident license: Annual: $18.00. Short-term: $10.50 (5-days).

Where to write for more information:
New Mexico Department of Game and Fish,
Villagra Building, Santa Fe, NM 87503

Licenses issued in a recent year: 250,000.

Most popular species:
Largemouth and smallmouth bass, channel and flathead catfish,
northern pike, walleye, kokanee and coho salmon, brown, brook,
cutthroat and rainbow trout.

It's true. New Mexico is something of a desert state, but it also has many major
water impoundments which have created huge fishing areas which hold a wide
variety of popular freshwater game fish. Among these the Navajo Reservoir is the
largest trout water in the entire state. It was also on the Navajo that Mrs. J.B.
Holloman captured the current state record kokanee salmon, a 3-pound, 10-ounce
dandy, in 1980. Unfortunately she is the only lady angler to hold a state record for
a major species.

The Rio Grande River is probably New Mexico's best-known fishing resource.
Along its route are Elephant Butte Lake and Caballo Lake, both of which offer
walleye, bass and catfish. Elephant Butte also recorded a monster striped bass catch
of over 48 pounds in 1989 .

Most streams in the state receive a substantial runoff from melting snows in
nearby mountains, and the cooler, food-bearing water provokes early spring action.
Later in the year, as the streams clear and slow down, more anglers take to them for
larger catches. The top brown trout catch on record is a 20 1/2-pound fish taken back
in 1946, but a 16-pound rainbow record was set in 1986. Heron Lake on the far north
produced a surprising 21-pound, 9-ounce lake trout catch in 1989. The top
largemouth catch to-date is a 12 1/2-pounder taken out of Bill Evans Lake in the far
southwestern area of the state.

With over 1500 lakes, streams, creeks and reservoirs to choose from, you won't
have trouble finding a good spot to try your luck when you take that trip to visit New
Mexico's famous Carlsbad Caverns.

Ever upward

Cost of individual resident license: $14.00.
Non-resident license: Annual: $28.00. Short-term: $16.00. (5-days).

Where to write for more information:
   Division of fish & Wildlife, N.Y. State Department of Environmental
   Conservation, 50 Wolf Rd., Albany NY 12233-4790

Licenses issued in a recent year: 1,100,000.

Most popular species:
   Largemouth and smallmouth bass, muskie, walleye, northern pike, panfish,
   Atlantic salmon, channel catfish, brook, brown, rainbow and lake trout.

With its 4,000 lakes, 70,000 miles of rivers and streams, access to Great Lakes fishing in Lake Huron and Lake Erie, and the saltwater action off Long Island, New York is truly the Empire State of angling. Because of these exceptional resources, I recommend that you write for their packet of descriptive brochures on where to go and what to fish for. They are of top quality and very helpful. But here are a few hints of some of the opportunities available to you:

-Trout fishing. Every fly angler has muttered the name "Beaverkill" at one time or another in his musing about legendary waters. And that is just one of the many challenging streams for the fabled brown trout. But trout are also caught, in larger sizes, in Lake Ontario and Lake Placid, and the Catskill Reservoirs. Catherine Creek in the Finger Lakes region is a favorite for rainbows, and draws large groups of anglers during its top weeks of the season.

-Bass, northern pike, walleye and muskie are found in many lakes and streams, with the Niagara River, Lake Chatauqua, and the St. Lawrence River providing heavy catches throughout most of the year.

-Lake trout are common to many of the deep water lakes such as Lake George and Lake Placid. The record state lake trout, a 32-pounder, was taken from Lake Placid in 1986.

-Great Lakes action includes large steelhead, huge rainbow and brown trout plus Atlantic and chinook salmon. A 47-pound chinook was taken in Ontario in 1980, and a near 27-pound rainbow in 1985!

-Saltwater fishing attracts hordes of anglers to its Long Island. Its charter boat ports offer daily adventures after tuna, flounder, bluefish, kingfish and monstrous sharks. Montauk, on the far east end, is especially known for its big catches, which include a 3,450-pound great white shark taken during August of 1986...on 150-pound test line!

NORTH CAROLINA

**To be rather
than to seem**

Cost of individual resident license: $15.00.
Non-resident license: Annual: $30.00. Short-term: $15.00 (3-days).

Where to write for more information:
  North Carolina Wildlife Resources Commission,
  512 N. Salisbury Street, Raleigh,-NC 27604-1188

Licenses issued in a recent year: 475,000.

Most popular species:
  **Largemouth and smallmouth bass, striped bass, muskie, brook, brown
  and rainbow trout, walleye...plus blue marlin, bluefish, dolphin, wahoo,
  sailfish and tuna off shore in the Atlantic Ocean.**

Trout fishermen will find over 2,000 miles of cold, clear streams in North
Carolina, many of them hatchery-supported, with brook, browns and rainbows in
abundance. The Great Smoky Mountains provide most of the run-off to keep these
waters productive and exciting for fly anglers during much of the year,
  The Nantahala and Fontana Lakes in the southwestern corner of the state provide
water for many streams which are natural spawning areas for all species of trout,
with the larger streams producing the biggest catches. Lake James heads the
Catawba River system and its cool water offers exceptional bass and walleye
fishing, as well as for a variety of panfish. Downstream, Rhodhiss, Hickory and
Wylie Lakes add to the variety of fish available for the visiting angler.
  Large catfish, channel and flathead, are found in these waters, and the Yadkin
River, further east, has produced a flathead that went over 62 pounds. In 1988 a 69-
pound, 4-ounce blue catfish established a new record, and was caught in Badin
Lake. Muskie fishing is getting more attention in North Carolina as larger catches
have been recorded at James Lake and in the Little Tennessee River.
  A 300-mile coastline provides access to some of the finest saltwater action along
the east coast. Large blue and white marlin are often caught in the Gulf Stream off
Hatteras Island, but wahoo, dolphin, kingfish and bluefish also delight charter boat
clients. Surf anglers also flock to the island in search of those schools which move
in on the flood tide. In 1991 Mrs. Stephen R. Hutchins took first place in the I.G.F.A.
annual fishing contest for bluefish with a 14-pound, 10-ounce fish taken out of the
Orgeon Inlet on November 16th. Hooray for her.

Liberty and union, now and forever, one and inseparable

Cost of individual resident license: $9.00.
Non-resident license: Annual: $2.00. Short-term: $13:00. (seven-days).

Where to write for more information:
State Game and Fish Department, 100 North Bismarck
Expressway, Bismarck, ND 58501

Licenses issued in a recent year: 150,000.

Most popular species:
Northern pike, walleye, sauger, muskie, rainbow and brook trout,
chinook salmon and channel catfish.

Over the past ten years this prairie state has become an exciting fishing destination, chiefly through the efforts of its enlightened stocking program for many important species. Harnessing the great Missouri River at the Garrison Dam has produced an immense fishery in Lake Sakakawea which now holds state records for catches of a 31-pound, 2-ounce chinook salmon, an 11-pound, 12-ounce saugeye, an 8-pound, 12-ounce sauger and a 37-pound, 8-ounce northern pike!

Walleye fishing has also prospered in a number of other state waters such as Devil's lake, the Missouri River near Bismarck, Lake Tschida and the Garrison Tailrace. Big northern pike are another of North Dakota's fishing attractions today and while the state record catch was made in 1968, a 32-pound wall-hanger was taken out of the Missouri-River in just a few years ago. Other whoppers have come out of Lake Darling, the Oahe Reservoir and the Pipestem Reservoir.

Rainbow trout are now being caught along the Missouri River system, and the state record 20-pound, 4-ounce catch was made in the Garrison Tailrace in 1984. A monster 25-pound, 4-ounce brown trout was taken out of these same waters in 1987. Muskie anglers are also pleased with the increasing availability of these cantankerous fish in the state. The 40-pound tiger which set a new state record is an exceptional catch anywhere.

The Red River, running along its eastern border, is probably best known for its catfish catches and produced the state record fish of 31 pounds in 1990.

But it is the northern pike which continues to provoke most fishing conversation in North Dakota and is the state's "official" fish. For many years its hatcheries have worked at producing larger numbers of fingerlings for stocking. The fish can now be caught throughout the state, and in ever-larger sizes.

**With God,
all things
are possible.**

Cost of individual resident license: $12.00.
Non-resident license: Annual: $19.00. Short-term: $12.00. (3-days).

Where to write for more information:
  Ohio Department of Natural Resources, Division of Wildlife
  1500 Dublin Road, Columbus, OH 43224

Licenses issued in a recent year: 1,300,000.

Most popular species:
  Walleye, largemouth, smallmouth and striped bass, muskie, chinook and
  coho salmon, brown trout, crappie and bluegill.

Most people I know always seem to be driving through Ohio, going somewhere east or somewhere west...and not stopping to "smell the flowers". But the Buckeye State has corking good waters almost everywhere to give you an exciting angling adventure. Perhaps the most remarkable of these is Lake Erie, rapidly becoming known as the "walleye capital of the world". Lake Erie also is known for its fighting steelhead and its fiesty brown trout. Along its almost 200 miles of Ohio waterfront anglers head out into the lake from many charter boat centers, and also enjoy the convenience of over twenty piers to fish from.

Of its 68 major inland lakes the Pymatuning Reservoir on its northeastern edge, is best known for its challenging muskies, large walleyes, largemouth bass and even channel catfish. West Branch Reservoir, also in the east, is now producing trophy muskie catches. Grand Lake St. Mary's, located southwest of Lima, is a mighty 11,000-acre home to many large channel catfish, striped and largemouth bass, plus real eating-size crappies.

Ohio's Hebron Fish Hatchery has been the beneficiary of almost $3,000,000 from revenues generated by the Dingell-Johnson Act. Those dollars have helped increase the hatchery's annual output by over 50%, now producing more than four million fingerlings for stocking its lakes and streams with the state's most popular game fish.

But Lake Erie is still the number one fishery for most of Ohio's anglers who rejoice in the continual abundance of bass, crappie, bluegill, northern pike, walleye and the exciting coho salmon. Its boat dockages are easily accessible from Interstate Highways 80 and 90, only a short drive out of your way as you are driving through. So take the trip, and "smell the flowers" of Ohio.

OKLAHOMA

Labor
conquers
all things.

Cost of individual resident license $10.25.
Non-resident license: Annual: $23.50. Short-term: $7.50 (3-day).

Where to write for more information:
Department Of Wildlife Conservation
1801 North Lincoln, Oklahoma City, OR 73105-4998

Licenses issued in year: 575,000.

Most popular species:
Largemouth and smallmouth bass; blue, channel and flathead catfish;
crappie; northern pike; rainbow trout and walleye.

The state of Oklahoma is part of the vast western territory included in the famous Louisiana Purchase when President Thomas Jefferson hoodwinked Napoleon into one of the greatest land deals of all times. Not only did that deal bring us the future states that would foster some of the finest football teams in the century ahead, but it also brought with it thousands of lakes, rivers and ponds that have kept bass fishermen giddy for more than fifty years.

Eufala Lake, west of Fort Smith, is a true angler's paradise, yielding scrappy 5- to 15-pound blue catfish, husky largemouth bass, crappies and even striped bass in its tailwaters. Over 100,000 acres in size, it has also produced notable flathead and channel cat catches. Texoma Lake, located on the Texas border, is considered by many as one of the nation's finest fishing spots for smallmouth, crappies sunfish and cats. Walleyes and Florida bass are also stocked in the lake to broaden its interest among the angling community. The state record flathead catfish, a 70-pound, 14-ounce giant, was boated and later released in Lake Keystone, an Army Corps of Engineers project located near Tulsa, in 1991.

Rainbow trout can be had in a number of rivers scattered throughout the state, but the record 10-pound, 4-ounce catch was taken from the Lower Illinois River, east of Muskogee.

Your inquiry to the Department of Wildlife Conservation will bring you a rich assortment of literature to help you plan your trip to the state, with recommendations on the "best" fishing areas for your favorite species. Daily limits are generous and you'll be among some of the friendliest people you could ever meet. Just don't ask any of them to join you for a catfish hunt on a football Saturday!

233

The union

Cost of individual resident license: $14.75.
Non-resident license: Annual: $35.75. Short-term: $21.25 (10-day).

Where to write for more information:
Oregon Department of Wildlife Conservation, 2501 S.W. First Avenue, Portland, OR 97201

Licenses issued in a recent year: 750,000.

Most popular species:
Largemouth and smallmouth bass; coho and chinook salmon, steelhead and rainbow trout.

Oregon is probably best known for the majestic Columbia River which marks its northern boundary. This awesome waterway attracts anglers from many areas of the country, most of them seeking the exciting action provided by the migrating salmon and steelhead. Indeed, the state record steelhead, a 35 1/2-pounder, was landed in the Columbia in 1970. But the Columbia has also proven the versatility of its resource with a record 15-pound, 2-ounce walleye taken just below its John Day Dam in 1990 by an angler from North Dakota. This same river also produced the state's top smallmouth catch in 1989.

Western Oregon is peppered with lakes, reservoirs and rivers which offer rewarding fishing almost year around. The best known waters of this area are the Umpqua and Willamette Rivers, which are a special magnet for trout and salmon anglers. The state's record chinook catch is an 83-pounder...83 pounds!...caught way back in 1910 on the Umpqua. And everyone who has fished there since has dreamed of beating that record. A 65-pound challenger was taken from the Trask river in 1987, and a 52 1/2-pounder came out of the Chetco River in 1982.

Oregon also has almost 300 miles of coastline on the Pacific Ocean which offers a unique mixture of both fresh water and saltwater fishing. If you are traveling along the coast on one of your future vacations you should make a point of stopping at some of the many harbors where large fleets of charter boats are docked, ready to take you out after salmon or halibut...and maybe an afternoon of whale watching.

Oregon is a beautiful state to visit, with almost 30 million acres of forested land, snow-capped mountains...and fishing adventures to broaden your library of stories to tell back home.

PENNSYLVANIA

Virtue,
liberty and
independence

Cost of individual resident license: $12.00.
Non-resident license: Annual: $20.00. Short-term: $15.00 (7-day).

Where to write for more information:
  Pennsylvania Fish Commission,
  P. O. Box 1673, Harrisburg, PA 17105

Licenses issued in a recent year: 1,100,000.

Most popular species:
  Smallmouth and largemouth bass; northern pike and muskies, walleye,
  coho and chinook salmon; brook, brown, palomino and rainbow trout.

The Liberty Bell and Constitution Hall are two national treasures located in
Philadelphia, and thousands of visitors flock to visit them every year. We learn
about them in school and tuck away in our memories that we ought to see them
sometime during our lifetime, and certainly bring the kids along. But Pennsylvania
has even greater natural treasures tucked away in its rolling hills and pleasant
mountains: wide-ranging river basins, clear water lakes and streams that will put
fish on your line and smiles on your face. Throughout the entire state you will find
challenging waters with launching ramps and marinas from which to plan a day or
two in pursuit of your favorite quarry.

The huge Susquehana River divides the state almost in half, and feeds many
creeks and rivers along its route which are home to surprising quantity of our most
popular fresh water game fish. To the north, Lake Erie adds its great waters to the
total fishing resource for eager anglers.

The Juniata River, out of the Susquehanna, is an exceptional fishery for
smallmouth, but there are literally hundreds of other streams and lakes which have
both the largemouth and smallmouth in abundance. The Delaware river on the east
has become popular with muskie zealots who seek the excitement provided by the
testy tiger muskie, and Conneaut Lake and the Pymatuning Reservoir in the west
lay claim to some of the most stirring action for the larger, Ohio-strain muskies.

Trout waters are almost everywhere, and now buttressed by the generous
availability of rainbows and palominos in Lake Erie. Coho and chinook salmon are
also now caught regularly from charter boats working Lake Erie out of ports in the
Erie area. Continuing large catches have made salmon fishing a top attraction in
Pennsylvania today.

RHODE ISLAND

Hope

Cost of individual resident license: $9.50.
Non-resident license: Annual: $20.50. Short-term: $10.50 (3-days).

Where to write for more information:
  Department of Environmental Management, Division of Fish and Wildlife,
  Washington County Government Center, Wakefield, RI 02879

Licenses issued in a recent year: 40,000

Most popular species:
  Largemouth and smallmouth bass; northern pike; brook, brown and
  rainbow trout; plus several saltwater species, including bluefish,
  flounder, tuna, and even white marlin.

I don't have to tell you that Rhode Island is our smallest state, and that most school kids have trouble finding it on a map. But it's there, hunkered in between Connecticut and the chin of Massachusetts, jutting out into Cape Cod Bay and Nantucket Sound. While the state has just 40 miles of coastline, its Narragansett Bay rambles over almost 400 miles of saltwater shoreline from which you can travel into protected saltwater fishing grounds...and fish without the need of purchasing a license.

Party "Head" boats take groups of from 35 to 100 persons out for bottom fishing from marinas on the south shore, and smaller charter boats carrying smaller groups ply out of Newport, Point Judith, as well as from Bristol, up in the bay.

Much of the fresh water fishing done in Rhode Island is confined to public ponds, twenty of which are classified as "Class A", indicating species availability and suitability of environment. Among these, Hundred Acre Pond produced the state record northern pike in 1987, a 35-pound trophy. Carbuncle Pond is a popular largemouth spot and yielded a 10-pound, 6-ounce catch in 1991, the largest caught to-date in Rhode Island. Pawcatuck River, which runs across the lower half of the state, produced a record ll-pound rainbow in the same year.

The largest fish on the books for Rhode Island is a 70-pound striped bass taken off Block Island in 1984. Ten ponds are restricted exclusively to fly fishing, and fourteen are reserved for fishing only by youngsters fourteen years of age or younger. Maybe one day they will reserve a few just for us ladies!

SOUTH CAROLINA

While I
breathe,
I hope.

Cost of individual resident license: $10.00.
Non-resident license: Annual: $35.00. Short term: $11.00 (7-days).

Where to write for more information:
South Carolina Wildlife & Marine Resources Department,
P. O. Box 167, Columbia, SC-29202

Licenses issued in a recent year: 400,000.

Most popular species:
Largemouth and smallmouth bass; bluegill; blue, channel and flathead
catfish, crappie, brown and rainbow trout; and walleye. Add to those
more than fifty saltwater species caught off the Atlantic shore.

The biggest fishing news in South Carolina during 1991 was the capture of a 109-pound, 4-ounce blue catfish in the Cooper River by George Lijewski. A true leviathan, the fish broke the state's earlier record by 23 pounds, and is now the largest blue on record for being caught anywhere. Large cats are not unusual in South Carolina, which also has a 58-pound channel and a 74-pound flathead in its record books.

But the most popular fish in the state is still the largemouth bass, with most of the heavy action for that species taking place in Lakes Marion and Moultrie, located in the south point of the state. The top largemouth to-date is a 16-pound, 2-ouncer taken way back in 1949. Bluegills and crappies also are very popular, and are both found in abundance in the same waters.

Lake Jocassee is a favorite with trout anglers, and has produced a record brown catch of almost 18 pounds. The top rainbow, of 9-pounds, 6-ounces, came out of Richard B. Russell Lake in 1985. With 167 miles of Atlantic coastline, South Carolina also offers an immense variety of saltwater fishing, much of it taking place over 23 artificial reefs established by the Wildlife and Marine Resources Department. A total of 65 different saltwater species records are listed for state anglers, with a 1780-pound tiger shark topping the list. Other notable catches include a 588-pound hammerhead shark, a 500-pound swordfish, and a 738-pound blue marlin.

Seatrout, snapper, grouper and Spanish mackerel are popular food fish which attract large numbers of anglers to the many coastal marinas throughout the year. No wonder South Carolina is one of our leading tourist-attracting states today!

SOUTH DAKOTA

**Under God
the people
rule.**

Cost of individual resident license: $9.00.
Non-resident license: Annual: $30.00. Short-term: $14.00 (5-days).

Where to write for more information:
South Dakota Game, Fish and Parks Department,
523 East Capitol, Pierre, SD 57501

Licenses issued in a recent year: 200,000.

Most popular species:
Largemouth and smallmouth bass; channel catfish; northern pike;
walleye, chinook salmon; rainbow trout.

In less than fifty years, the state of South Dakota has been transformed from a moderate agricultural resource to one of the most abundant fishing grounds in America. It all began with the Missouri River. Four massive dams built along its length during the 1940's to the early 1960's created over 900 square miles of open water and 3,000 miles of shoreline.

The reservoirs created by those dams include Lake Oahe, Lake Sharpe, Lake Francis Case and Lewis and Clark Lake, each holding heavy populations of walleye and bass, with assorted stocks of northern pike, channel catfish and chinook salmon mixed in to sweeten the pot. Further west, miles of mountain streams and 14 man-made lakes offer exceptional fishing for brook, brown and rainbow trout. The state record brown, a 22-pound, 3-ounce prize, was taken from Pactola Reservoir in that area. The Rapid, Castle and Spearfish Creeks are other favorites for fly anglers, all heavily stocked with browns and rainbows, and offering good access areas. The Glacial Lakes region in the northeast corner of the state includes more than 100 clear, blue water lakes holding walleyes, northerns, largemouth and smallmouth bass as well as a variety of panfish.

Throughout these areas there are launching ramps for your boat, if you've trailered it along. If you prefer O.P.B.s, you'll also find plenty of marinas with rentals offering boats equipped with all the gear you like to fish with. For those with muskies on their mind, Amsden Lake (also in the northeast) has built a reputation for record-breakers, yielding a 40-pounder in 1991, a 31-pounder in 1987, and a 32-pound, 9-ounce fish in 1988...all establishing new highs for the state. For brown trout enthusiasts there is even urban fishing in Rapid Creek, which runs through Rapid City.

Agriculture
and
commerce

Cost of individual resident license: $15.50.
Non-resident license: Annual: $26.00. Short-term: $15.50 (10-day).

Where to write for more information:
Tennessee Game and Fish Commission, P. O. Box 40747,
Ellington Agricultural Center, Nashville, TN 37204

Licenses issued in a recent year: 800,000.

Most popular species:
Largemouth and smallmouth bass; spotted bass; muskie, northern pike,
walleye and sauger, blue and channel catfish, brook and lake trout,
crappie.

Tennessee anglers enjoy the rare luxury of having 59 different fresh water species
to pursue in the wide-ranging waters of the state. Perhaps the most noteworthy catch
to be recorded there is the 25-pound walleye taken out of the Old Hickory Reservoir
back in 1960. There is also a 42 1/2-pound muskie on the books, coming out of the
Norris Reservoir, up in the northeastern corner of the state in 1983. Norris gets
additional attention for its mammoth striped bass, although the state record 60 1/2-
pound monster came out of Melton Hill Lake in 1988. The great Dale Hollow Lake,
a 27,700-acre reservoir, is probably Tennessee's best-known fishing resource. Its
deep, clear waters produce first-rate catches of lake trout, muskies and smallmouth...
including the 11-pound, 15-ounce world record smallie taken there in 1955.

Kentucky Lake, in the west, is considered the most productive impoundment in
the Tennessee Valley Authority system, with almost unlimited action for largemouth bass and crappie. The Hiwassee River, just southwest of the Great Smoky
Mountains National Park, offers 26 miles of big trout water, all of it open all year
around. Trophy browns of 15 pounds, and rainbows pushing 10 pounds have been
frequently reported there.

Catfish enthusiasts will find memorable action throughout the state. Two plus 60-
pounders are among current Tennessee records, a 68-pound blue taken from the
French Broad River in 1983, and a 65 1/2-pound channel cat caught a year earlier
in Barkley Reservoir. Nashville, with its Grand Old Opry attraction, is the state's
best known tourist mecca, although some of Elvis' followers would vote for
Memphis, the home of Graceland. If either of these cultural centers takes you to
Tennessee plan some extra time for fishing.

239

Friendship

Cost of individual resident license: $13.00.
Non-resident license: Annual: $20.00. Short-term: $10.00 (5-day).

Where to write for more information:
Texas Parks & Wildlife Department, 4200 Smith School Road,
Austin, TX 78744

Licenses issued in a recent year: 1,800,000.

Most popular species:
Smallmouth and largemouth bass, striped bass, blue, channel and
flathead catfish, rainbow and brown trout, plus amberjack, cobia,
flounder, king mackerel, snapper, marlin and sailfish...all in Gulf waters.

The largest of our 48 contiguous states, it seems only logical that Texas should be on the record books for at least one world record catch. The 98-pound flathead catfish caught in 1986 certainly qualifies for that honor, but there is also a 91-pound, 4-ounce giant on the books, caught in Lewisville Lake... the same waters that produced the larger fish. Both of these catches should give you an idea that Texans take their fishing seriously, almost two million of them! Fresh water action centers heavily on the largemouth bass and there are many lakes which will reward you with bigger bronze-backs than you ever dreamed of back home. When you write to the Parks & Wildlife Department you will receive their recreational fishing guide which does you the great service of identifying "Texas' 12 Best Fishing Holes", so I won't detail all of them here. One of them, Lake Fork, deserves special mention, however. Outdoor writers put in many days on it each year, then write glowing articles about its phenomenal bass action. The state's record 17-pound, 12-ounce largemouth came out of there in 1986, as well as most of those lunkers which win citations every year. Located near Quitman, east of Dallas, it can provide a fabulous fishing adventure on your next trip to the Lone Star state.

Mention must also be made of the great saltwater fishing readily available from ports along the 367 miles of Gulf of Mexico coastline. From Port Arthur on the east, to Harlingen and Brownsville on the south, all types of seaworthy charter boats will take you out to where the big fish play. Blue and white marlin, sailfish and mackerel, wahoo and sharks are out there waiting to make your acquaintance... and present you with thrills you will never forget. And there are marshes, bayous and barrier islands with more excitement, all for you!

Industry

Cost of individual resident license: $18.00.
Non-resident license: Annual: $40.00. Short-term: $15.00 (5-day).

Where to write for more information:
  Utah Division of Wildlife Resources,
  1596 W. North Temple, Salt Lake City, UT 84116-3154

Licenses issued in a recent year: 400,000.

Most popular species:
  Largemouth bass, channel catfish, perch, bluegills, crappies, northern
  pike, cutthroat and rainbow trout.

Until the bass boys took over it was broadly recognized that most of the classic writing about fishing was done by fly fishermen. They also did most of the reading. Much of that output was inspired by the delicate nature of their tools, plus the stalking nature of their pursuit. But just as much of their inspiration, I believe, came from the intoxication they felt in the wondrous natural beauty of the surroundings in which they did so much of their angling. Utah is one of those states which offers such surroundings. Its brilliantly-colored canyons in the southeast, the desert-like basins of the west, and those middle Rockies that divide the state almost right through its center provide fascinating scenery for any fishing adventure.

Over seventy percent of the total land area is public land, encompassing streams, rivers and lakes of crystal-clear water, managed and stocked to provide a continuing challenge to a variety of anglers. The largest of these waters is Lake Powell, formed by the Glen Canyon Dam and situated almost 4,000 feet above sea level. Once a major producer of trophy bass, catfish and walleye catches, it has suffered from a recent draw-down but still continues to yield king-size striped bass, like the 48-pound, ll-ounce state record taken there in 1991. Utah Wildlife Resources personnel now cite the Strawberry Reservoir, located some fifty miles southeast of Salt Lake City, as one of its more promising spots for many fresh water species. It was there that the state's biggest cutthroat trout of all time was caught in 1930. While this record is reported in its official "Hunting and Fishing Guide," they overlook mentioning that it was caught by a lady angler, Mrs. E. Smith! That same guide will be a great time-saver for trout anglers who will find over 75 well-stocked waters providing memorable rainbow, brown, brook and cutthroat trout fishing.

VERMONT

Vermont,
freedom
and unity

Cost of individual resident license: $18.00.
Non-resident license: Annual: $35.00. Short-term: $20.00 (5-day).

Where to write for more information:
Vermont Department of Fish & Wildlife,
130 South Main Street, Waterbury, VT 05676.

Licenses issued in a recent year: 150,000.

Most popular species:
Largemouth and smallmouth bass; landlocked salmon; rainbow, brown, brook and lake trout, northern pike, walleye and panfish.

Lake Champlain, located in the northeast corner of the state, provides deep-water fishing all along its 100-mile length for lunker lake trout and landlocked salmon, walleyes, northerns, and both largemouth and smallmouth bass. Its wide range of habitat and ample forage fish have produced state records for fifteen different species, such as the 32-pound, 4-ounce channel cat caught in 1974 and the 12-pound landlocked salmon taken in 1979.

But Vermont is also blessed with over 5,000 miles of rivers and streams alive with brook, rainbow and brown trout, as well as walleye and smallmouth bass. The Connecticut River, running along its eastern edge, is another popular trout fishery, but has also recorded the state record catch for both tiger muskies and walleyes. The Missisquoi River, winding along the northeastern border, draws many of the state's avid muskie anglers and has claim to the state record for that species with a 29 1/2-pounder brought to boat in 1978. Glen Lake, in the central west, holds the record for northern pike with a 30 1/2-pound giant taken in 1974. Relatively small, it also offers excellent walleye and panfish catches.

With 288 lakes of 20 acres and larger, plus hundreds of small ponds, Vermont can be a surprising and gratifying stop on your next trip through New England. And if you should happen to land one of those "pole-benders" that you have always dreamed about, you can contact a state game warden who will help you get it photographed (along with you), and you will receive a handsome certificate to show all the folks back home.

Your Vermont visit should also include a stop at the headquarters of Orvis, the pantheon of all fly anglers, located in Manchester in the southwest corner of the state. You should find it somewhere along Highway 7. And tell them that I sent you.

VIRGINIA

**Thus always
to tyrants**

Cost of individual resident license: $12.00.
Non-resident license: Annual: $30.00. Short-term: $6.00 (5-day).

Where to write for more information:
  Virginia Department of Game & Inland Fisheries,
  4010 W. Broad St., Richmond, VA 23230

Licenses issued in a recent year: 600,000.

Most popular species:
  Largemouth, smallmouth and striped bass; walleye and sauger; northern pike and muskie; bluegill, rainbow, brown and brook trout. Also bluefish, bluefin tuna, spotted seatrout, black drum and many other saltwater fish caught off its Atlantic coast.

Virginia's James River has a reputation for producing more notable catches each year than any of its many other excellent waters. In 1991 it yielded a 56-pound, 12-ounce blue catfish which set a new state record. But it also is known for its generous stocks of scrappy smallmouth bass and trophy muskies. Smith Mountain Lake, just southeast of Roanoke, is famous for its large striped bass, many going over thirty pounds, and a 42-pound, 6-ouncer which is still tops for the state. The lake is Virginia's second most popular fishing destination and is heavily-stocked each year to provide rewarding catches of largemouth bass, walleye and muskies. New River, in the eastern corner of the state, surprised many muskie enthusiasts with the 45-pound record catch taken there in 1989, but also yields good stringers of bass and walleye.

Then there is Hungry Mother Lake, a 108-acre state park resource, which has attracted a good deal of attention since it recorded a record 27-pound, 12-ounce northern pike catch in 1987. Trout anglers savor the 2100 miles of wild mountain streams, plus 600 miles of stocked waters, all of which receive well-deserved praise for their abundance of rainbows, brookies and browns. Indeed, Virginia offers more fishing for native brook trout than all other southeast states combined.

Offshore, along the 112 miles of Atlantic coastline, charter boats work the waters of Chesapeake Bay and out into the deep ocean where bluefish, black seabass, black drum and spotted seatrout can be had. Two Virginia ladies, Louise M. Gaskill and Diane Dattoli have their names in the I.G.F.A. record book for twin catches of 80-pound black drum (also known as "croaker").

243

WASHINGTON

By and by

Cost of individual resident license: $14.00.
Non-resident license: Annual: $40.00. Short term: $14.00 (3-day).

Where to write for more information:
   Washington Department of Wildlife, 600 Capital Way N.,
   Olympia, WA 98501-1091.

Licenses issued in a recent year: 900,000.

Most popular species:
   **Largemouth and smallmouth bass; bluegill, walleye, channel catfish,
   rainbow, golden, brook and brown trout; plus many saltwater varieties.**

I haven't tried to count them all, but I am firmly convinced that the state of
Washington has more lakes, rivers and streams for fresh water fishing than any
other. In addition, there is the tremendous fishery provided by Puget Sound, ranging
out to the Pacific Ocean by the Strait of Juan de Fuca, and...ultimately...the offshore
waters of the Pacific itself. What more could an enthusiastic angler wish for?

The Columbia River snakes down from British Columbia on the northeast corner
of the state, working its way down to Oregon south of Pasco. Along its route it
provides a rich mixture of bass, catfish, crappie and walleye fishing, with many of
its catches holding current state records. On either side of the Columbia there are
countless rivers fed by the snows off the Cascade range of mountains. Mount
Ranier, towering to a height of more than 14,000 feet, is snow-capped year around,
and is visible for many miles.

The E. F. Lewis River, feeding into the Columbia just north of Vancouver, lays
claim to the state's largest winter-run steelhead, a 32-pound, 12-ounce beauty taken
in 1980. The top summer-run steelhead was an even bigger 35-pound, 1-ounce
trophy caught in the Snake River, north of Richland in the eastern half of the state.
Bass, panfish and walleyes thrive in the clear, cool waters that are found almost
everywhere. Loon, Deer and Waitts Lake, all located north of Spokane, are known
for spectacular trout catches. The 22 1/2-pound record rainbow was taken out of
Waitts lake in 1957, and has not been threatened in recent years.

Visitors to Washington frequently have salmon on their itinerary, and travel
down to Astoria at the mouth of the Columbia, where they will find boats to take
them out to catch them...and then return them to canneries where the fish can be
packed for the trip home.

Mountaineers
are always
free.

Cost of individual resident license: $11.00.
Non-resident license: Annual: $25.00. Short-term: $5.00 (3-day).

Where to write for more information:
  West Virginia Department of Natural Resources,
  1900 Kanawha Blvd. East, Charleston, WV 25305

Licenses issued in a recent year: 250,000.

Most popular species:
  Largemouth and smallmouth bass; channel and flathead catfish;
  walleye, muskie, northern pike; brook, brown, rainbow and golden
  rainbow trout.

The Little Kanawha River, in the northwest, is one of West Virginia's most popular waters, offering channel and flathead catfish, muskie and bass. New River, the oldest river on the American continent, flows northwesterly through the Appalachians, with great walled canyons along its banks. Local experts predict that this river will one day produce the new state record smallmouth, and you might as well be one of those in the competition.

Muskies of the Ohio strain are native to West Virginia and are found in 41 streams running a total of 684 miles of the Ohio River drainage. They are also being stocked in other waters to help meet the increasing interest in this popular game fish. The state record is a respectable 43-pounder caught in the Elk River in 1955, but 1991 produced a new record tiger (hybrid) muskie of over 28 pounds in Sleepy Creek. Trout anglers can choose among almost 200 waters stocked from nine hatcheries which supply fingerlings of all varieties. The top rainbow catch to-date is a 11 1/2-pounder produced by the South Branch of the Potomac River, which also yielded the record brownie, a 16-pounder, in 1968.

If you fancy crappies you will be interested to learn that West Virginia produced one of just over four pounds in (where else?) Meathouse Fork of Middle Island Creek. Other large catches are reported from Bluestone, East Lynn, Sutton and Burnsville Lakes. I recommend that you write for the West Virginia packet of information on its fishing waters. It is heavily detailed and includes many recent articles on the best waters to fish, baits to use, and some dandy data on float fishing trips. These range from 3 to over 12 miles and sound like great sport...and certainly something you might never experience in your home state.

WISCONSIN

Forward

Cost of individual resident license: $12.00.
Non-resident license: Annual: $28.00. Short-term: $13.00 (4-day).

Where to write for more information:
  Wisconsin Department of Natural Resources, Box 7921,
  Madison, WI 53707

Licenses issued in a recent year: 1,500,000.

Most popular species:
  **Largemouth and smallmouth bass; crappie, northern pike, walleye,
  trout salmon...and muskie!**

Automobile license plates for Wisconsin motorists for years have carried the slogan: "The Dairy State". While it may be true that it is the leading producer of dairy products it is also true that it has one of America's largest groups of hospitable, enthusiastic fishing camp operators anywhere. While the state has only 3,620 lakes of 20 acres or larger in size, it makes up for that with the excitement created by the catches which come out of those waters every year. The fish which makes the biggest news each season is the muskie, and the state is now laying claim to the world's record catch, a 69-pound, 11-ounce whopper caught back in 1949. The Chippewa Flowage, with over 17,000 acres of surface, is its leading muskie resource and produced that contending fish. But up in the northeast section of the state Vilas County boasts of 1,327 lakes, most of them with lunker muskies lurking in them.

Lake Winnebago in the central-east is another massive lake which is teeming with walleyes caught all summer, and through the ice in winter. Wisconsin's "thumb" on the northeast is Door County, a popular family vacation area with a loyal following of vacationers who return every year to enjoy its broad range of recreational activities, including angling for large northerns in its bays, or venturing out into Lake Michigan for chinook and coho salmon. The big lake also attracts trout enthusiasts in large numbers, many of them seeking to top the state record brown, rainbow and tiger trout catches it has yielded over the past twenty years. While bass are found in many Badger State lakes, the Flambeau Flowage in the north is a major source of hefty smallies. The Wisconsin and Fox Rivers are prime catfish waters and are home to state records for both flathead and channel cats.

Any trip to Wisconsin should include a visit to the National Fresh Water Hall of Fame in Hayward, a fantastic museum and amusement park for the entire family.

WYOMING

Equal rights

Cost of individual resident license: $9.00.
Non-resident license: Annual: $50.00. Short-term: $20.00 (5-day).

Where to write for more information:
  Wyoming Game and Fish Department, 5400 Bishop Blvd.,
  Cheyenne, WY 82002

Licenses issued in a recent year: 245,000.

Most popular species:
  **Largemouth and smallmouth bass; walleye; northern pike and muskie;
  all varieties of trout.**

My statistical resources indicate that there are Wyoming state records for 27 different species of fresh water fish. The good news for us girls is that the biggest of all of these, an even 50-pound lake trout, is attributed to a lady: Doris Budge, who caught that trophy in 1983 in Jackson Lake. Located in the far west, just south of Yellowstone National Park, Jackson is also famous for its catches of cutthroats and browns. The state's largest other trout catch is a 25-pound, 13-ounce brown landed in the Flaming Gorge Reservoir in 1982.

The Boysen Reservoir, just south of Thermopolis, is one of Wyoming's best-kept fishing secrets with its heavy population of industrial-size walleyes, up to 14 pounds, plus dandy perch and rainbows. To the southeast, the Seminoe Reservoir offers similar excitement for the same species, plus cutthroat trout, and recorded the top walleye catch of 15-pounds, 5-ounces in 1988.

Rich in the natural beauty of its thrusting mountain ranges, Wyoming retains much of the true character of the Old West. Natural geysers, like "Old Faithful" in Yellowstone, are unforgettable sights. No wonder the state attracts millions of visitors each year. Its Grand Teton Mountains, reaching 13,000 feet in height, shelter some of the finest fishing waters anywhere. Some day in the future your vacation plans will take you there. The kids, those under 14 years of age, can fish with you free, if you hold the required non-resident license, even the 5-day bargain.

You'll discover an amazing medley of cold-water impoundments, warm-water - ponds and rushing streams in which to add to your total fishing adventures. You can find the distinctive grayling trout in the Gibbon River within Yellowstone, and the spectacular golden trout in Washakie Lake, Upper and Lower Titcomb, and Wall Lakes. And little Mead Lake, over near Wyoming Peak, holds title to the top grayling, just under 2 1/2 pounds. You would never catch a beauty like that back home!

CANADA ET AL

Some 800,000 anglers from the United States travel into Canada each summer in search of the legendary lunker walleyes, northern pike, bass and muskies for which the Dominion is famous. But less than 20% of those visitors are women anglers. One reason for this disparity may be that men believe those trips are too rigorous for us ladies...or that they just want to be alone. Whatever the reason, you can work to change that by learning all about the fishing adventures available in our neighbor to the north by just writing to the six agencies listed below, each representing one of those provinces which lie adjacent to our northernmost states. Remember to use a 30¢ stamp.

ALBERTA: Alberta Tourism 10155-102 St., Edmonton, Alberta, Canada T5J 4L6

BRITISH COLUMBIA: Dept. of Fisheries & Oceans, 555 W. Hastings, Ste. 400, Vancouver, B. C., Canada V6B 5G3

MANITOBA: Manitoba Natural Resources, Box 24, 1495 St. James St., Winnipeg, Manitoba, Canada R3H 0W9

ONTARIO: Ontario Ministry of Tourism & Recreation, 77 Bloor St.. W., 9th Floor, Toronto, Ontario, Canada M7A 2R9

SASKATCHEWAN: Tourism Saskatchewan, 1919 Saskatchewan Dr., Regina, Saskatchewan, Canada S4P 3V7

QUEBEC: Dept. of Hunting & Fishing, P. O. Box 22000, Quebec City, Quebec, Canada GlK 7X2

And here are a few other spots you will want to learn more about:

BELIZE: Write to Belize Tourist Board, P. O. Box 325, Belize City, Belize, Central America.

COSTA RICA: Some of the best fishing anywhere in the world! Write to Golfito Sailfish Rancho at International Reservations Center, Inc., P. O. Box 290190, San Antonio, TX 78280.

BAJA CALIFORNIA..and many other places you haven't even heard of: Write to PanAngling, Ltd., 180 N. Michigan Ave., Chicago, IL 60601.

Any of the areas listed above will expose you to first-rate fishing excitement and add gloriously to the stories you can tell the boys back home!

SUPPORT GROUPS...FISHING ORGANIZATIONS...NETWORKING

There are national organizations concerned with the promotion of fishing for individual species, as well as with the conservation of their fisheries. Many have local chapters with frequent meetings where you can get together to tell stories, meet other anglers, and just have a good old time. Here are just a few which you might want to write to for membership information.

FEDERATION OF FLY FISHERS: P. O. Box 1088, West Yellowstone, Montana 59758.

GREAT LAKES SPORT FISHING COUNCIL: 8244 North Monticello, Skokie, Illinois 60076.

INTERNATIONAL GAME FISH ASSOCIATION: 1301 East Atlantic Blvd., Pompano Beach, Florida 33060.

IZAAK WALTON LEAGUE OF AMERICA: 1701 North Fort Myer Drive, Suite 1100, Arlington, Virginia 22209.

NATIONAL FRESHWATER FISHING HALL OF FAME: P. O. Box 33, Hayward, Wisconsin 54843.

MUSKIES, INC.: 2301 - 7th Street North, Fargo, North Dakota 58102

SMALLMOUTH, INC.: 206 Buncombe street, Edgefield, South Carolina 29824.

TROUT UNLIMITED: 800 Follin Lane, Suite 250, Vienna, Virginia 22180.

WALLEYES UNLIMITED U.S.A.: 1203 Fern Drive, Mount Prospect, Illinois 60056.

And here is a new one just getting started, but already with chapters in ten states...and especially (only!) for us girls:

WOMEN FOR FISHING, HUNTING & WILDLIFE: P. O. Box 582342, Minneapolis, MN 55458-2342.

You may discover others in your community, all working to preserve and extend our fishing waters...as well as to help all of us increase our enjoyment of the Great Outdoors. Any one of them could produce a more entertaining evening than the P.T.A.. Drop in on one of their meetings and look around. You could make some warm fishing friendships, and even learn how to tie a few more knots!

BIBLIOGRAPHY

Periodicals:
Angler & Hunter
Bassmaster
Field & Stream
Fins & Feathers
Fishing Facts
Fishing Tackle
   Trade News
Fishing Smart
Fishing World
Glamour
Gone Fishin'

Gray's Sporting
   Journal
Health
In-Fisherman
International Angler
Journal of Psychology
Mayo Clinic
   Health Letter
Minneapolis Star
   Tribune
Newsweek
New York Times

North American
   Fisherman
Ontario Out Of Doors
St. Louis Post
   Dispatch
Self
The Splash
Sports Afield
Sports Illustrated
USA Today
Wall Street Journal
Wilson Quarterly

Books:

The Armchair Angler
   - T. Brykczinski & D. Reuther

The Compleat Angler
   - I. Walton & C. Cotton

The Dirty Half Dozen
   - Wm. Nagler, M.D.

Encyclopaedia Britannica

Fishing Moments Of Truth
   - E. Pepper & J. Rikhoff

A History Of Angling
   - C. Waterman

How Do You Go To The Bathroom
   In-Space? - Wm. R. Poague

The Incredible Journey Of
   Lewis And Clark
   - Rhoda Blumberg

McClane's Angling World
   - A. J. McClane

McClane's Standard Fishing
   Encyclopedia -A.J. McClane

National Survey of Fishing, Hunting,
   and Associated Recreation
   - U.S. Dept. of the Interior

Official World Fresh Water Angling
   Records
   - N.F.W. Fishing Hall Of Fame

Poker For Women
   - Mike Caro

A River Never Sleeps
   - Roderick L. Haig-Brown

Salmon And Women
   - W. Peterson & Professor P. Behan

Sport Fishing In Canada
   - Dept. of Fisheries & Oceans (Can.)

The Sportsman's Companion
   - Lee Wulff

The Successful Woman
   - Dr. Joyce Brothers

The War Against Women
   - Marilyn French

The World Almanac

World Guide to Fly Fishing
   - Jim C. Chapralis

World record Game Fishes
   - I.G.F.A.